Stylistic Deceptions in Online News

Also available from Bloomsbury

Contemporary Media Stylistics, edited by Helen Ringrow and
Stephen Pihlaja
Intercultural Crisis Communication, edited by Christophe Declercq and
Federico M. Federici
Keywords in the Press, by Lesley Jeffries and Brian Walker
Telecinematic Stylistics, edited by Christian Hoffmann and
Monika Kirner-Ludwig
The Discursive Construction of Economic Inequality,
edited by Eva M. Gomez-Jimenez and Michael Toolan
What Is Cultural Translation?, by Sarah Maitland

Stylistic Deceptions in Online News

Journalistic Style and the Translation of Culture

Ashley Riggs

BLOOMSBURY ACADEMIC
LONDON • NEW YORK • OXFORD • NEW DELHI • SYDNEY

BLOOMSBURY ACADEMIC
Bloomsbury Publishing Plc
50 Bedford Square, London, WC1B 3DP, UK
1385 Broadway, New York, NY 10018, USA
29 Earlsfort Terrace, Dublin 2, Ireland

BLOOMSBURY, BLOOMSBURY ACADEMIC and the Diana logo
are trademarks of Bloomsbury Publishing Plc

First published in Great Britain 2020
This paperback edition published in 2022

Cover design by Ben Anslow
Images: Black Grunge background © in-future / Getty Images,
Tabloid newspaper clippings © Sean Gladwell / Getty Images,
Dispersion of white light © petrroudny / Getty Images

Published with the support of the Swiss National Science Foundation. The open access
version of this publication was funded by the Swiss National Science Foundation.

A catalogue record for this book is available from the British Library.

Library of Congress Cataloging-in-Publication Data
Names: Riggs, Ashley, author.
Title: Stylistic deceptions in online news : journalistic style
and the translation of culture / Ashley Riggs.
Description: London ; New York : Bloomsbury Academic, 2020. |
Includes bibliographical references and index.
Identifiers: LCCN 2020026391 (print) | LCCN 2020026392 (ebook) | ISBN
9781350114173 (hardback) | ISBN 9781350114180 (ebook) | ISBN 9781350114197 (epub)
Subjects: LCSH: Bastille Day Truck Attack, Nice, France, 2016–Press coverage–Europe. |
Online journalism–Europe. | Online journalism–Political aspects–Europe. |
Journalism–Europe–Language. | Journalism–Translating. | Terrorism–Press
coverage–France–Case studies.
Classification: LCC HV6433.F7 R54 2020 (print) | LCC HV6433.F7 (ebook) |
DDC 070.4/49363325–dc23
LC record available at https://lccn.loc.gov/2020026391
LC ebook record available at https://lccn.loc.gov/2020026392

ISBN: HB: 978-1-3501-1417-3
           PB: 978-1-3501-8402-2
           ePDF: 978-1-3501-1418-0
           eBook: 978-1-3501-1419-7
           DOI: 10.5040/9781350114203

Typeset by Integra Software Services Pvt. Ltd.

To find out more about our authors and books visit www.bloomsbury.com
and sign up for our newsletters.

For Alan

Contents

Tables

Acknowledgments

Published with the support of the Swiss National Science Foundation. The open access version of this publication was funded by the Swiss National Science Foundation.

This kind of project is always a group effort. I am very grateful to the Swiss National Science Foundation (SNSF) for the generous grant which allowed me to conduct the project that culminated in this volume, and for funding its publication in Open Access format. At University College London (UCL), I was incredibly fortunate to be mentored by Federico M. Federici and to have access to workspace, facilities, and great interdisciplinary minds as a visiting research fellow at UCL's Institute for Advanced Studies. Thanks also to the team at University of Granada's *Facultad de Traducción e Interpretación* for facilitating my research stay, and especially to my *amiga-hermana* Elvira Cámara Aguilera for our discussions on Spanish metaphor, for her kindness, and for our friendship. While in Spain, I visited Esperança Bielsa, who gave me feedback on one of my articles, and María José Hernández Guerrero, who generously shared her time and her ideas. A whole host of colleagues at the *Faculté de traduction et d'interprétation* of the *Université de Genève* have provided invaluable advice, and I would particularly like to thank Lucile Davier for giving me suggestions for reading, and for sharing precious insights on everything from research design to career planning; Mathilde Fontanet, Valérie Dullion, Lucía Morado Vazquez, Samantha Cayron, and Véronique Bohn for discussing style and nuance in French and Spanish, and/or for the useful feedback they provided when attending mock presentations about my project. It was extremely helpful that my former supervisor, Professor Emeritus Lance Hewson, and my father, Larry Riggs, were available to read some of my material and help me improve it, and that Greg Giannakis was willing to take care of many not-inspiring, but nonetheless essential, tasks related to formatting and usage. It was a delight to work with Andrew Wardell and Becky Holland of Bloomsbury: I am grateful to them and their whole team for their professionalism and efficiency. Bloomsbury, as well as Roberto Valdeón at *Perspectives* and Alexander Kuenzli at *Parallèles*, also kindly gave me permission to use portions of material I had published with them previously. Finally, special thanks go to my mother for her company during a working summer, and to Alan for a better partnership than I could ever have imagined.

Abbreviations

Daesh   Acronym for the extremist organization also known as Islamic State

DT   The *Telegraph*

EM   *El Mundo*

EP   *El País*

LC   *Le Courrier*

LT   *Le Temps*

L2   Second language

TDG   *La Tribune de Genève*

TG   The *Guardian*

Introduction

On the night of July 14, 2016,[1] just after thousands of residents and tourists had finished watching a fireworks display in celebration of Bastille Day, a violent attack took place in Nice, France. The perpetrator, Mohamed Lahouaiej-Bouhlel, drove a truck through the crowds, killing eighty-six people and injuring 434 others. This attack came relatively soon after two other very serious attacks in France in January and November 2015, similar for their high number of fatalities—the so-called Charlie Hebdo and Bataclan attacks—which were still etched in people's minds and which had also determined security policies, such as a state of emergency, that were still in place in France but did not prevent this violent act.

I chose to study the way the attack was portrayed in the news of three European countries, the UK, Switzerland, and Spain, and to focus on stylistic features of the news texts, for three reasons. First, I had the same impression I had had when reading or watching news about the tragically momentous attacks of 2015: that from the earliest moment of the news cycle, there was an immediate and pervasive focus on Muslims and radical Islam, despite the fact that again there was very little information about the event. Second, the specific language choices, but in particular stylistic choices, on the part of journalists seemed to me to be playing a significant role in shaping the media's messages. Third, a number of factors had coalesced after the 2015 attacks, factors which continue to play a significant role in national and international public opinion, politics, and policy: the immigration "crisis" persists, with the accompanying debate on open borders, security, and jobs. Ethno-nationalist populism is on the rise across Europe. The referendum in favor of Brexit, which took place just a few weeks before the attack, was followed by an increase in hate crime in the UK, in particular against Muslims; at the time of writing, neither such acts nor the debate and controversy around Brexit itself have abated. The combination of separatist and divisionism movements appearing in Europe is reflected in both Brexit and the battle for sovereignty between Spain and Catalonia. Donald Trump, who is known for extreme positions on Muslims and immigrants, and who would soon fuel an international focus on "fake news," has done serious and potentially lasting damage to democratic processes as well as to international alliances in his three and a half years as president of the United States. Terrorist attacks in "the West" seem to be growing more frequent and anti-Muslim sentiment and violence more pronounced. At the same time, as the media landscape continues to evolve rapidly, there are many questions about the future of news, with journalism (appropriately or not) described as "in crisis." In many Western countries, ownership of the media seems to be falling into fewer and fewer hands, and they are powerful ones; this in turn raises questions about both the diversity of news content and the independence of journalists.

That said, while a wealth of research exists on the power of the media, the intersections between media and politics, or the role of the media in shaping public opinion, very, very few studies examine the influence of stylistic features of news in a comprehensive manner. While I cannot claim to be utterly comprehensive, the fact that in this book I examine the use of a number of different stylistic devices in the news of three different countries will provide a new and illuminating angle from which to view the "crisis" and to think about improving certain media practices.

Why did I not choose to analyze the stylistic features of news articles about the Charlie Hebdo or Bataclan attacks here? Not only did the events receive wide international media attention, but also, no fewer than eighty-three books were written about them between 2015 and 2016 (Amiraux and Fetiu 2017). The Nice attack is another event in the chain of which those prior attacks form a part; looking at the continuing trajectory of representation of violence as another piece of the puzzle, another link in the "event chain," shows how certain reporting choices have coalesced, but also, from an ethical perspective, that some choices, despite being common, are highly questionable.

Let me give one example of what might be called a questionable choice: as I watched the news about the Parsons Green "incident" unfold in London on September 15, 2017,[2] I was particularly struck by one tendency of the morning television shows. Multiple broadcasters, along with the experts or officials they consulted, used the following phrase or a very similar version thereof: "We are still in the early stages and we have to be careful not to jump to conclusions, but … " before going on to formulate hypotheses or draw on prior events to construct possible scenarios—that is, to draw some kind of preliminary conclusion. As is often the case in such situations, the news continued to focus entirely on this event for hours, even though, as is also often the case in the period immediately following such acts, there were few to no facts to report because the investigation was just getting underway. Also as usual, unsubstantiated rumors circulated, on Twitter in particular. The events and the reporting once again brought to the fore, for me, the question that was part of the impetus for this study, and that journalists, I know, grapple with: to report, or not to report, as such events unfold? I agree that this is "the way it's done"; but does it have to be? What argument should prevail: that the public has a right to be informed, an argument actually underpinned by the pressure on media organizations to "sell," to get the first scoop? Or that reporting should be factual, and therefore may well require a waiting period to get facts in place? Not to mention the importance of preserving the integrity of an ongoing investigation.

For reporting too soon can have costs. Canel (2012: 214) examined editorials published in the Spanish newspapers *El Mundo*, *Abc*, and *El País*[3] after the bombings that took place in Madrid in March 2004 and were wrongly attributed to ETA (Euskadi Ta Askatasuna, or "Basque Homeland and Liberty," an armed separatist organization in the Basque country) in the very early stages of investigation and reporting, in particular by media that supported the conservative government in power. Some maintain that this error lost the conservative government the election that took place immediately after the event. Interestingly, "[t]he *problem* definition in the editorials of March 11 was the 'treatment of terrorism' by different political parties" rather than the perpetrators (identified, at that stage, as ETA [Basque nationalists]) (Canel 2012: 218; emphasis in the original), and the newspapers made their judgments about actors' capabilities "with an eye on the election" (218). "The three newspapers" she examined "reacted to the evolution of the frame by going to battle for a specific political option" and against others. Importantly, they "went even further than the political parties they supported: *Abc* and *El Mundo* (right-leaning) were much more critical of the nationalist parties and of the Opposition than the government was, and *El País* was much more critical of the government than the Socialist Party was" (221).

For the author, this demonstrates that "partisanship is a feature of the Spanish press" (Canel 2012: 221), but it is first and foremost a feature of editorials, the text type she examines. For Piquer Martí (2015), in contrast, the media in general are supposed to be the guarantors of "the right to true, just and contextualized information." This right "also extends to citizens who belong to minority cultures such as, in this case, Muslims"[4] (138). The press is, according to Piquer Martí, the most trustworthy media, and "encourages reflection more than others; moreover, it is better able to foster, in citizens, certain values and frames of reference," although she warns that it is also "able to reproduce imperialist ideologies and conceptions of society" (Crespo Fernández 2008: 46; qtd. in Piquer Martí). Canel (2012: 221) makes the important observation that "unbalanced news comes not only or necessarily from individual journalists but also from the interaction of different factors, which include real world developments, cultural norms," the rules governing journalists' decisions, the government-media-public(s) triangle, and "each side's skills at frame promotion" (221). Unbalanced news happens, including when terrorism is the topic. As with violent and terrorist acts themselves, partisan news about terrorism has costs, and in both cases it is often Muslims or those believed to be Muslim who pay dearly, as I will demonstrate with the findings presented in this book. As we will see in much more detail in the chapters that follow, this minority group is often discriminated against both by the societies in question in this book and in their media, especially when terrorist acts or events believed to be terrorist in nature occur.

Such discrimination is widely qualified as Islamophobia. Runnymede Trust (2017) has provided both a short and a more developed definition of Islamophobia; the latter draws on the United Nations definition of racism. The first states that "Islamophobia is anti-Muslim racism"; the second, that

> Islamophobia is any distinction, exclusion or restriction towards, or preference against, Muslims (or those perceived to be Muslims) that has the purpose or effect of nullifying or impairing the recognition, enjoyment or exercise, on an equal footing, of human rights and fundamental freedoms in the political, economic, social, cultural or any other field of public life. (1; 7)

In the UK, social acceptance of Islamophobia, as indicated from poll results, is worryingly widespread:

> 37% admitted they would be more likely to support ... policies to reduce the number of Muslims in Britain (note this is worse than stopping Muslims from entering the country)
>
> On average, people think that Muslims make up 17% of the population, compared to the reality of less than 5%
>
> 62% agreed that Britain would lose its identity if more Muslims came to live here
>
> More than half of Britons regard Muslims as a threat to the UK. (Muslim Council of Britain 2016: 2)

These attitudes are showing up in schools as well:

> 35% of 10–14 year olds agree that "Muslims are taking over our country".
>
> Islamophobia is a particular issue in schools, … with young Muslims reporting that they are being called "terrorists" and "bombers" by classmates. (Muslim Council of Britain 2016: 2)

The Muslim Council of Britain (MCB) paper also provides examples and statistics of anti-Muslim hate crime and notes that "[t]he attacks seem to spike after major events linked to Muslims," including "terror atrocities abroad, and Brexit" (3).

As we will see, the media in all three countries in question here, the UK, Switzerland, and Spain, are sometimes blamed for their negative and disparaging portrayals of Muslims and Islam, which are particularly prevalent when terror events are the topic of news. In its 2016 report on country monitoring of the UK, the European Commission against Racism and Intolerance (ECRI) exhorted the UK media to "avoid perpetuating prejudice, in particular against Muslims," qualified the tendency as "reckless," and lamented the fact that press regulation measures were insufficient:

> ECRI regrets that a way has not been found to establish an independent press regulator and that, as a result, certain tabloids continue to publish offensive material … ECRI urges the media to take stock of the importance of responsible reporting, not only to avoid perpetuating prejudice and biased information, but also to avoid harm to targeted persons or vulnerable groups. (ECRI 2016: 23)

Regarding Muslims specifically and the way they are often linked to terrorism in the media,

> ECRI considers that, in light of the fact that Muslims are increasingly under the spotlight as a result of recent ISIS-related terrorist acts around the world, fuelling prejudice against Muslims shows a reckless disregard, not only for the dignity of the great majority of Muslims in the United Kingdom, but also for their safety. (23)

Particularly important for my research, with regard to media reporting on terrorism, ECRI

> draws attention to a recent study by Teeside University suggesting that where the media stress the Muslim background of perpetrators of terrorist acts, and devote significant coverage to it, the violent backlash against Muslims is likely to be greater than in cases where the perpetrators' motivation is downplayed or rejected in favour of alternative explanations. (23)

The year before, then High Commissioner for Human Rights Zeid Ra'ad Al Hussein exhorted the UK to "tackle tabloid hate speech," even making a comparison with Nazi media strategies after the *Sun* labeled migrants "cockroaches."[5]

So far, it is clear that among the major preoccupations of this book are UK, Swiss, and Spanish news about terrorism, the stylistic features of such news, and the anti-Muslim prejudice often present in such news, and in the societies in question. Translation, however, is also a key issue. How is it connected to the other themes in this book?

Notes on "Translation" and Terminology

I come from a Translation Studies background, and this has naturally shaped not only my vision of languages, cultures, and intercultural communication generally, but also my understanding of what translation means, and my method of analyzing stylistic features of texts. It is important to emphasize that in this book, I conceive of translation in a broader sense than some may be used to. This is not to minimize the importance of translation in its narrower sense—of source text to target text, of one language to another—nor in its more complex dimension where, for instance, news translation is concerned, in which case it may involve one or any combination of the activities of source-target translation, editing, adding, omitting, rewriting, and so on. News translation is a fast-growing area of Translation Studies and these issues are currently receiving a lot of attention. While the present study is also about news, translation is conceived of here as the process of re-presenting societies and groups for foreign readers, in this case, news readers from a different country than that of the societies or groups reported upon. Or, to turn it around, cultural re-presentation is translation.

That said, translation in the narrower sense does also feature in this book; for example, I have translated into English both segments of the French- and Spanish-language news articles examined, and excerpts cited from French- and Spanish-language academic sources. I want to make it clear that while I sought to make translations of academic references as fluid and idiomatic as possible, my strategy was not the same when I translated news segments. In many cases, I left them more literal or at least less smooth because remaining closer to the structure of the original excerpt would give readers a better idea of the content of the original segment and how it was presented.

Regarding terminology, I would like to point out that throughout this book, I have used the term "Daesh" to refer to the extremist organization that is often labeled "Islamic State" or "ISIS." "Daesh" is the equivalent of the Arabic acronym for the organization and is used less frequently in English than other acronyms or terms. I chose it for two reasons. First, I did not want to confer the legitimacy that a name that includes "State" confers. Second, the term allows me to avoid another, "Islamic," which encourages in people's minds an insidious blurring of boundaries between Muslims, Arabs, and Islamists (who are, despite the way the term gets thrown around, simply Muslims with political goals).

Remarks on Style

In this book, I examine stylistic features of news. What is meant by style, and why investigate it? It can be defined as "a choice of form ('manner') to express content ('matter')" (Wales 2001: 158). In *Marxism and the Philosophy of Language*, Vološinov summarizes the work of Vossler and Croce, who represent one major trend in the philosophy of language and who essentially assert that linguistics is "the study of expression par excellence," and that "[a]ny sort of expression is, at the root, artistic" (52). While one can query the all-encompassing nature of this affirmation, stylistic features, which are the result of personal choice and reflect the original, idiosyncratic features of an individual's way of expressing herself, are arguably artistic and therefore creative (this is most evident in the case of metaphor). Moreover, in Matejka's ([1929] 1986) Appendix to Vološinov's work, which he co-translated, he points out that for Vološinov, "the primary target of linguistic investigation should be exactly that which reveals the creative aspect of human language" (168).

The role journalistic style plays in conveying information and portraying events and cultures has been much overlooked and, I claim, its impact underestimated—especially where common yet influential rhetorical devices such as alliteration and assonance (which make particularly salient for the reader the content they accompany) and modality (which shapes reader belief and confidence in the information received) are concerned. Nevertheless, framing studies (see, for example, Baker 2006, 2007) and discourse analysis, both commonly applied in news translation research, indirectly justify this kind of focus. Reese (2001: 11) defines frames as "*organizing principles* that are socially *shared* and *persistent* over time, that work *symbolically* to meaningfully *structure* the social world" (emphasis in the original). Baresch, Hsu, and Reese (2012 [2010]: 641) cite the "War on Terror" as an example. In addition, "Reese's definition suggests that framing research not only examine the manifest or most salient content but also strive to catch the structure and pattern hidden in the media texts, and search for *what makes people take this latent structure and way of thinking for granted*" (Baresch et al. 2012 [2010]: 641; my emphasis). Discourse analysis draws upon stylistics (Schäffner 2013: 48) but has yet to take sufficient account of combinations of stylistic elements in media texts. I maintain that they play a role in encouraging people to subscribe to the "structure and way of thinking" that they encounter in news texts.

Indeed, while we may not pay particular attention to stylistic elements when we read news texts, they nevertheless wield a lot of power. Baresch et al. evoke, for example, the potential role of "allusion" or "situational irony" in constructing underlying, organizing principles (2012 [2010]: 644–5), observing that while "[t]hese devices will be difficult to spot," "the researcher must account for them" (645). Put otherwise, such devices are not obvious, they are under-researched, but they are nevertheless a vital force in the way in which we interpret information. Therefore, "[a]t this early stage in new media scholarship," researchers "must innovate methods for identifying, sampling, and analyzing data sets that will yield meaningful results" (645). Coming from a translation perspective, Boase-Beier, too, emphasizes the importance of "stylistically-aware analysis" (2006: 111). Not only does it help "the translator to describe and justify … stylistic decisions," but "we can go further, and argue that knowledge of stylistics will allow the translator to consider how such aspects of meaning as attitude, implication, or cognitive state can be recreated in the target text" (Boase-Beier [2011] 2012). Even when the aim is not translation in its narrower sense, that is, from source text to target text, but rather news analysis and the way its discourse translates events, cultures or groups for an-other audience, looking at style "will allow more detailed consideration of the interplay of universal stylistic features such as conceptual metaphor, culturally embedded imagery, and specific linguistic connotation" (Boase-Beier [2011] 2012). Working from a translation criticism perspective, Hewson (2011: 74–83) identifies alliteration and modality as two further key foci for analyses seeking to describe stylistic effects.

The stylistic features I chose to focus on in my analysis are alliteration and assonance, metaphor, and modality. Alliteration and assonance do not necessarily carry the same weight across languages. Nevertheless, as Van Hoof (2008), discussing both French and English, observes,

> rhyme, assonance and alliteration fulfill multiple functions: they work together to form rhythm, contribute to harmony, help to solidify ideas and help readers remember the content of verses. This is just as valid for other domains as it is for poetry. (899)[6]

Moreover, his examples demonstrate that alliteration is frequently accompanied by a marked rhythm.

Metaphor, omnipresent in the literary text, plays an important role in shaping impressions and interpretations and is often a challenge to translate. Metaphor is by no means unique to the literary text, however. Does it carry the same weight in other kinds of texts? How does it contribute to shaping their content and messages? This study is in part an opportunity to reflect on the discursive power of metaphor in a very different text type, the news article, and on how it may contribute to "translating" not only events, but also the people and places involved. I have nevertheless avoided including "dead metaphors," those that have become so ubiquitous that they are no longer recognized as being metaphors and, for the same reason, do not have the influence upon readers that other metaphors do.

In identifying and discussing modality, I will include instances of epistemic modality, deontic modality, and what Bednarek (2010) calls "mental process," with most emphasis on the first and last type, as there are more instances of these in the kinds of (ostensibly) informational news texts I examine. Drawing upon definitions from linguistics, Bednarek and Caple (2012) define epistemic modality as "the speaker's degree of confidence in the truth of the proposition" (158–9, note 3). For Halliday (1976), this type of modality covers possibility, probability, and degrees of certainty. Deontic modality, which Halliday terms modulation, covers inclination, permission, necessity, and obligation. Bednarek's (2010) "mental process" category incorporates

> expressions such as decide, imagine and speculate, which can be used to attribute statements to sources (e.g. Somebody working in the post room was injured in the hands and face as another parcel exploded. Some **speculated** it was linked to recent bomb scares. (ABC News Radio, 24 December 2010)). (Bednarek and Caple 2012: 159, note 4; emphasis in the original)

In this section, I have laid out justifications for investigating the stylistic features of news and described the specific features that are the focus of this study. In the following section, I present the corpus of news articles that I analyzed.

Corpus

The corpus of online news articles from the UK, French-speaking Switzerland and Spain contains just under 114,000 words (see Table 1): 27,850 from the *Guardian* and the *Telegraph* (thirteen and fourteen articles, respectively); 32,100 from *Le Temps* (twelve), *La Tribune de Genève* (twenty-six), and *Le Courrier* (ten); and 53,700 from *El País* and *El Mundo* (thirty-six and thirty-one, respectively). Articles were included in the corpus if they addressed the Nice attack, were published during the defined time frame, and appeared in the "News" section of the sources' websites. As is evident from the content, however, they do not qualify solely as "hard news," but rather as a combination of news- and news analysis-type articles. White (1997: 107) claims that "hard news" texts aim "to represent themselves as neutral and impersonal" and therefore avoid "explicit value judgments ... about the morality, competence, normality, etc. of participants, explicit evaluations of events and entities in terms of their aesthetics or emotional impact, inferences about the motivations and intentions of participants," and "contentious claims about causes and effects." Almost none of the news articles I analyzed fit all of these criteria, which demonstrates that appearing under the "News" section clearly does not equate with providing totally objective information.

These particular online newspapers were chosen because they represent contrasting parts of the political spectrum, had roughly comparable readership statistics from 2013 to 2016[7] (Ofcom 2017: 28–30), and are not tabloids. The situation in French-speaking Switzerland is slightly different, as its media tends to be center or center-left on the political spectrum. I added *Le Courrier* to the *Suisse-romande* subcorpus to ensure some variety, as it is widely seen to be more independent and non-partisan. That said, it has recently described itself as left-wing,[8] while *Le Temps* was recently described to me as neo-liberal. These discrepancies indicate that it is often difficult to ascribe a hard and fast political affiliation to a newspaper, and political leanings can also change over time. Moreover, the Swiss still favor print over digital news. *Le Temps* and *La Tribune de Genève* print versions have a comparable number of readers, whereas *La Tribune* has twice the number of online readers as *Le Temps*. I was unable to obtain data for *Le Courrier*.

Table 1 Statistics for the Full Corpus

Country/region	Number of words	Percentage of corpus
UK	27,852	24.5%
Suisse romande	32,064	28.2%
Spain	53,685	47.3%
Total	113,601	

Table 2 Corpus of Online Newspapers by Country and Political Affiliation

Country	Online newspaper	Probable affiliation
UK	The *Guardian* (TG)	left-leaning
	The *Telegraph* (DT)	right-leaning
Switzerland	*Le Temps* (LT)	mixed[9]
	La Tribune de Genève (TDG)	unclear
	Le Courrier (LC)	left-leaning
Spain	*El País* (EP)	left-leaning
	El Mundo (EM)	right-leaning

The time frame for the articles is July 15 to 18, 2016: the day after the terrorist attack in Nice took place and the following few days. I did this

1. to limit the corpus to a manageable size,
2. because a first dip in the number of news items occurred after July 18, and
3. to avoid a distinct news cycle about a later attack on July 26, 2016.

Because the corpus has been constructed according to these thematic and temporal criteria, it qualifies as "comparable" (Kenny 2001; Olohan 2004).

Table 2 presents the corpus by probable political affiliation, where this could be reasonably determined. I chose the *Guardian* and *El País* because they are known to be left-leaning; the *Telegraph* and *El Mundo*, because they are widely considered to be right-leaning. As indicated above, the political characteristics of the *Suisse romande* press are less clear-cut.

Finally, it should be noted that the *Telegraph*'s content, unlike the *Guardian*'s, is behind a paywall, and that this could affect both reader characteristics and journalistic content to some degree. The potential influence of the paywall could be tested with further research.

Methodology

Federici has called specifically for the kind of news study I propose, highlighting "the lack of a breadth of studies focusing on key stylistic features of online news." The present study and the larger project will contribute to closing this gap while also building bridges between literary and non-literary analysis. My approach is inspired in part by the close analysis of style that is characteristic of translation criticism (Boase-Beier 2006; Hewson 2011). Scholars including Brownlie (2010), Munday (2007), O'Halloran (2010), and Simpson (1993) have demonstrated the validity of studying monolingual corpora in part through stylistic analysis, even with non-literary texts, while Boase-Beier (2006) has shown how close consideration of style can aid in the actual translation of both literary and non-literary texts. Brownlie (2010: 53) identifies the "use and explanation of French phrases" by journalists as "a stylistic characteristic." According to O'Halloran (2010: 100), even in "hard news," the stylistic element of "metaphors can be ideologically significant" and "influence how people think about" events.

Some might ask why I describe my approach as "stylistic analysis" rather than "discourse analysis." In fact, "discourse analysis" itself means different things to different scholars and, according to some definitions, stylistic analysis is a subset of it: "Discourse analysts also use concepts (e.g. cohesion, coherence, speech act, genre, style, rhetorical purpose, transitivity) that have their origin in other sub-disciplines of Applied Linguistics, such as text linguistics, pragmatics, stylistics, rhetorics [*sic*]" (Schäffner 2013: 48). Specifically stylistic features of news and particularly combinations of these features have been under-researched up to now. I focus on them and do not claim to examine all of the other elements that Schäffner lists.

I chose to work on online news articles from three different countries and, in the case of Switzerland, only from the French-speaking region, and really from Geneva (although at least *Le Temps* is read more widely). There are various reasons for this. The most obvious is that my three working languages as a translator and Translation Studies scholar are English, French, and Spanish; therefore I can aptly analyze news in those languages. In addition, I have lived in Geneva for more than twenty years. But there are other reasons. The three countries are (geographically or politically) part of Europe. Spain and Switzerland are neighbors of France; the UK has many ties with France, not least historical ones. Thus the three countries are connected enough to France to be interested in what happens there, and at the same time sufficiently different themselves to make comparisons of their news reporting interesting, especially if one wants to question the concept of "European" or "transnational" news. In addition, the *Suisse romande* speaks the same language as France and Geneva, in particular, has certain cultural characteristics in common with France and various extremely close ties (not least of which are economic) while also sharing a kind of love-hate relationship with the country, common when close borders paradoxically mean that people of different nations want to distinguish themselves from each other.

In their study of online news from the *Guardian* and a Swedish newspaper, Karlsson and Strömbäck (2009: 8) provide a strong argument for analyzing British news: "The rationale for including Britain is that news sites from the United Kingdom are widely used not only by domestic audiences, but also by international readers, particularly when international news events such as wars and crises are happening." Esser (2012) instead argues that media research should not focus on national contexts and indicates that over the past few years prior to her study, the situation had improved as scholars took into account the transnational nature of the media in Europe. Nevertheless, my research suggests that the differing historical, political, economic, and social characteristics of the *Suisse romande*, the UK, and Spain may translate into differing treatment of both terrorist events and Muslims in their respective online news. I think it is precisely the comparative analyses I conduct, on national contexts, which can contribute to affirming or refuting the "transnational hypothesis" I alluded to above. In addition, after conducting their meta-study of English-language research examining the treatment of Muslims in the media, Ahmed and Matthes (2017) concluded that

1. as most studies involve English-language sources,[10] new research should branch out to include other languages, which my study does; and that
2. "cross-national comparative work" and cross-disciplinary research (237–8) are now essential. My study also meets these requirements.

I have emphasized the fact that stylistic features of news have rarely been studied. According to Zhang et al. (2015: 228), "[s]tudies on media translation [tend to] pay more attention to extralinguistic factors, in particular the issue[s] of power, ideology, and [the context of] translation in news media" than to discursive strategies. Studies that constitute exceptions to the prevailing focus on extralinguistic factors often concentrate on one specific aspect of language, for instance, metaphor (for example, Bazzi 2014; Schäffner 2014), neologism (Gallardo San Salvador 2012), or lexical borrowing (Le Poder 2012), or examine discourse types or positions of authority through analyses of reported speech in the news (see, for example, Baumgarten and Gagnon 2008; Davier 2013, 2017; Muñoz-Calvo and Buesa-Gómez 2010; Schäffner and Bassnett 2010). My focus on other aspects of journalists' language contributes to filling a gap in current research.

Before conducting my analysis, I formulated the following hypotheses. In terms of general themes,

1. references to the home country and/or its citizens, which journalists sometimes use to make an article relevant for the domestic audience (Freedman 2017: 215), would occur across the corpus, but right-leaning newspapers would center more on the home country and also portray it as superior (Brownlie 2010; Kelly 1997, 1998);

2. representations of French society and of Muslims and/or Islam would be more negative in right-leaning sources, given their alignment with conservative positions and policies, which are often anti-Muslim and also likely to find fault with the socialist government in place in 2016 in France. The conflation of Muslims with terrorism would be more pronounced in right-leaning news sources but nevertheless also visible in left-leaning ones.

The first hypothesis aligns with Cottle's assertion that "[w]hen reporting on distant disasters and humanitarian emergencies, … national news media often seek out stories populated by their own" citizens. "This stock news cast of *dramatis personae* serves to 'nationalize', personalize and 'bring back home' the meanings of distant events and tragedies" ([2011] 2012: 482). It is also based on Valdeón's (2009: 149) observation that news reporting is "heavily influenced … by the national narratives of the writers, which permeate the events themselves and offer domestic perspectives of European and world issues." In relation to the second hypothesis, "the global war on terror, inevitably, becomes reported through blood-flecked glasses tinted by national" and, I would add, political "interests" (Cottle, [2011] 2012: 483) and prejudices.

In terms of style specifically, my hypotheses were that

3. across the corpus, modal use would sometimes give suppositions a patina of factuality, and in ways that would be likely to heighten the sense of threat. In right-leaning sources, this phenomenon would also encourage distrust of Muslims;

4. alliteration and assonance would predominantly accompany negative content and serve to emphasize and reinforce it, thereby giving it more weight, in all news sources. This in turn would be likely to fuel readers' sense of threat and "*of a state of emergency*" (Federici 2016: 1; emphasis in the original);

5. metaphors would most often be negative, and a significant number would evoke war and violence specifically.

I chose to leave reported speech out of my analysis and concentrate on the journalists' own discourse. This affected corpus selection: texts about the attack were omitted if they contained too many quotes or were under 300 words. A final remark on the corpus concerns the dates of publication. While there are few *Guardian* articles from July 17 to 18, 2016, this is partly due to what appeared in the relevant search, and partly to a discrepancy in date indications between the search results and the date indicated online, rather than from any deliberate pre-selection.

I used the qualitative data analysis software QDA Miner for this study. This meant coding textual elements in an iterative process of category definition and attribution within the broader categories of lexis, grammar, syntax, and rhetorical devices, and under themes such as "French society" or "attitudes of/ to Muslims." In other words, I established categories under which to classify textual segments according to what I found in the texts themselves (albeit with an interest, from the beginning, in segments containing references to Muslims, Islam, and French society).

I tallied instances of alliteration and assonance across the corpus and classified them as negative, positive, or neutral, depending upon the connotations of the content they accompanied. How is connotation understood here? It is true that various definitions of the term exist and take into account broader or narrower parameters. For instance, according to Osgood, Succi, and Tannenbaum (1957), interlocutors react to words in terms of how positive or negative, strong or weak, active or passive the words are. Twenty years later, Chuquet and Paillard (1987), working from the perspective of a translator aiming to render a target text and the pitfalls she might encounter when dealing with connotation, restricted their concern to the positive *versus* negative dimension. Don Bialostosky (2017) echoes common criticisms of such linguistic conceptions of connotation, which treat it as objectively classifiable and fail to take into account key factors in how words are interpreted, that is

> the kinds of situations and the kinds of utterances in which they are typically used, the kinds of speakers who use them, the kinds of hearers who hear them, and the kinds of emotional-evaluational tones with which they are used in those situations. We need to locate our individual associations in shared or at least shareable situations. (Bialostosky 2017)

Nevertheless, I chose to use a narrow conception of connotation in this study based on the positive and negative dichotomy. It is relevant to the topics being addressed and makes it possible to parse textual elements meaningfully, without being unwieldy. Moreover, I believe that the majority of readers of these news articles would make the same positive and negative associations. They share awareness of these news topics; knowledge of the news sources in question, their language, conventions, and political leanings; and have chosen to read them. The assumption of shared associations could nevertheless be tested with further research.

Vološinov (1986 [1929]) not only emphasizes the socially constructed nature of meaning and connotation, but insists that all words carry connotation or, as he labels it, "evaluative accent": "Any word used in actual speech" carries not only referential meaning, "but also value judgment: i.e., all referential contents produced in living speech are said or written in conjunction with a specific *evaluative accent*. There is no such thing as [a] word without [an] evaluative accent" (103; emphasis in the original). Moreover, he goes so far as to argue that the distinction commonly made by linguists between referential meaning and evaluation or connotation "is totally inadmissible," as

> [r]eferential meaning is molded by evaluation; it is evaluation, after all, which determines that a particular referential meaning may enter the purview of speakers—both the immediate purview and the broader social purview of the particular social group … The separation of word meaning from evaluation inevitably deprives meaning of its place in the living social process (where meaning is always permeated with value judgment). (105)

Metaphors were coded as

1. positive (e.g., "none can rival Nice when it comes to conjuring up images of the sun-kissed good life" (TGObs17)),
2. negative (e.g., "a cancerous obstacle" (DT26)), or
3. neutral (e.g., to be "in the spotlight" (TG1)).
4. relating to terrorist violence specifically;
5. not relating to terrorist violence specifically.

Where applicable, metaphors in the fifth category were also coded as

6. violent nonetheless.

Shortcomings

To be sure, my methodology glosses over the characteristics of online news which distinguish it from traditional print news: the convergent nature (Davier and Conway 2019), interactivity, and immediacy of online news which in turn make it "liquid" (Karlsson and Strömbäck 2009). "Online, the order in which news stories are presented can be constantly rearranged," while "in the offline environment, news is presented in a linear sequence making it clear where one news story ends and another starts." In addition, "on the news site-level of analysis, modifications in news content or context are not necessarily highlighted" (Karlsson and Strömbäck 2009: 15). Nevertheless, these observations apply mainly to the extralinguistic level of news content; the constellation of micro-level textual characteristics being analyzed here is more likely to correspond in significant measure to what a reader would have seen around the time of the event.

On the linguistic level, I had to make a selection of stylistic features; I could not cover all possibilities. It nevertheless became clear to me in the course of the study that a feature like prosody is also a key aspect of news style, and that it might be even more relevant in the French and Spanish texts than in the English ones. In any case, further research on stylistic features is sorely needed and would do well to include analysis of prosody.

Finally, visual content is an intrinsic part of "making" online news texts "mean." Given the scope of this study, I could not analyze it in this book, but I look forward to developing an article on this aspect of my current corpus.

The Chapters

I close this chapter by briefly explaining the content of those that follow. Chapter 2 explores how concepts and approaches from Translation Studies can be brought to bear in the analysis of "European" news about terrorism, discussing in particular the usefulness of the notions of cultural translation and cosmopolitanism for defining the role of the journalist. She is conceived of as an intercultural mediator and, indeed, a translator; news about terrorism, as a narrative of "crisis." The chapter goes on to present some of the key journalistic principles and guidelines of the online newspapers examined, as well as some examples of how they sometimes fall short of these principles and guidelines; and common forms of media regulation in the three countries in question. Chapter 3 contextualizes the three societies and in particular their attitudes to Muslims through an overview of their linguistic, legal, political, and social characteristics, their experiences with and responses to terrorism, and some features of their respective news landscapes. Chapter 4 presents the stylistic analysis proper, and Chapter 5 draws comparative conclusions about the findings. Chapter 6 includes reflections on the usefulness of this kind of study for Translation Studies and for journalism; changes that journalists and media systems could implement, and ideas for best practice; and closing remarks.

Terrorism in "European" News: What Role for Translation Studies?

This process of coming to see other human beings as "one of us" rather than as "them" is a matter of detailed descriptions of what unfamiliar people are like and of redescription of what we ourselves are like. This is a task not for theory but for genres such as ethnography, *the journalist's report*, the comic book, the docudrama, and, especially, the novel.

(Rorty 1989: xvi; qtd. in Maitland 2017: Fol. 103; my emphasis © Cambridge University Press. Reproduced with permission of The Licensor through PLSclear).

The presence of terrorism in contemporary societies and the related debates on immigration, integration, security, (counter)terrorism, Islam, and Muslims make the present study highly topical. The attacks of September 11, 2001 generated a wealth of scholarship in these areas. Scholarly and journalistic works alike also affirm that the 9/11 attacks were a kind of watershed moment[1] leading to the normalization of anti-Muslim discourse in the social, political, and media arenas (see, for example, Ahmed and Matthes 2017; Bielsa and Hughes 2009; Birkenstein, Froula, and Randell 2010; Burchardt and Michalowski 2015; Fiddian-Qasmiyeh and Qasmiyeh 2010; Ogan, Willnat Pennington, and Bashir 2014). The propensity of "media discourse" in particular to construct "meanings and identities of Muslims as the 'others' in liberal societies" (Ahmed and Matthes 2017: 235) has become more pronounced. The negative views and actions of the public are apparently widespread: A YouGov poll of British adults found that those who believe that "there is a fundamental clash between Islam and the values of British society" ranged from 44 percent to 59 percent between January 2015 and June 2017.[2] A survey of UK school children conducted by the charity Show Racism the Red Card in 2015 found that 35 percent of respondents "agreed or partly agreed" with the statement "Muslims are taking over England," and estimated the percentage of Muslims in the UK population to be 36 percent, whereas the 2011 census showed this figure to be under 5 percent.[3] Statistics from the Metropolitan Police[4] show that Islamophobic hate crime is very prevalent.

Moreover, according to Fiddian-Qasmiyeh and Qasmiyeh (2010: 310), as Europe grapples with the migrant "crisis" and terrorism, "religion has increasingly become a tool used by the media and politicians as a common denominator underlying new policies and the trans/formation of public opinion" in the UK and in Europe more generally. In the media, "Muslim migrants," in particular, "are largely presented as a threat to *national cultures* (Hussain 2007)," whatever that might mean (Ahmed and Matthes 2017: 234, my emphasis). "Most have found these media stances to obstruct societal integration of Muslim immigrants" (Ahmed and Matthes 2017: 234). In sum, the media participates in a discourse of "Us" *versus* "Them" that contributes to the polarization of communities and societies. If we observe in detail how journalistic language contributes to such a stance, we can perhaps learn how to counter it.

The fact that the event in Nice was qualified as a terrorist attack very early on in the news cycle is important for this study. As Freedman puts it,

> Terrorism has long been described as a 'symbolic act' (Thornton 1964: 73) … Terrorism, therefore, has to be made to mean, and who better to 'interpret' these life-changing events … than storytellers, mythmakers, media people, journalists? Symbol makers have a unique ability to shape the political agenda by organising the discursive frameworks through which the public comes to understand acts of violence. (Freedman 2017: 211)

It is essential to point out here that the terrorism that is "made to mean" in the European press is above all terrorism that happens *in Europe* and other so-called Western countries. Terrorism in other countries gets vastly less press. Take Nigeria: As Freedman (2017) and Owunna (2015) point out, during the same week as the Charlie Hebdo attacks, the terrorist organization Boko Haram killed more than 2,000 people in Borno State. The Charlie Hebdo events "generated more than 50 times more news stories worldwide". Why is this important? Because violent attacks that take place in the West and are reported upon in the West take on huge significance for the Western reading public, whereas the vast majority (some estimations say up to 99.5 percent) of terror attacks actually occur in non-Western countries and the vast majority of the victims of terror around the world are Muslim. Indeed, just five countries—Afghanistan, Iraq, Nigeria, Pakistan, and Syria—experience the majority of terrorist acts and deaths from terrorism. Thus, according to the most recent figures from the Global Terrorism Index (Institute for Economics & Peace 2019), Afghanistan, which "has replaced

Iraq as the country most affected by terrorism," saw a 59 percent increase "in terrorism deaths to 7,379 in 2018," and has seen a 631 percent increase in such deaths since 2008 (2). In stark contrast, Europe and the MENA (Middle East and North Africa) region "recorded the biggest *improvement* in the impact of terrorism, with the number of deaths falling by 70 percent and 65 percent respectively" (2; my emphasis).

The fact that there is no agreed international definition of terrorism—as of 2019, the UN had spent nineteen years working on one, to no avail—means that there is all the more room for interpretation. Price (2017: 166) criticizes the fact that "the working definition of (post-9/11) terrorism, circulated by the public authorities of 'advanced' states, emphasizes certain political characteristics at the expense of other modes of interpretation," a state of affairs which led authorities and the media to avoid labeling the Germanwings crash, for instance, in which a pilot deliberately crashed his aircraft, killing all 149 people aboard, as terrorism: "the Germanwings crash of 2015 was not described as an act of terrorism, because it was not the consequence of belief-driven activities" (168). Perhaps a larger part of the explanation than the author overtly admits, however, is that "the problem lies with the tendency to amplify the cases of anyone who has an apparent affiliation with 'Islamist doctrine'" (167). In the case in question here, however, such affiliation was not unequivocally *apparent*. It was certainly not in the attacker's *background*.[5] But Tunisian-born Mohamed Lahouaiej-Bouhlel, the man responsible for the attack in Nice, was neither white nor European. I aim to demonstrate that some of the tendencies in the linguistic, and in particular, stylistic, choices made by journalists covering the event were influenced by this fact.

Indeed, in the present study, the "Other" constitutes French society, but also Muslims or those perceived as Muslim. Why be so concerned with Muslims and Islam here? After all, I am simply studying an event that was labeled a terrorist attack. It is because my early perusal of the news about the attack suggested that the reporting might be another example of the way that terrorism and Muslims/Islam are constantly conflated in the media (see, for instance, Ahmed and Matthes (2017); Baker, Gabrielatos, and McEnery (2013); Birkenstein, Froula, and Randell (2010); Fiddian-Qasmiyeh and Qasmiyeh (2010); Khiabany and Williamson (2012); Ogan et al. (2014); Piquer Martí (2015); Rane, Ewart, and Martinkus (2014)). According to the *Observatorio de la Islamophobia en los Medios*, the majority of the Spanish Press is Islamophobic.[6] The British media's Islamophobic reporting is being blamed for the recent increase in hate crimes against Muslims (Versi 2016a). While there is little research on Islamophobia in the news of the *Suisse romande*, I wondered whether it would be less present there by virtue of the fact that the regional government and media tend center-left. Indeed, in their study of the intersections between Islamophobia, media coverage, and political ideology in Europe and the United States, Ogan et al. (2014) found that negative attitudes toward Islam and Muslims "strongly and consistently" correlated with "political conservatism" in both regions, while political liberals saw them in a less negative light (40). In her article about the discourse surrounding Islam in French and Spanish news, Bugnot (2012: 988) observes that in multiple Spanish news sources, "the emphasis is … placed on France's significant Muslim population, the largest in Europe." In Chapter 4, we will see that in European news, the emphasis is still present, is often negative, and contributes once again to conflating Islam/Muslims and terrorism; and we will see many examples of how this transpires. These processes are part of media's "othering"; how journalistic style contributes to such "othering," however, has not been sufficiently examined up to now.

Translation Studies and, in particular, news translation and translation criticism provide useful concepts and approaches for exploring the role of stylistic features in the news: news translation, because it conceptualizes both journalist and translator as "cultural mediators"; translation criticism, because it draws extensively on comparative stylistics and involves close textual analysis. Translation Studies have also begun broadening the definition of translation, for example, by considering cultural representation as translation (Maitland, 2017) or incorporating theories of cosmopolitanism (Bielsa, 2016a, 2016b, 2018), irrespective of whether interlingual translation (from one language to another) is involved. Where news analysis is concerned, I find the conception of translation as cultural representation, coupled with empirical analysis of style, to be more compelling than, for example, Baker's (2006) focus on narrative strategies, because stylistic choices are the building blocks of those strategies. Therefore, in the subsequent sections, I defend the chosen approaches and conceptualizations and combine them with media research on "making terrorism mean" (Freedman 2017: 211), including the frequent conflation of terror and Muslims/Islam, to justify stylistic analysis. I also demonstrate that discrepancies between news outlets' guiding principles and journalistic practice prove that such analysis is necessary.

Piquer Martí (2015) enumerates and describes a number of discursive strategies employed by the Spanish written news (they are certainly more widespread): (1) "the tendentious selection of topics" (142); (2) photographs (especially when photos from the archive are employed completely out of context); (3) euphemisms; (4) metaphors; (5) headlines. I would argue that she also implicitly includes two further discursive strategies: (6) the tendentious selection of voices, and (7) neologisms.[7] Such strategies often tend toward evaluation rather than simple recounting:

> The media construct the figure of the immigrant using an evaluative vocabulary, that is, a non-neutral language that has a significant capacity to influence the opinions of readers and to shape their vision of reality. (Crespo Fernández 2008: 48) (148)

Thus evaluations, often conveyed through the choice of connoted over neutral language, are employed in news texts, despite the ostensible goal of most journalists (as attested by most newspapers' guidelines) to be "objective." In addition, the limiting of topics to, and the use of the vocabulary of, violence and conflict when Muslims or Islam are the topic "shapes readers' image" of the Muslim collective (also a tendentious concept) "as a dangerous social group" (Piquer Martí 2015: 142). As we will see, this is one way in which news about Muslims feeds "a discourse of fear" (142). At the same time, "toned down" language, such as euphemism, can also be "indirectly discriminatory" (148). For instance, Piquer Marti discusses an example from *El País* in which a writer who was actually known for being racist and xenophobic was simply described as "critical" (148).

Another contributor to the discourse of fear is the tendentious focus on "jihad" and related terms. Cembrero (2016: 160) observes that both the Qur'an and the concept of jihad which is defined and addressed in it have generated many interpretations and much debate, including among scholars and theologians. For example, for some, there are ten occurrences that are linked with violence; for others, there are just three. Cembrero explains that the term also has a "spiritual meaning," that of improving the self as one follows the path chosen by Allah (2016: 234). For the author Tarek Osman, it means "exerting the soul against one's sins/weaknesses" (personal communication). He is among those who maintain that there are just three instances of jihad in the Qur'an that are linked to violence, but unlike Piquer Martí or the *Guardian* guidelines (see below), he maintains that the distinction between a "major" and "minor" jihad was only made much later by philosophers, and is not really useful.

The easy adoption and simplification of the term by "the West," in most cases without knowing much about Islam or having ever read (a translation of) the Qur'an, are therefore questionable at best. Nevertheless, as Piquer Martí demonstrates with examples from the Spanish press, it uses *ŷihād* frequently without ever explaining what the term means *to a Muslim*. For instance, in a 2013 news article, a *La Razón* journalist discussing a manual drafted by Al-Qaeda "takes the liberty of adding in parentheses, after the words *yihad individual*, his own definition: 'criminal actions undertaken alone." While this may be a "minority group's (Al-Qaeda)" interpretation, it is "radically different from the meaning that the majority of Muslims attribute" to the same term. "The press has transformed the term *jihad* into a synonym of *Islamic terror*" (148; emphasis in the original).

In a similar vein, the press sometimes creates extremely insidious neologisms; Piquer Martí (2015) highlights those of *Londonistán*, used in an *El País* article in 2013 that portrayed London as a "jihadist paradise" (146), and *Eurabia* in *La Razón*, used to convey the supposed threat of a Muslim invasion of Europe. Such choices are all the more insidious for the way they are sometimes combined with images. The *El País* text, biased enough on its own, is accompanied by a photograph devoid of any context, in which a Muslim man appears, praying on a rug on the ground, [supposedly] on a street. Because the image is not contextualized, one can have no idea if this particular man is in London, or if he has been radicalized; nevertheless, the association between Muslims praying, extremism, terrorism, and threats to public safety, is clearly made (146–7). In an article about France in *La Razón*—note the name of the paper, "Reason"—a picture of an armed soldier flanked by an injured man, coupled with the text, effectively conflates in a hugely misleading—one can go so far as to say dishonest—manner, French action in Mali (where the photo was actually taken) with the *internal* effort of expelling radical Imams (the topic of the article) (147). Regarding images, Piquer Martí adds that the ones chosen from the archive often show traits reflecting "physical difference (for example, the Arab style of dress) or scenes of poverty and violence," which only reinforce "existing stereotypes of Islam and Muslims" (146).

Another discursive strategy discussed by Piquer Martí (2015: 151–2) is that of selecting who is heard (and, by extension, who is silenced). The press selects not only what and how, but who. Often, a partial and stereotypical image of "the immigrant" and "the Muslim" is provided; in addition, a voice is most often given to radical Islam rather than to ordinary members of Muslim communities, so that Muslims, whom society already considers "other," come to be seen as not only different, but dangerous. Moreover, in practice, information selection and the choice to give a voice, in the "*Us*" group, only to people and bodies of power, silence the dominated, silence certain social groups, "silence immigrants in general and Arabs, Muslims, in particular" (152). El-Madkouri Maataoui and Taibi (2006: 134) also discuss multiple ways the press effectively silences these groups.

Finally, on the topic of headlines, Piquer Martí provides various examples of glaringly derogatory and sensationalistic ones. She also discusses work by Granados Martínez (2006: 61), who found that "the headlines of Spanish newspapers insist on identifying foreigners and, what's more, quantifying them in terms denoting invasion, occupation, etc." (Piquer Martí 2015: 153). Indeed (and here she cites Granados Martínez directly), when foreigners are "news," they are such because they

> cause disturbances in the neighborhoods where they live and in the places where they gather, both in the eyes of neighbors and in the eyes of local authorities. They are news because experts and political officials consider or predict that presence to be an invasion that Spanish society will have a hard time digesting. (Granados Martínez 2006: 63; qtd. in Piquer Martí 2015: 153–4)

The above has presented means of engaging in cultural (mis)representation. The next section argues that those who re-present other cultures are engaging in translation, even if there is no direct passage from one language to another.

Cultural Representation As/Is Translation

Translation Studies no longer conceives of translation predominantly as interlingual transfer and allows for conceptualizing translation as *the transfer of culture*. The burgeoning sub-discipline of news translation has played an important role in enlarging the definition (Bielsa and Bassnett 2009; Bielsa and Hughes 2009; Conway 2005, 2012, 2015; Davier 2013, 2015, 2017; Schäffner 2012; Schäffner and Bassnett 2010; Valdeón 2007, 2010; Van Doorslaer 2010a, 2010b, 2012), and in tracing the linguistic and cultural influences of cross-cultural communication (see, for example, Brownlie 2010; Conway 2010, 2012; Davier 2013, 2015, 2017; Davier and Conway 2019; Hernández Guerrero 2010; McLaughlin 2011; Muñoz-Calvo and Buesa-Gómez 2010; Valdeón 2007). In her analysis of English-language newspaper reporting on the 2007 French elections, Brownlie (2010: 32) uses "translation" in part to mean "explaining and communicating events from one cultural and political sphere to another." Conway's (2012) study of a Canadian website that presented stories about Muslim women, academics dealing with issues of secularism or immigrant communities, and an advocacy group, published in the series *Derrière le voile* by

Radio-Canada, understands "these stories as acts of *cultural translation*" (1001; emphasis in the original).

Thus, the role of translation in its contemporary, broader sense is to "provid[e] the means for the articulation of cultures and intercultural interchange" (Sousa Ribeiro 2004). What, then, is culture? The *Oxford English Dictionary* online (2017) defines culture as "[t]he distinctive ideas, customs, social behaviour, products, or way of life of a particular nation, society, people, or period. [...]" Culture is what *distinguishes* one group from another. Does this mean that it naturally engages in othering?

Not necessarily. If we, or those who provide us with information, engage in cultural translation, othering can be overcome. Maitland's (2017) "approach to cultural translation is interested in the ethical dilemmas posed when texts, human actions and human productions exercise power over people"; it is valid and valuable, I argue, to think in her terms about the writing of journalists who inform us about cultural "Others." According to Maitland's conception, all of the elements of the world that we encounter and seek to understand are source texts, and anyone who engages with them is a translator. In the situation at hand, this of course includes journalists, *a fortiori* when they are reporting on an event—and therefore, indirectly, also on a population and a society—abroad. According to Maitland, who also draws significantly on Ricœur, "the process of cultural translation starts with a demand to *understand*" in the face of the "realization that others exist and that they construct the world differently." As we struggle—successfully or not—to understand, the process allows us to "start to view the identity of groups, cultures, people and nations not as immutable substances or as fixed structures to be accepted *or* rejected, but instead as 'recounted stories' from which we would receive a sense of 'narrative' identity which is," in fact, "mobile." Accepting the storied nature of identity means "we renounce the idea of a fixed 'truth' and with it the implacability of the ideologies by which we organize our realities." At the same time, the ethical issue at stake is that the translator, in the broader sense of the term, must achieve a delicate balance: "to navigate our anxieties of otherness by making difference accessible while also protecting the 'other' from appropriation." Moreover, translation produces "'representations' of otherness and, as Tymoczko warns, participates in a process in which the self-same representations 'come to function as reality.'" Therefore, translating others comes with risk and responsibility, and can also result in cultural mistranslation.

Maitland also emphasizes the ability of translation to serve as a critique of ideology. This requires that agents of translation be interpreting subjects, that they demonstrate that their view is not the only one, and that they demonstrate why their view better merits belief. In the context of news writing, this would involve, for instance, allowing conflicting interpretations to be presented and digested, for example, through balanced and contextualized reporting. But to be effective, that is, to achieve cultural translation rather than cultural mistranslation, education and critical thinking on the part of both journalists and news readers are required, not least because "[m]apping the unfamiliar other out in terms we already recognise risks simply reproducing what we know while ignoring their specificities – which ... often constitutes an act of (colonial) violence" (Hodgson 2018). In a similar vein, Kapsaskis (2019: 4) points out that the creative appropriation required for cultural translation to occur could turn out to be not only "emancipatory," but a means of achieving "the 'wrong' goals (e.g., racist or oppressive)." "This point is particularly relevant at the current political juncture when a culture war rhetoric is increasingly being used to steer the discussion away from real issues and progressive policies, in many parts of the world" (4), and when certain minorities are being reductively and stereotypically defined as problematic, backward, and dangerous.

The Journalist as Intercultural Mediator

Enter the journalist-as-translator. D'hulst et al. (2014: 1255) place both within the category of cultural mediator, that is, "a person active across linguistic, artistic and geographical borders and as the carrier of cultural transfers." I understand journalists to be intercultural mediators upon whom it is incumbent to "optimize communication between cultures" (Chesterman 1995: 149). However, some would argue that this is more easily said than done. As Valdeón (2009: 149; also quoted in van Doorslaer 2012: 1051) observes, journalistic reporting is "heavily influenced ... by the national narratives of the writers, which permeate the events themselves and offer domestic perspectives of European and world issues." Indeed, articles are necessarily shaped by journalists' backgrounds, experiences, and worldviews, as well as multiple external factors including information sources, time pressures, "the editorial conventions and policies of the media, ... the expectations of the readership" (Valdeón 2018: 7), "real world developments, cultural norms," the political leanings of the newspaper, and "each side's skills at frame promotion" (Canel 2012: 221). At the same time, the media are expected to act as guarantors of "the right to true, just and contextualized information" (Piquer Martí 2015: 138). As we will see, the guidelines set out for journalists convey the same message. Importantly for the present study, this right "also extends to citizens who belong to minority cultures such as, in this case, Muslims" (138).

With the above in mind, cosmopolitanism provides a useful perspective from which to examine foreign news. Defined as openness to the other, the cosmopolitan outlook is constructive and positive, as it both relies upon and fosters engagement with the foreign. Second, and importantly for someone coming from the discipline of Translation Studies, cosmopolitanism is

> the product of a view of translation that implies much more than the linguistic transfer of information from one language to the other, appealing rather to an experience which mobilises our relationship to others as well as our conception of ourselves. Cosmopolitanism, understood in these terms, comes very close to a conception of translation that challenges translation as [linguistic] transfer. It puts in the centre, a view of translation as the experience of the foreign. (Bielsa 2016a: 144–5)

Can we hope for news to become more cosmopolitan?

As we have seen, many studies have found that, instead, journalists often engage in "othering" (Allan, [2010] 2014) and sometimes both rely on and perpetuate prejudices, in particular where foreign countries, Muslims, and Islam are concerned (e.g., Brownlie 2010; Bugnot 2012; Kelly 1997, 1998; Ogan et al. 2014; Piquer Martí 2015; Rane, Ewart, and Martinkus 2014). Investigating journalistic style sheds light on *how* this occurs[8] and it may, in turn, encourage reflection and changes in practice. The work on cultural translation (Maitland 2017) and cosmopolitanism (Bielsa 2016a, 2016b, 2018) discussed above has demonstrated the value of considering media output as a means for readers to engage with the foreign.

As her audience's interlocutor, as a purveyor of cultural knowledge, all the more so when writing about an "other" culture, and as the author of an interpretation of events, the journalist wields a certain power. In deciding who is interviewed or not, who is quoted or not, what information is included or left out, how thoroughly that information is verified, as well as in making linguistic choices which will convey images, connotations, judgments, suggestions, and so on, journalists simultaneously reflect and contribute to shaping cultural debate, public opinion, and even politics and policy. This is not to ignore other agents who wield power (government or media magnates, for example). As Conway (2010: 202) points out, "[w]hile individual journalists might not be responsible for the system of transformations under which they operate, that system and the power relations that shape it do have an influence on the stories they produce."

In addition, "the effects of media power are cumulative, working through the repetition of particular ways of handling causality and agency, particular ways of positioning the reader" (Fairclough 1989: 54), that is, of framing events. It is in part by investigating such strategies and their prevalence that we can better understand the media's influence.

News as Narrative

Terrorism is doubly symbolic: first, because it is perpetrated for political ends and to elicit reactions—in particular, fear (Freedman 2017, p. 211); second, because the word stands in for other ideas and/or becomes inextricably tied to them in various types of discourses. Because it is symbolic, and because there is no clear, internationally agreed legal—not to mention moral—definition of "terrorism" (Kundnani 2017; Warsi [2017] 2018), it "has to be *made to mean*" (Freedman 2017, p. 211; emphasis in the original), and indeed, within the definitional void, uses (or telling instances where the term is avoided) of the term—not to mention consequences—proliferate, whether in everyday discourse, law and its application, the political sphere or, importantly for this study, the media.

Freedman (2017: 211) groups journalists with "storytellers, mythmakers," and other "[s]ymbol makers," observing that they "have a unique ability to shape the political agenda by organising the discursive frameworks through which the public comes to understand acts of violence." Terrorism is thus an event which is interpreted, rather than simply an act or a fact. Muslims and Islam, because they are commonly conflated with terrorism, are therefore also rendered symbolic. I will discuss the notions of event and interpretation further now.

According to Eyerman, individual happenings become events "[t]hrough a dialectic of actions and interpretation. Actions occur in time and space, events unfold" (note the metaphor) and become meaningful "in the interplay between protagonists, interpreters and audience, as … meaning is attributed and various interpretations compete with each other" (Eyerman 2008: 22; also qtd. in Titley 2017: 5). Put otherwise, the process of imbuing a happening with meaning constitutes a "struggle" during which, eventually, "various accounts stabilize, with perhaps one achieving some kind of hegemony, but counter interpretations or stories may continue to exist alongside" (Titley 2017: 5).

The Nice attack was an event in this sense, and also because in the process of meaning-making, it was associated with other terrorist acts. The *Guardian* article that I have labeled TG9 shows this linkage clearly in the first phrase of its headline: "From Charlie Hebdo to Bastille Day." Indeed, the Nice attack is part of an "event chain" that may include, depending upon the journalist, readership and context of publication, the Charlie Hebdo events, but also the Bataclan attacks, the killing of a priest in Normandy, or the actions of Mohammed Merah in 2012, in France; 7/7 (the London bombings of summer 2005), the killing of a British soldier on the streets of London in 2013, the recent Westminster Bridge and Manchester attacks, among others, in the UK; 9/11, for these and many other national contexts.

The journalist, then, does not simply hold up a mirror to a happening to "show" it objectively and transparently, but rather constructs and conveys her interpretation of that happening (which thus becomes an event). She does not provide "the truth," but rather begins or continues a narrative. Importantly for this study, if she reports on an event occurring abroad, her reporting has, as we saw in the discussion of Maitland's (2017) approach to cultural translation above, a particular translational dimension, not only because of the "transediting" (Schäffner 2012; Stetting 1989) activities likely to be implicated in such work, but also because when she narrates or re-presents events taking place abroad, she also re-presents, to some degree, the country, culture, and population in question. While she may not currently be required—nor, many would argue, have the time—to engage in all the aspects of "ethical reflection" Maitland (2017) describes, one might hope that she would; some would argue that the lack of such reflection has contributed to the current, so-called "crisis" in journalism and a prevalent lack of trust in the news.

News texts are frequently discussed and analyzed in terms of framing. However, as the title of this book indicates, I will look instead at stylistic features. Why? Such features are situated at a more micro level than framing, so how significant can they really be? They are generally considered key aspects of literary texts, not pragmatic texts, not least because they are what makes a text an "aesthetic object," in which form is at least as important as content and the "interrelation" of the two is what gives the text meaning (Culler 1997: 33). And yet, to ask how journalistic texts "make terrorism mean" (Freedman 2017: 211) is to ask, as one does for literary texts, "about the contribution of its parts to the effect of the whole" (Culler 1997: 33). Like literary texts, journalistic texts create meaning through the use of evocative language. Journalism studies have sometimes recognized the key form-content relationship in such texts, with Ettema (2012 [2010], 296) even asserting that "the formal features of news, as much as (or more than) its content, are a source of whatever socio-cultural authority that journalism retains."

Similarly to Culler (1997) on literary texts, then, Ettema goes so far as to suggest that the aesthetic/stylistic features of the text are one source of the power the journalist wields. They are also the result of free choice. They are marked; they are remarkable. They have effects upon the interpretations that readers are likely to construct (Hewson 2011). In other words, I will argue, they are a non-negligible aspect of "making terrorism mean" (Freedman 2017: 211). Furthermore, stylistic features of news texts have been under-researched up to now, with a few notable recent exceptions—primarily involving metaphor, but mainly in financial/economic journalistic texts (see, for example, Ravazzolo 2017; Schäffner 2014).

Another key exception, where reporting on Islam and Muslims specifically is concerned, is identified by Piquer Martí (2015: 149–50): the frequent use of two types of metaphor, which also serve to sensationalize: natural disaster metaphor and war metaphor. The first type often involves "waves," and evokes "chaos, the uncontrollable" (149); an example of the second type that the author provides is that of describing the increase in numbers of Muslim residents in cities as a "time bomb" (150), a discursive choice which also claims a relationship of cause and effect between this demographic change, on the one hand, and the risk of a rise in "radicalization" and violence, on the other.

Clearly, there is a "narrative aspect of identity" (Grieves 2012: 15), and in the case of Muslims, journalists have told a predominantly negative story up to now. This is part of the violence of being rendered symbolic. In Chapter 4, we will see how this process plays out in the present corpus.

Terrorism as "Crisis"

Irrespective of the controversy surrounding violent attacks of the past few years, including those that occurred in France in 2015 and 2016, reporting on them qualifies as what is commonly called crisis communication. Indeed, according to Canel (2012) and Canel and Sanders (2010), terrorist attacks can be considered cases of crisis communication, as they involve risk and uncertainty, "an important communication dimension, and … the reputation of organizations" (Canel 2012, p. 215).

I argue for the use of this label while also remaining fully cognizant of Zelizer's (2015) novel and convincing arguments that problematize the very term "crisis." Although she predominantly criticizes the recent trend of talking about the "crisis in journalism," her definitions and her position are also important to think about with respect to reporting on a violent event abroad. Crisis is "[c]haracterized by some combination of perceived suddenness, disruption, urgency, loss, and the need for external assistance in order to offset helplessness and reach recovery" and thus "seems to possess an extended set of attributes" (Zelizer, 2015: 890). It is a point where "a sense of challenge looms so large that it takes over" (888). Uncertainty is a key aspect of the crisis moment, which it is in our nature to try to minimize and combat:

> In Bauman's words (Bauman and Bordoni 2014: 7), when discussing "crisis of whatever nature ... we convey first the feeling of uncertainty, of our ignorance of the direction to which the affairs are about to turn—and secondly the urge to intervene." (Zelizer 2015: 890)

Indeed, although there are various definitions and points of view on what "crisis" encompasses, "at the heart of most perspectives is the aspiration that one can reach its other side" (890).

Nevertheless, what I am concerned with here is a type of crisis *communication*, that is, the journalistic reporting that occurs, urgently, in the context of violent attacks. Whether or not these events and their ongoing nature *should* be termed crises, for the moment, they *are*. Moreover, Zelizer's critique reminds us of the power the press wields in its role as crisis communicator: "Though crisis is a phenomenon with material dimensions—factories close, people die, infrastructures collapse—it is shaped too by discourse: We name it, we flesh out its details with words, we give it identity through comparison and analogy and metaphor" (Zelizer 2015: 892).

Zelizer's analysis also gives insight into how the press may play a better role in crisis communication. One way is by questioning that "extended set of attributes":

> [E]ach of them is easily debatable when probed closely: Is a crisis that ensues following long periods of neglect as sudden as we make it out to be? Why is disruption more deserving of attention than what precedes it? Do environments without the capacity to learn through mistakes or problems escape discussion about crisis? What precisely is so attractive about the promise of a noncrisis moment? These questions, and others, begin to hint at how partial and precarious the idea of crisis may in fact be. (Zelizer 2015: 890)

With regard to terrorism reporting specifically, Philip Seib (2017) highlights related questions that he believes the media is failing to ask as it reports on terrorist attacks:

> [I]t became clear that for all the breathless headlines about IS-inspired terror attacks, many know little about the complexities of terrorism and Islam. Who

are these people who murder so wantonly? Why do they do it? And, most importantly, how might such attacks be stopped?

Journalists can and should ask key questions like Zelizer and Seib's about terror-related events and about how they themselves approach reporting on such events. If they do so, they will be more likely to fulfill their role as cultural mediators. Particularly valuable is the idea that focusing on a violent moment or event may mask the fact that it was not really so sudden and impossible to predict, that previous conditions of "neglect" (890), negligence, excess, or other (societal) trends may have actually set up the current moment. In addition, as Zelizer herself highlights, they need to think carefully about the intricacies of their language, and its likely effects. Finally, while a crisis is often seen as something having gone wrong, as a problem to be solved, Zelizer points out that it can actually be a very productive moment.

"Bringing the Story Home"

Before moving on to the section on journalistic principles and guidelines, I would simply like to highlight one other characteristic of news about violence abroad that is mentioned in the literature and also present in my corpus: the strategy used by many journalists of "bringing the story home" (Cottle [2011] 2012; Freedman 2017), that is, tying it to the experience of the domestic audience so as to make it more relevant for them. As we will see in the results of the corpus analysis, this can have at least two key effects: encouraging a heightened feeling of fear and sense of threat, and portraying the home country as superior (Kelly 1998; Riggs 2019b).

Journalistic Principles and Guidelines

In analyzing the news that journalists produce, it is important to take into account the principles and guidelines that underpin—or are supposed to underpin—their work. McBride and Rosenstiel (2014) present the journalistic principles drafted by The Poynter Institute[9] (United States) in the 1990s and widely accepted as core values, and then propose their new set of principles, which build on the preceding ones to "meld the core values of journalism with the democratic values of the digital era" (2). The original Guiding Principles for Journalists revolved around three key concepts—Truthfulness, Independence, and Minimize Harm—and were organized as follows:

1. Seek truth and report it as fully as possible.

- Inform yourself continuously so you can in turn inform, engage and educate the public in a clear and compelling way on significant issues.
- Be honest, fair and courageous in gathering, reporting and interpreting accurate information.
- Give voice to the voiceless.
- Hold the powerful accountable.

2. Act independently.

- Guard vigorously the essential stewardship role a free press plays in an open society.
- Seek out and disseminate competing perspectives without being unduly influenced by those who would use their power position counter to the public interest.
- Remain free of associations and activities that may compromise your integrity or damage your credibility.
- Recognize that good ethical decisions require individual responsibility enriched by collaborative efforts.

3. Minimize harm.

- Be compassionate for those affected by your actions.
- Treat sources, subjects and colleagues as human beings deserving of respect, not merely as means to your journalistic ends.
- Recognize that gathering and reporting information may cause harm or discomfort, but balance those negatives by choosing alternatives that maximize your goal of truth telling. (McBride and Rosenstiel 2014: 3–4)

The authors go on to present and comment on their revised version. "Where we once argued for independence, we now advocate transparency. Independence is part of that principle" (4). They see this move as a stronger guarantee of principled actions and accountability, another key principle, on the part of journalists. In addition, they re-envision the principle of minimizing harm as one of "engaging community" (5). Thus, minimizing harm goes along with "a promise to act in the interests of informing a community and upholding democracy," as well as "acknowledging that community itself has a substantial ability"—and also a right, as was underscored at the 2019 Conference of the International Association for Media and Communication Research (IAMCR) in Madrid—"to contribute to the conversation." They consider that these values elevate "respect for the community" and, in turn, "guide us toward an ethic of diversity" (5). Importantly for the present study, they also maintain that such values lessen "the temptation to manipulate through fear and sensationalism" (5).

The code of principles of the International Federation of Journalists[10] formulates similar requirements related to accuracy, avoidance of harm, and discrimination:

"3. The journalist shall report only in accordance with facts of which he/she knows the origin."

"5. The journalist shall do the utmost to rectify any published information which is found to be harmfully inaccurate."

"7. The journalist shall be aware of the danger of discrimination being furthered by the media, and shall do the utmost to avoid facilitating such discrimination based on, among other things, race, sex, sexual orientation, language, religion, political or other opinions, and national or social origins." Let us now look at how these principles are reflected in the guidelines of the newspapers in the corpus studied here.

The Guardian

The *Guardian's* Editorial Guidelines[11] reproduce the Press Complaints Commission's (PCC) Code of Practice. This body has been replaced by the Independent Press Standards Organisation (IPSO; see section "'Regulation' of News Outlets" below). The opening summary of the Guidelines immediately addresses concerns related to transparency, albeit in other words: "our most important currency is trust." The Code also states that journalists are responsible for protecting the newspaper's reputation for independence. Among the instructions related to accuracy in the Code are (1) "[t]he Press must take care not to publish inaccurate, misleading or distorted information, including pictures"; and (2) "[t]he Press, whilst free to be partisan, must distinguish clearly between comment, conjecture and fact." In a similar vein, the guidelines stipulate that

> If you are employed as a columnist—with your views openly on display—you may have more latitude than a staff reporter, who would be expected to bring qualities of objectivity to their work. (*The Washington Post's* Code has some sound advice: "Reporters should make every effort to remain in the audience, to stay off the stage, to report the news, not to make the news.")

The *Guardian* quotes a similar, left-leaning news source from another country, the United States, to reinforce its point. Moreover, a paragraph specifically devoted to race states:

> In general, we do not publish someone's race or ethnic background or religion unless that information is pertinent to the story. We do not report the race of criminal suspects unless their ethnic background is part of a description that seeks to identify them or is an important part of the story (for example, if the crime was a hate crime).

Finally, the document stipulates that "[i]t is essential that an agreed code be honoured not only to the letter but in the full spirit." The analysis below will show that this is not always the case in practice. Interestingly, unlike some of the other news sources (see below), the document stipulates that the guidelines do not "form part of a journalist's contract of employment, nor ... of disciplinary, promotional or recruitment procedures." Nevertheless, adherence to the Code is part of the terms of employment.

The *Guardian*'s Style Guide[12] addresses potentially contentious terms. For example, definitions are given for, and distinctions made between, "jihad," "jihadi," and "jihadists." The document indicates that the noun "jihad" is "[u]sed by Muslims to describe three different kinds of struggle: an individual's internal struggle to live out the Muslim faith as well as possible; the struggle to build a good Muslim society; and the struggle to defend Islam, with force if necessary." "Jihadi" is a noun or adjective which journalists should "[o]nly use ... in the most general sense to apply to a Muslim pursuing jihad, in particular the first two kinds of struggle. *If referring to the third struggle, jihadist is preferable*" (my emphasis). The final term is defined as a noun or adjective referring to

> [a] person who believes in jihadism, ie, the fundamentalist pursuit of violent jihads to defend the Islamic faith. It can be used to refer to members of formal organisations, such as Islamic State or al-Qaida, as well as those who are not. For example, *the Charlie Hebdo killers or Woolwich murderers would be referred to as jihadist terrorists*. (my emphasis)

Where available, the guidelines for problematic terms in the style guides or comparable documents of the other newspapers in the corpus are included below.

The Telegraph

Unlike the *Guardian*, the *Telegraph* is officially regulated by IPSO (see section "'Regulation' of News Outlets"). The newspaper provides its journalists with

Editorial and Commercial Guidelines[13] based on that body's Editor's Code and includes a direct link to the full Code on the webpage. The Guidelines underscore the newspaper's "commitment to integrity" as well as "the core journalistic values of accuracy, fairness and fearless reporting in the public interest." On accuracy, the *Telegraph* webpage states, "The Editors' Code of Practice administered by the Independent Press Standards Organisation (IPSO) stipulates that the press must take care not to publish inaccurate, misleading or distorted information." The page also briefly addresses independence, transparency, and "enforcing these guidelines," a process which does not go beyond the internal level. However, the guiding principles do "form an ongoing part of training for all staff." In line with the fact that *Telegraph* content is behind a paywall, the content of the guidelines is, as the title indicates, bound up with commercial and financial situations. For instance, in the section on transparency, the webpage maintains that

> [i]t is perfectly proper for journalists to write content that is paid for commercially, provided that it is clearly marked as such. In undertaking such tasks, journalists should do nothing to compromise their ability to write for our audience objectively, fairly and honestly.

Contrary to the *Guardian*, the *Telegraph*'s style book[14] includes no entry for "jihad" or any derivative.

Le Temps

Information about the editorial guidelines of *Le Temps* states that they constitute an "integral part of the contract that binds the publisher and each journalist at *Le Temps*"[15] (3), and interns must also respect them. The guidelines insist on the need to "distinguish fact from commentary" (4) and written content from advertising content. The document states that *Le Temps* strives to uphold "liberal values," but this seems to be closely connected to economics, as its own wording suggests: it seeks to uphold "the principles of the market economy" (5). That said, among the seven causes it has chosen to uphold are the climate, and an "inclusive economy" (10). Article 4.5 states explicitly that the newspaper respects and defends the French language and will therefore avoid using Anglicisms.

Le Courrier

Here is a rare instance where stipulations about editorial principles are readily available on the homepage of the newspaper's website; in the case of *Le Courrier*, a link to the *charte rédactionnelle* (editorial guidelines) is the first one under the rubric "About Us." According to these guidelines,[16] the newspaper is based on a "humanist vision" which includes defending "the poor and disadvantaged" and "encouraging dialogue among religions and between the religious and non-religious," for example. It also clearly states that it is not always neutral: it takes positions on different issues when this is justified, without being politically partisan. Journalistic independence is paramount, it says; at the same time, it clearly emphasizes that "independence does not mean neutrality." Nor does it mean engaging in "partisan politics," however. The guidelines lay out the details of how the newspaper guarantees neutrality. One key aspect is that the editorial team of the newspaper and the overarching body in charge of it, the nonprofit organization *Nouvelle Association du Courrier* (NAC), are separate, although the former sends delegates to represent it at meetings of the latter. The Association of Readers of *Le Courrier* and some individuals are members of the NAC, demonstrating the importance and weight of public opinion. All members of the NAC must sign the guidelines, and they are appended to *Le Courrier* journalists' contracts.

La Tribune de Genève

No information about ethical principles or style is readily available, and my e-mail and telephone queries were unsuccessful.

El País

In the voluminous style guide (*El País* 2014: 32) of the newspaper, Chapter 1 is entitled "Ethical Principles." Key points in its "Treatment of Information" subsection include: "rumors are not news"; "the journalist provides his/her readers with information that has been verified, and avoids including personal opinions with this information"; "when content has not been sufficiently verified, the writer will avoid expressions such as 'apparently', 'it could be [that]', 'cannot be ruled out', or similar formulations unless supporting data is included." In the vocabulary section, the entry on "jihad" (*yihad*) is as follows: "In Arabic, 'holy war'. Should not be used without explanation of its meaning or if the context does not make its meaning clear" (528). The vocabulary section defines "Muslim" (*musulmán*) as "A person who professes Islam. Is not a synonym of Arab or Moor" (409).

Referring to the 2002 version of the guidelines, Piquer Martí (2015: 146) notes the warning that journalists should be "extremely careful when publishing archive photos ... journalists and editors must make sure that as they are taken out of their original context, any illustrations inserted do not harm the image of the people who appear in them" (146). We saw earlier in this chapter that the newspaper does not always conform to its own recommendations.

Piquer Martí (2015) also underscored the fact that headlines are another significant and powerful discursive strategy, as they grab the reader's attention and help her decide whether to read an article. It is not surprising, then, that the Style Guide "devotes a section to this issue. The first two paragraphs include the following recommendations: 'Headlines are the prime element of information. They serve to attract the attention of the reader and impose their content upon him/her'; and 'Headlines must be unambiguous, concrete, accessible to all readers and devoid of any kind of sensationalism'" (Piquer Martí 2015: 153). However, such headlines as "¡Que le corten la cabeza!" (Off with His Head!) or "La ira del Bin Laden birmano" (The Fury of the Burmese Bin Laden) or "Vuelve el fantasma de Londonistán" (The Spectre of Londonistan Returns), appearing, as Piquer Martí points out, in the self-same newspaper in 2013, certainly do not appear to have followed these instructions.

El Mundo

According to an e-mail response I received from *El Mundo*, no new edition of the style guide has been issued since 1996. In this guide, it is Chapter 8 that addresses professional ethics. The opening paragraph indicates in bold that morality and democracy "are the foundations of journalism" (105). It immediately discusses the origins of this position:

> From 1644, the year *Aeropagitica* by John Milton was published with the subtitle *For the liberty of unlicenc'd printing*, freedom of the press was the constant—albeit often disrespected—slogan of democratic development in England and, later, in the rest of the world. Its enshrining in the First Amendment of the United States Constitution is an as yet unsurpassed legal milestone.While everything that is published [in the press], except that which directly falls under crimes such as calumny, libel or defamation, should be defended according to the principles of freedom of the press, not everything that is published is journalism. This activity is distinctive not only for its freedom, but also because it comes with a civil responsibility. (106)

In addition, the Style Guide cites the Statutes of the Editorial Board and the Federation of Press Associations as effective modes of autoregulation (106; also see sections "'Regulation' of News Outlets" of this chapter and "(Regulatory)

Bodies with Teeth?" of Chapter 6). Journalists and editors have voluntarily signed up to the latter, and this requires them to respect the ethical code set out by the organization, on both a personal and a moral level. In the Style Guide, it is argued that coercive and binding legal limitations are not the answer to regulation as they can easily end up threatening press freedom, not to mention the type and quality of information that the public receives (106). The text also highlights *El Mundo's* policy of publishing "the most critical opinions of the newspaper itself expressed by its readers" (106) and its dedication "to publishing everything that is newsworthy and unquestionably relevant to the public" (110).

Moreover, *El Mundo's* Style Guide includes specific instructions regarding attitudes to minorities. Among its "ideological principles" is the following: "*El Mundo* is particularly sensitive to the rights of minorities" (117). Specifically,

> pejorative statements about ethnicities, religions or specific groups are prohibited, and particular vigilance must be used in cases in which content that is not ostensibly racist would end up proving so in the context, for example, specifying that prisoners are 'gypsies' or 'Moroccan' in cases where the origin of those involved is as irrelevant as if they were from Aragon, blond, or Adventists. (111)

Other foundational principles include "The aim of *El Mundo* is to be a progressive newspaper" (117), and "press independence, objectivity, rigor and the non-manipulation of content are basic objectives of the Editorial Board of *El Mundo* and the fundamental rights of its readers" (118). On terminology, the Guide provides the following definitions. "*Yihad*: In Arabic, 'holy war'. Should be written in italics. Should not be used without explaining its meaning in parentheses" (297); "Muslim: person who professes Islamism. May or may not be Arab" (252).

The above sections show that newspaper principles and guidelines, while they may differ on some points, emphasize accuracy, independence, and avoidance of sensationalism and discrimination; and that the sources do not always follow recommendations. The following section provides some brief indications about how media in the UK, Switzerland, and Spain are regulated.

"Regulation" of News Outlets

The press industry believes strongly that it should be allowed to self-regulate, and democratic governments are typically reluctant to impose reforms or other forms of regulation for fear of being accused of limiting press freedom. This phenomenon was particularly pronounced in Spain in the twentieth century, as the development of the sector followed a history of dictatorship and change of regime, and the country subsequently defended democratic principles fiercely in various sectors. In the area of media regulation and accountability, various categories of media accountability instruments (MAIs) exist, and they have developed enormously over the last two decades in conjunction with the rapid and far-reaching changes that have taken place in the media sector. Two distinctions can be made, between "journalism-internal and journalism-external MAIs on the one hand," and "institutionalised and non-institutionalised MAIs on the other hand" (Eberwein, Fengler, and Karmasin 2019: 6). As the terms indicate, "media actors" may be held to account by "traditional institutions within the journalistic profession" (6) (press councils, ombudspersons, and codes of ethics, for instance) or by external bodies "such as media research" organizations, "NGOs or viewer/user associations" (6). However, Miranda and Camponez (2019) pinpoint the inadequacy of such categories with their critique of the frequently used category of self-regulation, which would appear to echo the "journalism-internal" mode of regulation. Indeed, according to the authors, the functioning of the UK PCC (also see below), often "presented in the literature as a system of journalism self-regulation," shows that the notions of "self-" and "journalism-internal" regulation "can ultimately be applied to describe arrangements that do not include direct intervention or the representation of journalists" (19).

The idea that regulation in the UK qualifies as "journalism-internal" "self-regulation" is faulty for another reason: according to Ramsay and Moore (2019: 85), the press sector in the UK is characterized by "the existence of powerful and coordinated industry representative bodies dominated by proprietorial interests, and a culture of close contact between political parties, governments and newspaper groups." The authors explain that these issues are behind a long history of failures on the part of the industry to improve self-regulation. For instance, when the Calcutt Report of 1990 called for the establishment of a PCC and also set a deadline for its creation, the press industry "disbanded its self-regulator and set up the PCC" (86), but the new organization was accompanied by a funding body "through which the industry exercised extensive powers over the self-regulator" (86–7), and in reality, the new system respected few of the Calcutt recommendations. Most recently, in the aftermath of the Leveson Inquiry, the recommendations were again largely ignored.

That inquiry began because "large sections of the press" (87) were engaging in illegal activity by breaching existing data protection legislation, in particular during the so-called *News of the World* Scandal. When the Information Commissioner sought "a strengthening of legal penalties to disincentivise such behaviour" (87), he was met with staunch resistance not only on the part of the press lobby, but also on the part of the PCC itself (87). As Leveson noted in his scathing critique, the body was not a regulator at all, first and foremost because it was not independent of the powerful players in, and wielding strong influence on, the industry itself (*Leveson Inquiry* 2012: 12). What little was salvaged of Leveson's recommendations in subsequent proposals on regulation was roundly rejected by the five main publishing groups that had taken over negotiations following the Inquiry. They finally created "their own self-regulatory body to replace the Press Complaints Commission," IPSO (Ramsay and Moore 2019: 92). These authors' review of the scheme found that "of the 38 recommendations laid out in the Leveson Report that were directly applicable to the self-regulator, IPSO satisfied just 16" (93; Moore and Ramsay 2013: 26–40). Perhaps most significantly, "IPSO was dependent on the industry at almost every level" (Ramsay and Moore 2019: 93).

Sorsa (2019) provides more details about IPSO's shortcomings. When it was created in 2014, it "was being entirely funded by the Regulatory Funding Company, which is dominated by a handful of national and regional publishers that write the rules which dictate what IPSO may or may not do" (Sorsa 2019: 141). In response to this, the National Union of Journalists "called for greater interaction between the public, editors and journalists in the appointment of the Code Committee" of the organization (141). Nevertheless, IPSO remains profoundly beholden to the industry as its functioning remains highly reliant on big media players. The Muslim Council of Britain (2017) and its Assistant Secretary General, who is also Executive Director of the Centre for Media Monitoring, have pointedly highlighted the inaccuracy of the adjective "independent" in the Organization's name, given the conflicts of interest that exist due to members who are newspaper editors.

Moreover, a review of the organization, labeled "external," was in fact set up by IPSO itself, as it "set the parameters of the review, selected and paid the reviewers, and hosts the report on its website" (Ramsay and Moore 2019: 95). As of December 2017, IPSO had "not launched a single investigation into the industry that it is supposed to regulate," "despite evidence of patterns of reporting by IPSO members that appear to contravene the Standards Code" (95). Nor had it set up, as of 2016, a hotline that journalists could use to report breaches of the standards (Sorsa 2019: 141). In addition, and importantly for this study, "potentially inflammatory coverage of immigrants and Muslims (Sherwood 2017)" has "been flagged by observers" in IPSO members' reporting (Ramsay and Moore 2019: 96), with, again, no investigation. Today, post-Leveson, "regulatory coverage" in the UK "is less comprehensive than it was before Leveson" (96).

Partly in response to this, another UK press regulator, IMPRESS, was established in 2016. As of autumn 2019, it regulated 131 publications, but as Sorsa (2019: 141) explains, "[i]ts members are mainly local publishers and do not currently include publishers of national publications," which suggests that its reach and influence remain limited so far. Nevertheless, it differs from IPSO in four important ways which may extend its influence in the longer term. First,

> it is funded by the Independent Regulation Trust instead of the industry organisations, and is therefore free to set its own rules and a Code of Practice independently from industry intervention. Second, IMPRESS can launch an investigation when a code breach is serious *or* systemic, while breaches of both conditions are required for IPSO to launch an investigation. Third, IMPRESS appointments – from the original appointments panel to the chair, board complaints and code committee – are independent and transparent. … Fourth, IMPRESS offers greater protection for whistleblowers, as it is not under control of the industry it is supposed to oversee. (Barnett 2016) (Sorsa 2019: 141)

As I said, IMPRESS has yet to make its mark. Moreover, as of 2017, "[t]hree legacy print publishers, covering the *Guardian*, the *Independent* and the *Financial Times*, remain outside any external system of self-regulation, and have instead instituted their own internal complaints mechanisms" (Ramsay and Moore 2019: 95). The British press remains extremely powerful and extremely under-regulated. Importantly, as the authors argue, "[t]he vulnerabilities inherent in the industry's regulatory system" also "risk further reputational damage to the principle of self-regulation," as the system fails to adequately uphold the basic principles of independence and accountability (97).

In Switzerland, the media regulation authority introduced "a semi-governmental 'Swiss model'" of regulation in 2008. It focused "on local commercial broadcasters," represented "a form of regulated self-regulation (Wyss and Keel 2009: 115; Wyss 2013: 112)" (Saner and Wyss 2019: 150), and made compulsory the establishment of an "editorial quality management system (EQMS) to obtain public funding" (Saner and Wyss 2019: 150). Saner and Wyss (151) point out that "[i]n such a co-regulatory system, the public authorities accept that the protection of societal values can be left to self-regulatory mechanisms and codes of conduct."

While the above appears to focus on broadcasters alone, Saner and Wyss's study also looked at print media and presents results for this sub-sector. They found that where the development of quality policies is concerned, "the proportion in the print media … decreased significantly" (Saner and Wyss 2019: 155) between 1998 and 2015. In terms of charters that guarantee newspapers' editorial independence, there has also been a decline (155–6). In contrast, when they looked at ethical guidelines, they saw an "enormous and thorough increase in all types of media and in total number" (156). Both in Switzerland and in most democratic countries, "[e]thical standards and guidelines are codified by professional associations, with press councils monitoring compliance and publicly reprimanding violations of the codes of conduct" (156). Not only are such guidelines meant to aid journalists to be as ethical as possible in their professional activities, including by providing clear rules regarding "ethically sensitive decisions," but they also exist to prevent external control (156). The researchers' longitudinal study demonstrates, however, that in order for media organizations to actually reach the point of implementing effective forms of self-regulation, "a critical public debate and regulatory efforts are needed" so that "instruments of self-control" are properly developed and can actually become institutionalized (157). Unfortunately, the authors also observe that "[d]ue to the continuing tense economic situation of the print media, these players, in particular, are experiencing a considerable deterioration in the existence of basic editorial documents" (158). Moreover, print media allow for "institutionalized internal criticism" and agree "fewer performance targets" for journalists than their sector counterparts. Saner and Wyss (158) conclude by advocating "the extension of a government-induced EQMS regulation for newspaper newsrooms, as well as for new journalistic players on the media horizon and online media in general." In addition, as EQMSs have been "proven to promote MAIs," their implementation "may also have a positive effect on (perceived) journalistic quality" (158).

Development of MAIs is one of the consequences of the Leveson Inquiry, as it prompted efforts to find "alternative forms of keeping journalists and media organisations accountable for their actions" (Cheruiyot 2019: 285). Prime among these are "instruments that give a greater role to citizens (Bertrand 2000; Fengler et al. 2014)." Indeed, very recent MAIs include media journalism,[17] which in our case would involve "journalism about journalism," and social media debate and criticism. However, some very recent studies are not particularly optimistic about the effectiveness of MAIs. Many, from scholars to researchers to practitioners, doubt the real impact of MAIs because most of them "lack the direct power to sanction any breaches of established journalistic standards" (6). Effectiveness actually varies from one country or context to another, however, as do the predominant MAIs in place.

With respect to the countries that occupy us here, we have addressed the UK; Switzerland has a national press council, whereas Spain has regional organizations (8) rather than a state regulatory body (Rodríguez-Martínez, Mauri-De los Ríos, and Fedele 2017: 61). This is part of the reason that Spanish press models also vary from region to region (Suárez-Villegas et al. 2017). As was the case for MAIs, the verdict from studies of press councils and their ethical codes (Eberwein, Fengler, and Karmasin 2019: 11–13) is often negative. For the moment, it is clear that "non-state means" of ensuring that the press fulfils its responsibility to the public are favored by the industry, as they can monitor press actions while, it is hoped, also safeguarding media independence and vitality. These days, however, the ability of such instruments to truly protect press freedom and "media plurality is often questioned," including by "media practitioners" themselves (13).

Miranda and Camponez's (2019) focus on mechanisms in which journalists *do* effectively participate provides useful information on the contexts studied here. For instance, the UK has an Ethics Council of the National Union of Journalists (EC/NUJ) whose twelve members are "nominated and elected from among the unionised journalists." In addition,

> only unionised journalists may file complaints about transgressions to the NUJ's code of conduct. The EC/NUJ issues opinions on the conduct of journalists …
> The council's direct sanctions involve the disclosure of decisions and warnings and it may recommend to the union's national council fines, suspension or expulsion of the offenders. (Miranda and Camponez 2019: 21)

They also note that in Spain, Catalonia has played a key role in journalism "self-regulation," establishing the first body in Spain to resemble a press council. While that organization does not solely comprise journalism professionals, the *Comisión de Arbitraje, Quejas y Deontología del Periodismo* (CAQDP), which was set up by the Spanish Press Federation of Journalists Associations in 2004 and became a foundation in 2011, "is composed only of the representatives of journalism organisations" (23). Other Spanish regulatory bodies these authors identify are the Information Council of Catalonia, and the Working Group for Defence and Professional Ethics of the Professional College of Journalists of Catalonia.

With respect to self-regulation and MAIs in the Spanish context, "leading print and broadcast media all have introduced ombudspersons since the mid-1990s, and maintained at least several of them until now" (Eberwein, Fengler, and Karmasin 2019: 9). Social media have also "emerged as an important platform for deliberation about media accountability" there (10). They certainly do not have comparable clout in Switzerland, for example (10). Social media are an example of how citizens play a role in press accountability, and this role is becoming more and more recognized and valued within the industry. Ramon, Mauri, Díaz del Campo, and Rodriguez (2019) recently presented the results of their study on "Spanish journalists' and citizens' perceptions of in-house traditional and innovative instruments" at the 2019 IAMCR conference in Madrid. These researchers insist on the notion of ethics and/as accountability, and consider accountability to be composed of three dimensions: transparency and self-regulation, but also audience participation. Using surveys, interviews, and focus groups in a number of Spanish regions, they looked at Spanish journalists' perceptions of the effectiveness of MAIs used in-house, and at citizens' knowledge of those mechanisms. The Spanish journalists clearly preferred accountability to regulation, but found the existing tools only moderately effective at best. For instance, stylebooks were considered the most effective tools, but with a score of only 5.82 out of 10. Indeed, they are valued but underutilized due to lack of time, a resource which is invaluable to journalists, but also very scarce. Furthermore, the journalists recognized that non-compliance with stylebooks is not penalized, which may explain the perceived lack of effectiveness. In addition, the researchers found differences according to age and experience: older journalists rated stylebooks and ombudspersons higher, while newcomers embraced accountability most and were more likely to find website sections such as corporate information particularly important. From the point of view of citizens, the focus groups highlighted the lack of visibility of MAIs and the need to better promote them. One approach that was suggested was to put the ethical code on the front page of print news or online news websites.

In sum, both groups were well aware that criticism is healthy. Visible, easy contact between journalists and the public is needed, and both groups recognized that this would help journalists do their jobs better. Significantly, the journalists valued reader comments, and letters to the editor in particular. That said, solutions such as chats, digital meetings, or error correction buttons were largely unfamiliar to the two groups. In the light of their findings, the researchers recommended that news outlets revise and update their MAI portfolios.

Miranda and Camponez (2019) note that the Spanish bodies whose practices they studied are better than others at taking public opinion into account. For instance, their statutes stipulate that "public representatives" who sit on the boards "must come from the areas of education, ethics, culture or law" (25; 28). Nevertheless, "sanctioning power" is "mainly of a moral nature" (28). The authors also highlight the recent efforts of Spanish journalists to "reorganise themselves into professional colleges" (32).

Finally, *El País* and *El Mundo* are both part of The Trust Project,[18] whose logo appears on their websites. The Trust Project, as its own website states, is "a consortium of top news companies" that is working to develop transparency standards, called Trust Indicators, to help news consumers "easily access the quality and credibility of journalism." Trust Indicators are defined on the site as "standardized disclosures about a news organization's ethics and other standards for fairness and accuracy, a journalist's background, and the work behind a news story. Leaders from 100 news organizations" were involved in creating them. The two Spanish news sources analyzed here were among "the first to display and test the Trust Indicators."

In sum, different constellations of regulation exist in the different countries in question, including external regulation (although the label often belies the reality), self-regulation, or contribution to regulation by the public. In addition, such regulating sometimes occurs on the regional level, sometimes on the national level. Newer forms include the different types of MAIs recently developed and implemented, in particular in the wake of the Leveson Inquiry, although experts do not always agree on their effectiveness. Finally, the public needs to be made more aware of the different forms of regulation, as this will ensure accountability and foster quality reporting on the part of journalists.

Comparing British, Spanish, and Swiss Societies: Politics, Social Attitudes, Language, and the News

In Chapter 2, we saw that when terrorism and other violent attacks are reported upon by the media and the perpetrators appear to have a connection to Muslims and/or Islam, this potential connection often becomes a major focus of the news. At the same time, the voices of those most affected—or maligned—often go unheard. This can, in turn, affect the way that academics working on the language of the press analyze news texts. Indeed, Ahmed and Matthes (2017: 236) issue an important warning for (Western) scholars who critically examine media discourse: because Muslims are not sufficiently involved in the production of media discourse, "academic discourses," in turn, "run the risk of using pre-constructed media categories when studying Muslims and Islam." In order to counter this tendency, it is important to include, in research, "the range of rapidly shifting social, political and religious contexts" (Ahmed and Matthes 2017: 236) involved. For this reason and because the news articles I analyze come from British, Swiss, and Spanish news sources, I discuss in this chapter the place that terrorism occupies in these countries and explore how related issues such as migration, integration, or religion may shape attitudes in divergent ways in the national and regional contexts in question, due to their particular historical, political, social, and linguistic characteristics. For instance, this chapter will briefly examine Spain's evolution from a "país de emigrantes" [country of emigrants] to a "país receptor de inmigrantes" [country that takes in immigrants] (Piquer Martí 2015: 139) and the resulting shift in societal attitudes toward migrants, including Muslims; the devalorization of a previous policy of multiculturalism by the Conservative government in the UK in favor of "British values," a "hostile environment policy" vis-à-vis migrants, and stringent laws in the name of counterterrorism; the rise of anti-Islam opinions and policies in Switzerland despite the fact that the country has never experienced the types of attacks that have occurred in the past two decades in France, the UK, Spain, or the United States. Degrees of devolution and of linguistic diversity are also explored. Finally, some characteristics of the news landscapes are discussed, although my primary focus is the textual product.

In their introduction to *After Integration: Islam, Conviviality and Contentious Politics in Europe*, Burchardt and Michalowski write: "Islam is mainly an immigrant religion in Europe" (2015: 11). Given how long Muslim communities have been present in some European countries, and the fact that demographics are changing rapidly, it is high time this idea was challenged. In the meantime, though, this widespread attitude has all kinds of ramifications, across Europe but also by country, in terms of where Muslims stand with other members of society; how they are viewed, how they view themselves; what space they can occupy, what rights they have; how they are treated, how they treat others; what roles they play. Among other issues, in examining European societies, Burchardt and Michalowski (2015) point out, one must recognize and try to take into account the complex interplay between secularity (and its varying definitions and roles) and social, political, and economic history. The role of secularity in the functioning of the societies in question will therefore also be addressed here.

Linguistic Issues, including Linguistic Diversity

English is the official language of the UK. However, following the UK's ratification of the European Charter for Regional or Minority Languages in 2001, it now has an impressive number of recognized minority languages, although the way they are treated in practice varies enormously. These languages are Welsh, Scottish Gaelic, Scots, Ulster Scots, Cornish, and Manx (language of the Isle of Man) (Vacca 2013). When the last official census was conducted in England and Wales in 2011, more than 90 percent of respondents said English, the official language of the UK, was their first language (Office for National Statistics 2018). More recently, it has been estimated that more than 95 percent of people in the UK are monolingual English speakers.[1] In 2011, after Welsh, with 562,000 speakers, Polish was the third most spoken language, with 549,000; then Punjabi, with 273,000; Urdu, with 269,000; Bengali, with Sylheti and Chatgaya, 221,000; Gujarati, 213,000; Arabic, 159,000 (Office for National Statistics 2018). These languages do not receive any special recognition. And yet, demographics are changing significantly—at the time of the last census in 2011, 13.4 percent of the residents of England and Wales were non-UK-born, compared to just 4.3 percent in 1951 (Office for National Statistics 2013). In 2018, the figure had risen to 14 percent.[2] In terms of speakers of *recognized* minority languages, Scotland had 1.54 million Scots speakers and 57,602 Gaelic speakers, while 184,898 people in Northern Ireland indicated some knowledge of Irish and just 16,373 spoke Ulster Scots. Only 557 people declared Cornish to be their main language (Office for National Statistics 2018). As of 2015, some 1,800 people claimed to have knowledge of Manx.[3] As of 2013, Wales had "the strongest legislation on minority languages in the UK" (Vacca 2013: 89).

In Switzerland, German, French, Italian, and Romansh are the official languages; Romansh is an official language mainly at the cantonal (see below) level, but also at the federal level when the government communicates with Romansh-speaking citizens (*Encylopaedia Britannica* Online 2019). According to statistics compiled by the Swiss government,[4] as of 2017, 62.6 percent of the Swiss population was German or Swiss German native speakers; 22.9 percent, French native speakers; 8.2 percent, (Swiss) Italian speakers; and 0.5 percent, Romansh speakers. The geographical zone where each language is spoken is generally close to the neighboring countries that speak the same language, Germany, France, and Italy; Romansh is a Rhaetian romance language spoken in parts of southern and eastern Switzerland, and parts of northern Italy. That said, the Swiss, in their tendency to "emphasize difference," reinforced by the country's "rugged topography" (*Encylopaedia Britannica* Online, 2019), as well as the fact that they value regional and even local identity above the national, very often insist on the distinctions between themselves and the populations of these neighboring countries, as well as between themselves and residents of Switzerland's other linguistic regions. At the same time, given the linguistic and cultural characteristics Swiss regions share with the neighboring countries as well as their interest in these countries' national media, Germany, France and Italy naturally also influence the Swiss regions closest to them.

The fourth- and fifth-most-spoken languages in Switzerland are English (5.1 percent) and Portuguese (3.7 percent). Albanian (3.1 percent) and Serbo-Croatian (2.4 percent) follow; their presence is due to the arrival of many migrants and refugees from Bosnia and Herzegovina and from Kosovo during the violence of the 1990s. With Turkish residents, these groups make up a significant portion of Switzerland's Muslim population.

The official language of Spain is Castilian,[5] and 99 percent of Spanish citizens speak it as a first or second language. The Spanish constitution also allows its seventeen *comunidades autónomas* (autonomous communities; see below) to recognize regional languages as "co-official" (*Encylopedia Britannica* Online 2019), and six of the seventeen have done so: Catalonia and the Balearic Islands for Catalan, Valencia for *valenciano*, Galicia for *gallego*, and the Basque Country and some parts of Navarra for *euskera* (Basque). In addition, "[a]lthough not named a co-official language of Asturias, Bable (Asturian) is protected and promoted under the community's statutes, as are local Aragonese dialects in Aragon. ... Aranese, spoken in the Aran Valley, is safeguarded in a provision by the region's government, the autonomy of Catalonia" (*Encylopaedia Britannica* Online 2019). It is in such areas, and particularly in Catalonia, Galicia, and the autonomous cities of Ceuta and Melilla (see below), that Castilian is more often residents' second language. In Catalonia and Galicia, regional and local government bodies and administrations conduct their affairs in the respective regional language.[6] In the Basque Country, the Balearic Islands, and the *Comunitat Valenciana*, the regional language and Castilian are co-official (*Encylopaedia Britannica* Online 2019).

Where a regional language is official or co-official, teaching in that language is enshrined in law, regardless of the fact that the percentages of people across Spain who speak, for instance, Catalan/*valenciano*, *gallego*, or Basque are small (as of 2018, 17 percent, 7 percent, and 2 percent, respectively[7]). In stark contrast, in the autonomous cities of Ceuta and Melilla, Castilian is the one official language and also the language of prestige, whereas 50 percent of Ceuta's inhabitants are of Moroccan origin and 40 percent of Melilla's, of Berber origin. While it was difficult to find current data on the language specificities of these cities, a study of high school students in Ceuta (Antón 2011) found that 18 percent were Castilian-mother-tongue and 67 percent considered Arabic their first language; 27 percent of the latter group said they were more competent in Arabic than in Spanish. Cembrero (2016) maintains that language issues (294) are responsible for the 25.2 percent school dropout rate in Ceuta and Melilla (258).

Political and Legal Issues

In this section, I discuss political and legal aspects of the UK, Switzerland, and Spain which may shape attitudes toward those considered "Others" in the three countries. Just as we saw in the section on linguistic characteristics above, this necessitates some discussion of levels of regional diversity, and attention to the complexities of the Swiss cantons and of the *comunidades autónomas* in particular. That said, it is beyond the scope of this text to go into detail about levels of devolution in the UK and the countries that comprise it.

Politics, Law, and Religion

As indicated above, and given one of the issues inherent in this study—Muslims as "Others" in the media and in society—it is important to look at the interplay between politics, laws and regulations, and religion. One key component, then, is the relationship between church and state. Bassets (2017) distinguishes between *laicidad*, a position that "defends the separation between religion and the state," and *laicisimo*, a position that "actively aims to exclude religion from public spaces."

The policies of European democracies generally tend toward *laicidad* (secularity); in some cases, this has been true for over a century. More recently, in conjunction with a hardening of opinion against Muslims, they are also tending toward *laicismo* (secularism), which has manifested itself in controversies, bans, or proposed bans of headscarves in schools or state institutions and administrations, or efforts to ban the burka in all public spaces, for instance. However, according to Cembrero (2016: 385–6), "secularism [*laicisimo*] is starting to be questioned in some European countries that practice it ... In her academic articles, Zoila Combalía, Professor of Ecclesiastical Law at the University of Zaragoza, warns of the 'dangers of a repressive secularity [*laicidad represiva*] that could hinder the integration of Islam in European societies.'" In addition, for this reason, "she is 'surprised' that some propose for Spain a form of secularity [*laicidad*] inspired by the French model, when France itself is abandoning it because it doesn't work'" (Cembrero 2016: 385–6).

Despite the European tendency toward secularity (at least ostensibly; we will see that the claim of such a policy often belies a different reality), there is a parallel countercurrent which, in strong contrast, emphasizes and even instrumentalizes religion. According to a professor of sociology at the Universidad Complutense de Madrid quoted in *El País*, "[t]here is a far right in Europe which, even though it is not religious, uses the Christian identity to ... counter the appeal of emigration and globalization" (Abad Liñan 2018). The journalist adds that "these Catholic, Protestant or Orthodox ultras, who stand for a 'pro-Western and extremely xenophobic' idea of Europe, present religion as a key aspect of identity to fulfil an aim that is not religious but rather 'political and cultural'" (Abad Liñan 2018). Given, among other factors, European populations' distrust of Muslims and fears about rising immigration, parties that rely on this kind of discourse are making gains across the region. One example is the *ultramontano* or radically conservative VOX in Spain. While in 2016, Cembrero characterized the far-right party as marginal, its status is changing rapidly: it recently won seats in Spain—specifically, twelve seats in the parliament of Andalusia in the December 2, 2018 regional elections—for the first time in forty years. In addition, in the national elections of April 28, 2019, it won twenty-four seats in Spain's Congress of Deputies (*Congreso de los Diputados*, lower house of parliament), where previously it had none. Moreover, a recent survey confirms that VOX is the fastest-growing political party in Spain, and some believe that the ongoing "Catalan conflict" will strengthen it further (Llaneras 2019).

The fact that the UK is made up of four countries and its legal system, of three main sub-systems, means that religion is managed in various ways. That said, the constituent countries have been dominated by various forms of Christianity for some thousand years, and the Church of England remains England's official state church. Weller and Cheruvallil-Contractor (2015) point out that because the legal system of the UK is based on common law and has no constitution, there is significant room for "adaptability" (or inconsistency) "in matters … concerning the relationships between religion, state and society" (312). Non-negligible examples of this, as Fiddian-Qasmiyeh and Qasmiyeh (2010: 296–7) illustrate, include the misleading and inconsistent labels applied by the Home Office to indicate the origins of asylum-seekers and refugees, suggesting both a major focus on and a major misunderstanding of ethnicity and geopolitical identity—not to mention actual geographical provenance—of certain groups arriving in the UK. In defining the migrant "Other," the Home Office engages in generalization, labeling, and *mis*labeling. In stark contrast, from the inside, in this case the points of view of interviewees who were asylum-seekers or refugees, "multiple re/presentations of religious identification" emerge which "reflect not only the heterogeneity of the category 'Muslim', but also the multiple ways in which people define themselves and present themselves to others" (302). Ambivalence about one's own identity can also arise as one's understanding of it evolves, a process which is necessarily affected by life in the host context (302–3):

> [T]ransformations in religious practice and identification may be instigated by the political and social environment in which individuals are currently located, with their real or imagined visibility leading to their hiding or modifying their approaches to Islam. Indeed, while individual descriptions of religiosity and practice may of course reflect personal feelings and preferences, they may in addition be determined … to a large extent by the national and international realities framing the topic under consideration. (303)

Another significant contrast, then, is revealed here: self-representations by Muslim asylum-seekers and refugees are often not only personal, but fluid, malleable, aware of, and sensitive to change; other representations are often not only general but rigid, static, unaware, and misinformed, not just in terms of geography, but also, in the case of the UK, in the separation between (more established) Asian Muslims[8] (even if this label, too, is a generalization) and newly arrived Middle-Eastern Muslims (304).

The Rushdie affair[9] was a "watershed" moment (Weller and Cheruvallil-Contractor 2015: 313) in the history of Muslims' relations with British society, and for their public status within European societies more generally. Legal decisions made in relation to blasphemy in the wake of the controversy surrounding publication of *The Satanic Verses* convinced many Muslims "that legal protection from blasphemous libel extended only to Christian sensibilities," thereby "underlining the perception among Muslims of a deeply rooted religious disadvantage and discrimination" (313). Subsequently, Muslims provided the major impetus for UK-wide laws against religious discrimination, the first accomplishments being to extend anti-blasphemy laws beyond the Church of England and to revisit hate speech legislation. At the same time, however, the episode cemented for various European governments the idea that Islam is fundamentally incompatible with their societies. In addition, in the UK, despite the establishment of the Racial and Religious Hatred Act in 2006, the constellation of legal changes that occurred around that time, including the abolition of existing blasphemy laws in 2008, actually kept the focus on racial or ethnic, rather than religious, issues: "discriminatory bias was created against religious (as opposed to racial or ethnic) groups, and at the disadvantage of Muslims in particular" (Maussen 2015: 98).

Is the UK a secular nation? On the one hand, if secularity means a population that does not believe in God or engage in any religious practices, the fact that in the last decades more and more people have claimed lack of belief and church attendance has plummeted suggests the country is becoming more and more secular. On the other hand, if secularity means absence of religion from state institutions, the label clearly does not fit. Take just one example—the significant role the Church plays in Parliament:

> The UK Parliament automatically awards 26 seats in the House of Lords to bishops of the Church of England. These bishops are able to (and do) vote on legislation, make interventions, and lead prayers at the start of each day's business.[10]

The same source observes that the only other country "to award clerics of the established religion votes in [its] legislature" is the Islamic Republic of Iran.

Another interesting issue is that of religious education in the UK. Offering it is mandatory in all state-funded schools. The Church of England supports this requirement, including where Islam is concerned, because it deems religious literacy to be important. Just how the content is to be delivered, however, remains woefully undefined. Furthermore, *attending* is not mandatory; and in the past couple of years, parents across the UK have been rebelling against the possibility of their children learning about Islam, pulling them out of school—they have the legal right to do so under a 1998 law—or refusing to let them go on field trips that involve visiting a mosque, for instance.

Finally, it is worth noting that in contrast to Muslim populations in Switzerland and Spain, Muslims in the UK have played an important role in achieving law and policy changes, community building, and educational endeavors. This may be in part attributable to such factors as mastery of the national language and stable, long-term status in the UK, particularly of the large and well-established Muslim population of Indo-Pakistani origin. Muslims became more politically active as of about the 1990s, "especially through the Labour Party,[11] leading to the election of a significant number of Muslim elected local councilors (see Purdam 2000, 2001)" (Weller and Cheruvallil-Contractor 2015: 317). Moreover, as of the late 1980s, Muslim media organizations were created (i.e., *Muslim News*, *Q-News*, and the *Islam Channel*, a TV station, in 1989). "Such media have provided an alternative image of Muslims and Islam in comparison with the predominantly negative one found in the mainstream national media" (317).

Switzerland is made up of twenty-six cantons and some 3,000 *communes* (municipalities). The legal, political, and social landscape of Switzerland is complex in part because these cantons have a lot of autonomy. Each has its own constitution, parliament, government, and courts. Any powers that have not been expressly attributed to the Confederation are the remit of the cantons; these include health, education, and policing. Moreover, it is the *commune* that grants citizenship, which in part explains why Swiss identity is much more closely tied to this substructure than to the Confederation.

One area of policy that different cantons may manage in very different ways is that of religion. The Confederation states that it guarantees freedom of religion and equality before the law and that, as long as the cantons respect this principle, they may manage religious matters and the relationship between church and state as they see fit, including deciding which religious entities receive state support. One example of religious matters that cantons regulate in different ways is that of levying a church tax. For instance, payment of the tax is theoretically obligatory for all church members, but it is actually voluntary in the cantons of Geneva and Neuchâtel, the two cantons that have most clearly separated state from church; and businesses must pay it in twenty-one of the twenty-six cantons

(Geneva is not one of them). That said, it is important to be aware that the only boxes the taxpayer can check that will lead to payment of the tax are Christian Catholic, Roman Catholic, and Protestant/Reformed. Thus, cantonal taxation policies in the area of religion show a clear bias that disadvantages people and entities associated with minority religions, including Islam. There has also been extensive debate, just like in other European countries, around the questions of religious education for Muslims or the viability of allowing headscarves in schools, whether to allow halal meat (the mode of killing required is considered cruel to animals), and the establishment of Muslim cemeteries (which the cantons of Neuchâtel, Zurich, Geneva, Basel, and Berne have made possible by changing their laws) (D'Amato 2015: 291–3). In terms of wearing visible signs of the Muslim religion, Gianni, Giugni, and Michel (2015) and Cembrero (2016: 96) all highlight the fact that the Swiss canton of Ticino was the first European region to ban the full Islamic veil in all public places.

The anti-minaret ban of 2009 (also see section "Social Issues, including Religion and Attitudes to Religious Minorities"), which received 57.5 percent of the vote, is a particularly well-known example of the Swiss public's reaction to the presence of Muslims and Islam in the country:

> In 2009 the passage of a referendum to outlaw the construction of minarets (towers that feature in the design of many mosques) highlighted widespread misgivings about the presence of Muslims in Switzerland. The minaret ban had been promoted by the conservative Swiss People's Party. (*Britannica Academic Online*, 2019)

The Swiss People's Party's campaign included posters featuring a Swiss flag from which many minarets—really resembling swords or knives, and therefore very menacing—protrude, with a figure in the foreground wearing a black burka, the word "Stop!," also in black, and the exhortation to vote "yes" on the minaret ban. Moreover, "the local Catholic and the local Protestant Church" both "publicly supported local protests against the building of minarets" (Michalowski and Burchardt 2015: 120). The contrast between the acceptance of Muslim cemeteries (required for religious reasons) in some cantons and the ban is a single but telling example of the lack of "a unitary approach to Muslims in Switzerland" (D'Amato 2015: 299)." Indeed, "[r]elations—between cantons and religions, between Muslim and non-Muslim communities—are fragmented according to the opportunity structures provided by the institutional and political settings of the different cantons" (299). On the issue of minarets, given the region and press in question in this study, it is important to note that of the four sole cantons that voted against the ban, three were in the *Suisse romande*: Geneva (by almost 60 percent), Vaud, and Neuchâtel.

As we have already seen, Spain is made up of seventeen autonomous communities. It is important to realize that these regional autonomies took different paths to becoming so. The constitution of 1978 which accompanied Spain's transition from dictatorship under Franco to constitutional monarchy allowed for autonomous communities of two different types, "each of which has a different route to recognition and a different level of power and responsibility" (*Encyclopaedia Britannica* Online 2019):

> The three regions that had voted for a statute of autonomy in the past—Catalonia, the Basque provinces, and Galicia—were designated "historic nationalities" and permitted to attain autonomy through a rapid and simplified process. Catalonia and the Basque Country had their statutes approved in December 1979 and Galicia in April 1981. The other regions were required to take a slower route, although Andalusia was designated as an exception to this general rule. It was not a "historic nationality," but there was much evidence, including mass demonstrations, of significant popular support for autonomy. As a result, a special, quicker process was created for it.
>
> By May 1983 the entire country had been divided into 17 *comunidades autónomas*.

In 1995 the two autonomous cities of Ceuta and Melilla, both geographically part of Morocco on the North African coast, were added. Catalonia was given the status of nation in 2006 under Zapatero's socialist government, but Spain's Constitutional Court has since ruled that this term has only historical and cultural import and carries no legal weight.

What of the relationship between church and state in Spain? Comparing and contrasting France and Spain, Bugnot (2012: 982) observes that the notion of *laïcité* in Spain is "relatively recent and constantly developing." In addition, the country's "non-confessional" nature, enshrined in the Constitution of 1978, "has to cohabitate with a powerful Catholic hierarchy" that "controls a prestigious primary and secondary school network that extends across the country." As we will see below, this "cohabitation," coupled with the country's long history of strict Catholicism, actually goes some way to undermining Spain's supposed "non-confessional nature."

That said, Spain's shift away from the despotic and rigid aspects of Franco's totalitarian regime and its later adoption of the multicultural model of integration, in particular in the last two decades of the twentieth century, fostered a certain openness, including to other religions. An important step took place in July

1989, when "the Advisory Commission for Religious Freedom unanimously approved the recognition of Islam as a firmly established religion [*religión de notorio arraigo*] in Spain" (Cembrero 2016: 206). There followed the creation of the Islamic Commission of Spain (CIE) and the signing of the Cooperation Agreement between this body and the Spanish state in 1992.

Spain's *official* recognition of Islam "is probably unique in Europe" (Astor 2015: 259). Nevertheless, the benefits have largely remained on paper only, as Cembrero (2016) amply demonstrates. He presents a long list of issues and inconsistencies, including, to give just three examples, the availability of public funding for Christian, but not Muslim, peregrination; the fact that the shirts of soldiers' (including the significant number of Muslim soldiers) uniforms have a cross on them (355–6); as is the case in Switzerland, the possibility for citizens to attribute a portion of their tax to the Church, but not to other religious organizations (381). The numerous examples Cembrero cites highlight "the inconsistency of the State, given that Article 16 of its Constitution states that 'there shall be no national religion'" (356). (While Cembrero (2016) holds up France as the model for genuine secularity, as—he believes—its 1905 law established a clear separation of church and state, France's recent politics, too, nevertheless demonstrate that such laws remain insufficient when the Judeo-Christian tradition remains the exclusive—and exclusionary—religious yardstick used by members of society, including politicians.) Furthermore, Astor recognizes "a general disinterest among public officials in taking concrete steps to accommodate the ordinary needs of Muslim communities, especially when doing so comes with political risk" (2015: 262). The author points out that Muslims "have had great difficulty establishing mosques, obtaining land for Muslim burial grounds, arranging for Islamic religious instruction in schools, and attaining other measures of accommodation" (262), despite allowances set out in the Agreement.

According to Cembrero (2016: 376), if the measures of the Agreement have only been partially rolled out, this is also in part "due to the divisions and apathy among Muslims themselves." Apparently (203) the infighting of the two leaders of the previous rival associations that make up the CIE has actually impeded the enforcement or securing of recognition of the rights that are guaranteed under the Agreement. The author also maintains that Muslims—presented, unfortunately, as a monolith—remain in a mindset where they relate to Spain as Muslim foreigners, not as Muslims of Spain. This is a generalization; to the extent to which it applies, it may have a lot more to do with how society defines and treats them than with how they see themselves (see, for example, Barbero 2016).

It may also have to do with the fact that the governance[12] of Islam in Spain is decentralized. Catalonia is the major exception and is working to institutionalize it "and religious diversity more generally" (Astor 2015: 258). This is all the more significant as the autonomous region is home to the largest Muslim population in Spain. For its initiatives, Barcelona's Office of Religious Affairs (OAR) "has drawn heavily on examples from British, American, and French cities," not only because they have "longer traditions of regulating religious diversity," but also for linguistic reasons: OAR employees "have greater fluency in English and French than in other European languages" (259). The *Generalitat*'s Directorate General of Religious Affairs (DGAR) operates at the regional level (259). Moreover, Cembrero (2016: 117) attributes to Catalonia a vested interest in attracting immigrants—as well as encouraging them to learn Catalan directly, rather than Castilian—the idea being that they would then support the separatist movement. But one has to question the influence of Cembrero's own ideology in making this assertion, as the separatist movement is an incredibly polarized, divisive, and emotional issue for Spaniards. I do wonder whether the volatile question of Catalan independence gets bound up with generalizations about the greater concentration of Muslims there and (extremist) violence. The question warrants further research.

Despite the efforts of local and regional organizations such as the OAR, "social tensions surrounding Islam's presence in the region have persisted" (Astor 2015: 259). Barbero (2016) also provides useful insights about how the legal framework in Spain addresses immigration and Muslim immigrants in particular, and how regulation of citizenship contributes to "othering" the Muslim community. For him, Spain's approach is part of a larger strategy of "orientalization" of this group by government, politicians, and the media, which in turn legitimizes the "securitization of immigration," and relies on the construction of an image of the "immigrant as criminal" and of the "Muslim immigrant as terrorist." According to Barbero, such attitudes are longstanding, as Muslim otherness is a historical matter for Spaniards[13] (363) and closely tied to the construction of the "Spanish identity."

Politics, Law, and Terrorism

Given the focus on terrorism of the news articles in my corpus, it is important to look at how the issue is addressed in the countries in question. In the UK, Section I of the Terrorism Act of 2000 defines terrorism as "the use or threat of action" "to influence the government or an international government organisation or to intimidate the public or a section of the public", or to advance "a political, religious or ideological cause." The action is terrorist in nature if it "involves serious violence against a person" or "serious damage to property," "endangers a person's life, other than that of the person committing the action," "creates a serious risk to the health or safety of the public or a section of the public," or "is designed seriously to interfere with or seriously to disrupt an electronic system".[14]

Over the last two decades and in particular since 9/11, a complex web of anti-terrorism laws and measures, too extensive to be presented in detail here, has been progressively introduced in the UK and progressively fine-tuned as new violent events have occurred. What can be said is that these policies are widely considered to be increasingly restrictive of civil liberties, increasingly invasive in terms of citizens' privacy, and increasingly likely to result in racial profiling—which means they disproportionately affect people of color, Muslims, and people believed to be Muslim. One of the prime targets of criticism currently is the Prevent strategy, so I will discuss it briefly here.

Prevent is one of four so-called strands of the UK's official counterterrorism strategy CONTEST (along with Pursue, Protect, and Prepare), and the most vehemently criticized. A minor aspect of the larger strategy introduced under New Labour (Blair) in 2003, Prevent has since been reinforced, including after the London terror attacks of July 2005 and after the killing of Lee Rigby in 2013. The official aim of this strand is "to stop people becoming terrorists or supporting terrorism." A worthy goal, as was the "first pillar" of Prevent: "to tackle disadvantage, inequalities and discrimination" (Warsi [2017] 2018: 87). Other pillars aimed to foster "civic challenge and debate" (88) and to challenge extremist ideologies. Again, worthy goals. However, two main problems developed. The first is related to the vocabulary of extremism: "'radicalization' became the new buzzword for the discussion of all things that led up to the actual violent act of terrorism"; it was defined as "the process someone goes through in becoming a terrorist," not as "a reason or a root cause" (89), and as a result, reasons and root causes could be more easily ignored (89). Moreover, the government defined extremism as "[v]ocal or active opposition to fundamental British values, including democracy, the rule of law, individual liberty and mutual respect and tolerance of different faiths and beliefs" (95). The argument that developed was that all Islamists—itself a misused term, as it simply refers to "Muslims with political goals" (93)—are extremists, and that their values are diametrically opposed to "British values."

The second problem is that in 2015, it became compulsory for schools, universities, National Health Service (NHS) employees, and local authorities to essentially police their respective environments, as they were made responsible for identifying signs of extremism and reporting them. This has eroded trust within various institutions, including by challenging fundamental relationships such as those between teachers and students or doctors and patients; made easier and more legitimate the profiling and stigmatization of certain groups; and threatened the "robust debate" (105) and free speech that are part of the *raison d'être* of institutions of higher education. As we can see, the climate this creates actually works roundly against the original principles of the Prevent strategy.

Switzerland does not have a specific law pertaining to terrorism; it qualifies as a criminal act. For Jean-Paul Rouiller, head of the Terrorism Joint Analysis Group at the Geneva Centre for Security Policy and a former analyst for the Swiss intelligence services, Switzerland "has not integrated [into its law] the close relationship between intention and action. Legally speaking, both should be punished" (Misson 2014). However, according to another expert quoted in the same article,

1. a crime is punished once it is committed, and
2. incorporating the notion of intent would make the law more difficult to apply and also potentially lead to abuses.

As of 2014,

> [t]he penal code punishes preparatory acts in certain cases; they must be at a relatively advanced stage. They do not constitute a crime unless they correspond to one of the infractions listed in the Penal Code. "In a case where a [would-be] perpetrator of a terrorist act changed his mind, it would be important to determine the extent to which his acts were premeditated." [Nesa Zimmerman, Phd student in law at the University of Geneva.] Otherwise, according to the law, he would be exonerated if he decided not to go through with the act (art. 260a of the Penal Code). (Misson 2014)

Article 573 of the most recent version of Spain's penal code defines terrorism as "any serious crime against life or physical integrity, freedom, moral integrity, sexual freedom and indemnity, property, natural resources, the environment, public health" or "the Crown," "involving catastrophic risk, fire, falsifying documents," amassing or trafficking arms, with the aim of "subverting the constitutional order, ending or gravely destabilizing the functioning of the political, economic or social institutions of the State," forcing state institutions to engage in certain actions or to "abstain from doing so," "gravely altering the public peace, gravely destabilizing the functioning of an international organization," or "provoking a state of terror within the population or a part of the population."[15] Both the variety of types of acts labeled terrorism and the level of detail may well be tied to Spain's history of organized violence. While Catalonia and the Basque Country were the first autonomous communities to receive the status, their histories have been marked by strong militant activity, including violence widely considered to be terrorism, on the part of the Basque separatist group ETA and, on the part of Catalonia, the volatile and hugely controversial movement for independence, which turned particularly violent in autumn 2019. "[T]he militant Basque nationalist movement … has sought total independence and used terrorism as its principal method. As a result, domestic terrorism is a major concern of the Spanish police" (*Encyclopaedia Britannica* Online 2019).

In 2012, still a time of economic upheaval following the 2008 financial crisis, separatists made great strides in elections in both regions; given the significant Muslim population in Catalonia, I will give this region more attention here. In addition to economic factors, Catalonian separatists were also spurred on by the reversal in 2010 by Spain's Constitutional Court of a number of measures agreed in 2006 that had given the region greater autonomy. *Independentistas* began to act on their promise to gain independence by holding a referendum in November 2014, despite the fact that secession is illegal under the constitution of 1978. Support was very high, but voter turnout was not. "[E]xactly one year later the regional parliament narrowly approved a measure to implement a 'peaceful disconnection from the Spanish state.' Rajoy responded to the move by making an immediate appeal to the Spanish Constitutional Court" (*Encyclopaedia Britannica* Online 2019).

Following the Brexit referendum in the UK, Catalonia's independence movement gained ground, with polls showing majority support in Catalonia for the first time in 2016. In the end,

> Rajoy's government was unable to contain the Catalonian drive for independence, and a new referendum was held on October 1, 2017. Spanish police confiscated ballot papers and engaged in violent clashes with voters, leaving hundreds injured. Although widespread irregularities marred the polling, the Catalan parliament interpreted the result as a mandate to declare independence from Spain, and it voted to do so on October 27. Within minutes of the declaration, Rajoy invoked Article 155 of the Spanish constitution, stripping the Catalan parliament of power and imposing direct rule from Madrid. (*Encyclopaedia Britannica* Online, 2019)

Madrid dissolved the regional parliament and held snap elections. Rajoy's move was popular with the Spanish electorate,[16] which hints at the deep and bitter divisions that continue to exist in Spain between unionists and separatists.

How does militant or terrorist activity relate to perceptions of Muslims in Spain? Scholars differ on the extent to which the terrorist attacks in Madrid in March 2004 (called 11-M in Spain) hardened public opinion against Muslims. According to Astor, the attacks fueled "public anxieties regarding Spain's growing Muslim population" (2015: 256). Cembrero (2016) does not frame it this way at all, however. He claims the event "hardly provoked any xenophobic reactions against the Muslim population, not even against those who had the same nationality—Moroccan—as the material perpetrators of 11-M" (81). The period even saw more Spanish tourists visiting Morocco (82). "While it may seem paradoxical," he goes on, in Spain, "there was more aversion to Muslims following the two series of attacks that spilled so much blood in Paris, in January and November 2015, than after 11-M" (83). It is perhaps not really paradoxical, though, as a lot had changed in between the two events (see section "Social Issues, including Religion and Attitudes to Religious Minorities"). In addition, the section of Cembrero's own text that directly follows these observations explains that Catholic priests in Spain attributed blame to all Muslims after the France events (84) and evokes a security force memorandum targeting people who looked North African (84). The author also observes (146–7) that around the time of the Paris attacks, both the minister of the interior at the time and the conservative newspaper *La Razón* equated *independentismo* with terrorism and crime. Catalonia is another paradox: while pro-independence people have allegedly worked to attract Moroccans there, the discourse of the right is particularly harsh toward them (122).

Regarding José Luis Rodríguez Zapatero and the post-11-M period, Astor (2015: 257) observes that Zapatero's socialist government, which came to power immediately after the attack, naturally worked on bolstering national security; in addition, the integration of Muslims returned to the administration's agenda after having been ignored by José Maria Aznar's conservative government. For example, a new Foundation for Pluralism and Coexistence provided significant funding to religious minority associations and federations (257), as well as developing "initiatives aimed at promoting public awareness and toleration [*sic*] of religious diversity, improving data on the presence of religious minorities, and facilitating access to resources" for those "involved in religious governance" (257). Today, however, support of this Foundation is far from unanimous, including among Muslim leaders. It is even seen by some as a tool for "controlling and domesticating Islam" (257).

Finally, in the wake of the "Charlie Hebdo" events, the Rajoy government tried to put into place something akin to the UK Prevent[17] program, *id est* "mobilizing all public administrations as well as civil society to detect" and report "suspicious behavior before it results in acts of terrorism" (Cembrero, 2016: 169). After the Bataclan attack, the Interior Ministry launched *Stop Radicalismos*, part of a larger initiative launched at the beginning of 2015 "that goes significantly further than the measures in place in other European countries." It "consists of encouraging citizens to signal via email, a specific website, a free telephone number or a mobile application (Alertcops), signs of radicalization or the disappearances of individuals who may have gone to conflict zones" (172). The contact information for *Stop Radicalismos* is provided in a number of the Spanish articles in my corpus.

Even though the government's plan hasn't been comprehensively put into practice, because it is modelled on the counterterror initiatives of other European countries, certain measures can be quite invasive. It follows that criticism of it is similar to that leveled at, for instance, Prevent (Cembrero 2016: 169). First of all, needless to say, "Muslim officials are angry about the plan," as Muslims weren't included in its elaboration and are already more than sufficiently stigmatized (170). In addition, there are certain risks. For instance, Cembrero maintains that among Muslims—but why not others?—"people could be tempted to refer someone to Stop Radicalismos out of vengeance or spite" (173). This is all the more likely as "informers" can remain anonymous (unlike in France, for instance, where citizens have to provide their contact information). Furthermore, the measures "are reminiscent of the anonymous denunciations" made between 1936 and 1945 "of teachers and professors accused of opposing the new regime of Franco" (173). Nevertheless, despite these risks and the concerns of the Muslim community, there was generally little criticism of the plan when it was implemented, perhaps because anxiety had risen, along with the terror alert level (4 out of 5), according to a Pew survey in June 2015 (173).

Social Issues, including Religion and Attitudes to Religious Minorities

This section will be particularly concerned with attitudes to minorities and the extent to which minorities, and in particular Muslims, benefit from cultural and religious rights (Burchardt and Michalowski 2015), an issue which is closely tied to the model of integration that predominates in each country in question. Burchardt and Michalowski (2015: 9) maintain that "in general, rights related to

Islam have actually expanded significantly in most Western European countries over the past two decades." As we will see from more detailed analysis below, this is definitely a generalization; it also masks the fact that there is a long way to go before various European democracies actually offer the degree of equality they claim to support.

Graphs presented by Michalowski and Burchardt (2015: 108–9) indicate that between 2002 and 2008, the ten European countries studied in the *Indices of Citizenship Rights for Immigrants* (ICRI) project became more restrictive on cultural rights for immigrants,[18] but especially the UK, the Netherlands, and France, with the Swiss shift fairly pronounced as well (despite very different migrant, and Muslim, populations, very different histories of terrorism, and so on). Spain only became slightly more restrictive. In contrast, religious rights[19] appear to have expanded significantly in the UK, France, and Spain, but not at all in Switzerland.

Integration is a central issue in Europe and often comes to the fore in political and media discourse when terrorist attacks occur. Despite the fact that the term is used often and as if everyone knows what it means, integration is also a complex notion that has multiple and conflicting definitions (on the thorniness of the concept of "integration," also see Riggs 2018; Wagman 2006). As Gianni, Giugni, and Michel (2015) explain, policies of integration vary according to country (see discussion of assimilationist vs. multiculturalist policies below). Moreover, integration happens in different spaces (school, the workplace) and depends upon different factors, which may be institutional/political (for instance, ease of obtaining nationality; the right to vote); sociocultural (ability to speak a national language or access to language courses, for example); economic (levels of discrimination in the workplace, for instance). The aforementioned examples are objective, but integration may also be subjective: an individual may *feel* integrated in one setting or aspect of her life and not in another.

At the level of national policies and institutions, two main approaches to integration exist. The first, assimilationist, corresponds to this description by Piquer Martí (2015: 150; she also cites Wagman (2006: 209)), although she does not use the term: "In many cases, the concept includes the idea that for immigrants to be able to 'integrate', they have to alter their behavior and their values in order to acquire other values that are considered 'superior', that is, those of the host society ('ours')." Note that in this scenario, the adjustment required is unilateral: the host society does not need to adapt. Access to citizenship is not facilitated and requires proof that the applicant has adapted to the national lifestyle and values, whatever that might mean and however it might be evaluated. Gianni, Giugni, and Michel's (2015) findings, discussed below, actually show that the assimilationist model "plays an important role in creating a demarcation between nationals and foreigners as well as between immigrant groups" (2015: 79). Importantly, the authors point out that in countries— their example is Switzerland—where this approach prevails, "the concept of assimilation has been replaced by the term integration in official discourse" (21).

The second approach, multiculturalist, is based on the view that in a society composed of various cultures, races, and ethnicities, differences—in particular of minority groups—should be acknowledged, respected, and even protected, because they enrich society as a whole. This necessarily involves the state intervening proactively in various ways, for instance, by providing special protection or allowances under the law for the practices of a given cultural group or granting it autonomous rights of governance. This model also facilitates access to citizenship (Gianni, Giugni, and Michel 2015: 19). A major criticism of the multiculturalist approach is that it allows and even encourages different groups to exist and evolve in separate bubbles rather than requiring their interaction, and therefore does not lead to effective integration after all. (Emblematic of the criticism and of the recent backlash against multiculturalism in Europe are Angela Merkel's declaration in 2010 that the multicultural approach in Germany had "utterly failed" and David Cameron's speech to the Munich Security Conference in 2011, during which he stated that "Under the doctrine of multiculturalism," the UK had "allowed the weakening of our collective identity" and "even tolerated" what he described as "segregated communities [...] living apart from each other and apart from the mainstream" "behaving in ways that run completely counter to our values."[20] What is not mentioned is how multiculturalism was defined, operationalized in law and policy, and measured.)

In line with Modood (2007), Gianni, Giugni, and Michel (2015) instead conceive of integration as a mutual, reciprocal "two-way process of social interaction" whose success depends on *both* immigrants/ethnic minorities *and* citizens/the majority, so that the former "cannot alone be blamed for failing (or not trying) to integrate" (Modood 2007: 48). This is the kind of integration that a cosmopolitan outlook or the approaches inherent in cultural translation would foster.

In the UK, the concept of integration was for a long time inextricably tied to a policy of multiculturalism, but as reflected in Cameron's speech, this began to change significantly around 2010. In France, the notion of integration is closely connected to a notion of French identity (whatever that means) which itself relies on *laïcité*: the secularity of the State (see, for example, Doyle 2011; Vaarakallio

2010). Nevertheless, the value placed on multiculturalism in the UK was still reflected in the previous coalition government's conception of integration provided by a House of Commons parliamentary report (Women and Equalities Committee 2016). It stipulates that policy should "focus[] on what we have in common rather than our differences," ensure that "[p]eople of all backgrounds have the opportunities to take part, be heard and take decisions in local and national life," and provide "[a] robust response to threats, whether discrimination, extremism or disorder, that deepen division and increase tensions" (Women and Equalities Committee 2016: 9). The same report, however, formulates strong concerns about the UK government's integration policy, which is inextricably bound up with counterterrorism efforts and especially with tackling extremism (recall the Prevent strategy). It encourages racial profiling and discrimination, in particular against Muslims or those perceived as Muslim:

> We do not underestimate the challenges the Government faces in tackling extremism, but the conflation of integration with counter-extremism has exacerbated inequalities experienced by Muslims. The Government needs to tackle the disadvantages faced by Muslims in their own right, not through the lens of counter-extremism. (5)

As we have already seen, and as Lee Jarvis, a prominent author on UK counterterrorism and security policy and editor of *Critical Studies on Terrorism*, has also noted, "counter-radicalisation policy … in the British case relies heavily on claims around fundamental or mainstream 'British values'" (Antichan and Jarvis 2017). This term, like "integration," is used frequently, particularly on the right, but not defined. Like the current tendency to conflate integration and counterterrorism measures, it poses a challenge to multiculturalism. It suggests that there are "others" who fall outside the realm of "Britishness" (also undefined) and who are assumed to not share those "values." Moreover, as the term "values" is morally focused, it claims superiority over those judged un-British while also intimating that they are a potential threat, since they do not share "our" moral code.

Fiddian-Qasmiyeh and Qasmiyeh (2010) highlight the heterogeneity of the "Muslim experience" through their focus on more recently arrived refugees and asylum-seekers of Middle Eastern origin living in the UK. What they say is valid for these groups more generally and the way their (varied and various) identities get equated with violence and danger. Their identities

> have been transformed in/by the public imagination, moving from an emphasis on their "refugee-ness" and categorization as either "bogus" or

"genuine" asylum-seekers, to a primal concern with their Muslim identity, which is equated with a threatening identity. (295)

Such tendencies, coupled with the specificity of their experience, contribute to their marginalization:

Muslim asylum-seekers and refugees' lives, whether practicing or not, are marked by physical and psychological alienation from both their country of origin (due to their request for political asylum) and the country which they hope will offer them protection (because of the impediments they face upon and following their arrival). This alienation is not only embodied in the specificities of their asylum journey, but also in the current political setting that incriminates and forcibly categorizes them as a threat to national security. (Fiddian-Qasmiyeh and Qasmiyeh 2010: 310)

Thus, they "find themselves exposed to three intersecting vulnerabilities: firstly, their uncertain legal status; secondly, their voluntary or imposed religious identification as 'Muslims'; and lastly, their exclusion from established Muslim communities in the UK" (294).

And yet, these individuals are regular human beings with regular, and noble, goals. In the interviews these authors conducted, asylum-seekers' and refugees' self-described identification and experience included a strong desire to be a productive member of society and to ensure the best outcome for their children's futures; confusion about which cultural norms to follow; sometimes a rejection of Islam, sometimes an intensification of interest in it, either for comfort, for points of reference and a kind of anchoring in the very uncertain circumstances of the asylum-seeker/refugee existence, or to provide children with a sound basis on which to make decisions/lead their lives; or being simultaneously (often marginalized) observers of, and active participants in, the host society (Fiddian-Qasmiyeh and Qasmiyeh 2010). The authors conclude that the overriding sentiment of this sub-group of asylum seekers and refugees is ambivalence, both in relation to the "within" and to the "without."

While notions of Britishness were becoming much more inclusive leading up to the 2000s, Weller and Cheruvallil-Contractor (2015) maintain that in the wake of, in particular, "the summer 2001 northern mill town disturbances involving young Muslims,"[21] 9/11, and then the 7/7 London bombings in 2005, "there has been a move away from earlier forms of multiculturalism" (320). They were writing in 2015; in the current climate, this is an understatement. At the same time, their conclusions are quite optimistic, in particular the notion that the younger generation, encompassing a Britishness that is inseparable from the Muslim part of its identity, as well as being well-educated and confident (according to the authors; this seems a generalization), will succeed in making inclusive multiculturalism the norm. Instead, recent articles indicate that part of the Conservative government's "anti-radicalisation strategy" will include inculcating "British values."[22] Weller and Cheruvallil-Contractor's optimism also seems to rely heavily on the fact that Britain is part of Europe, but soon it will not be, at least not politically. The moves to leave Europe are already affecting multiculturalism. Findings reported in 2017 are also cause for alarm:

> More than half of Britons see Islam (the mainstream religion, not Islamist fundamentalist groups) as a threat to Western liberal democracy. Over 30 percent of young children [i.e. the next generation] believe Muslims are "taking over England" and hate crime against Muslims continues to rise, up by 70 percent [from 2015 to 2016], according to the Metropolitan police. (Versi 2016a)

Thus, the fact that in 2014 the UK ranked fifteenth out of thirty-eight countries on the Migrant Integration Policy Index[23] suggests that the way policies are measured, who is consulted about integration of migrants and how integration is defined, may mask a more negative reality. It will be interesting to see what happens to the ranking post-Brexit.

The findings of the EURISLAM Project,[24] finalized in 2012, are particularly illuminating with regard to attitudes toward Muslims. The project, which examined approaches to the cultural integration of immigrants, and particularly of Muslims, in six European countries, began with the research question: "How have different traditions of national identity, citizenship and church-state relations affected European" "countries' incorporation of Islam, and what are the consequences of these approaches for patterns of cultural distance and interaction between Muslim immigrants" and/or "their descendants, and the receiving society" (Hoksbergen and Tillie 2012)? In all countries studied, "the non-Muslim majority group perceives the most cultural distance between Muslims and non-Muslims". In the UK, the Muslim community that perceived the most cultural distance between these two groups was Pakistanis; this is despite their greater mastery of the official language—as we have seen, a key factor in integration—than other Muslim communities (Hoksbergen and Tillie 2012). Across Europe, despite the popular claim that "Muslim values" are incompatible with democracy, Muslims showed "strong support for democracy," the sole exception being those of ex-Yugoslav origin in the UK (Hoksbergen and Tillie 2012). In the media, "[o]verall, more is said about Muslims by non-Muslims than by Muslims themselves" (Hoksbergen and Tillie 2012). In addition, in relation to media treatment of Muslims and integration, the report observes that while positive stances do exist, it is the negative content that is most salient. For this reason, a significant "segment of Muslim leaders feels that they need to defend Islam and the position of Muslims, followed closely by those who wish to interact and get into a discussion with non-Muslims" (Hoksbergen and Tillie 2012). Moreover, and importantly for this study, the researchers observe that "the UK case suggests" that positive input to the media increases "when the number of Muslim actors increases" (Hoksbergen and Tillie 2012).

In terms of social interaction and acceptance among Muslims and non-Muslims, it was in the UK and the Netherlands that "the majority population have close Muslim friends" (Hoksbergen and Tillie 2012). In the UK, Muslims, "except ex-Yugoslavs," "know more people from the majority population through associations than through their neighbourhood" (Hoksbergen and Tillie 2012). Because members of the majority population of the UK do "not have strongly pronounced religious identities," those of all Muslim groups are much stronger (Hoksbergen and Tillie 2012). That said, in line with Fiddian-Qasmiyeh and Qasmiyeh's findings, "[b]elonging was often described in contextual ways, and identity was also context-dependent"; that is, "individual respondents described their sense of belonging as being related mainly to their social networks and lifestyle choices they had been socialized into," rather than to the context of the country of origin (Hoksbergen and Tillie 2012). Muslims' feelings of acceptance are low (although this is less true of Pakistanis and ex-Yugoslavs in the UK). Put otherwise, "perception of out-group distance is the highest in the United Kingdom" (Hoksbergen and Tillie 2012). While this is subjective, the researchers also found that it was in the UK where "the national majority shows least acceptance of immigrants" (Hoksbergen and Tillie 2012). Interestingly, majority populations in all the countries except the UK had more problems sharing space with Muslims in public spaces than at social events. Disturbingly, in all countries except France, the majority population was very negative about hiring Muslims or working with them.

Finally, the report criticizes the fact that in Europe "the debate is merely characterized by a bi-directional communication between the states and Muslims [*sic*] organizations. Civil society actors as a relevant addressee are quite absent from it" (Hoksbergen and Tillie 2012). In line with Gianni, Giugni, and Michel's (2015) findings and the conception of integration as a mutual effort, one of the researchers' key conclusions is that "[p]olicies to stimulate dialogue should not only target Muslims, but also the majority population, since they perceive far more cultural distance than the Muslim groups in our study and have lesser bridging social capital [social networks that include both Muslims and non-Muslims and therefore 'bridge' the cultural gap] than the Muslim population" (Hoksbergen and Tillie 2012). Media and their portrayals of different societal groups have a key role to play in this.

The Muslim religious minority is relatively new in Switzerland. It was in the late 1960s that the first group[25] of Muslim immigrants arrived. Like in Spain, they came mainly for economic reasons: in this case, to resolve labor shortages. While some Muslims have always come from the Middle East, people in this early group were mainly Turkish and Yugoslav, aimed to stay only for short periods, and remained "invisible" (D'Amato 2015: 286) in religious and cultural terms. A second group appeared in the 1970s within the framework of a "policy of family reunification" and therefore no longer intended to go back to the country of origin. The third group was predominantly made up of asylum-seekers: those continuing to arrive from the Middle East were joined by Balkan Muslims in the 1990s as well as groups from sub-Saharan Africa and North Africa.

Today, the Muslim population of Switzerland also includes "descendants of the first waves and an increasing number of Swiss citizens who are converting to Islam (Gianni 2010)" (D'Amato 2015: 286). That said, just 4.5 to 5 percent of the Swiss population identifies as Muslim (286). In addition, *only 10–15 percent of that total number is actually practicing Muslims* (297; citing Gianni 2010: 14; my emphasis), or about 50,000 people and yet, this is the group the media focuses upon. There are more Muslims in the German-speaking areas (4.9 percent vs. 3.9 percent in the French-speaking *Suisse romande*), while those with passports reside mainly in the French-speaking part (287). Given the provenance of the news articles discussed here, it is important to note that the canton of Geneva is the only non-German-speaking canton in which the percentage of Muslims surpasses the national percentage (it was 5.4 percent in 2018).[26] In stark contrast to the French, UK, and Spanish Muslim populations, about 90 percent of Muslims in Switzerland have come from other parts of Europe. As the results of the survey by Gianni, Giugni, and Michel (2015) show, Muslims in Switzerland are mainly of Turkish, ex-Yugoslav, and North African (the Maghreb) origin, and the researchers insist on the major differences between them. There are significantly more Muslims from the Maghreb—language is certainly a factor in this—in the *Suisse romande*, the region of particular concern for us here, than in other parts of Switzerland.

In 2000 and then through a federal law in 2005, the Swiss government expressly "recognized the presence of foreigners and affirmed that their integration was a priority" (Gianni, Giugni, and Michel 2015: 22). Article 4 of the Federal Law on Foreigners stated the following, as summarized by Gianni, Giugni and Michel (2015: 22–3): "the integration of foreigners is intended to foster coexistence of the Swiss and foreign populations in accordance with constitutional values and mutual respect and tolerance; integration should allow foreigners whose residence status is legal and stable to participate in social, cultural, and economic life; integration means that foreigners are willing to integrate and that the Swiss population is open to foreigners; it is essential that foreigners familiarize themselves with the Swiss way of life and in particular that they learn a national language". Despite these principles, the authors observe that Switzerland ranked twenty-third out of thirty-eight countries on the Migrant Integration Policy Index of 2011 (the most recent data, from 2014, ranks it twenty-first), and that discrimination is rampant in Switzerland (Gianni, Giugni, and Michel 2015: 23).

It is important to look at the specificities of North African Muslims in Switzerland, both because they are the majority Muslim population in the Swiss region of concern here, and because, due to their physical appearance and provenance, they are part of the Muslim population in Europe that is most likely to be stereotyped as extremists/terrorists. It is Muslims from the Maghreb who tend to have the least stable residence status in Switzerland, whereas it is this group that is most likely to have one of the national languages as its mother tongue (Gianni, Giugni, and Michel 2015). The researchers also highlight the fact that many of the Muslims in their sample were multilingual, something which is rarely emphasized in the literature about migrants, but is a particular asset in this country of four official languages (36–8). In addition, while foreigners in Switzerland tend to have a lower level of education than Swiss citizens, that of immigrants from the Maghreb is in fact higher (38). Despite these qualifications, they have difficulties finding employment. This is in part due to lack of recognition of foreign diplomas and in part due to discrimination (44). Swiss residents from the Maghreb also have a higher rate of mixed marriages (25 percent) than the other Muslim groups. (The majority of Swiss citizens are married to Christians (48).) In a similar vein, respondents from the Maghreb had interpersonal networks that were more ethnically and religiously heterogeneous than those of other Muslims. The Swiss citizens' networks were the most homogeneous (49). If we consider that integration as a mutual process also depends on the efforts of the host society to establish intercultural contact, this tendency is "likely to hinder the process of integration" (51).

Despite the tiny number of practicing Muslims living in Switzerland, a significant portion of the Swiss population has been led to believe that Islam is threatening to overtake the country. The saga of the Swiss minaret ban (see, for example, Davier 2013; D'Amato 2015: 292–3) aptly demonstrates the significant role that fear-mongering on the part of both certain Swiss politicians and the media has played in swaying public opinion. In stark contrast to the fear in the country "that Islam could be politicized in the near future" is Gianni's observation that "Muslims in Switzerland do not interpret their presence and citizenship politically" (D'Amato 2015: 297). Indeed, the author considers that "the voting on the banning of minarets has shown how badly Muslims are organized at the national level" (296). This is similar to how Astor (2015) and Cembrero (2016) describe the situation in Spain. (It must be noted, though, that political agency is largely tied to citizenship, which, as Gianni, Guigni, and Michel (2015) discuss, is very difficult for non-Europeans to obtain in Switzerland. Eighty percent of the Muslims they surveyed said they would vote in local elections if they had the right. In addition, respondents from the Maghreb were actually more interested in politics than Swiss citizens (67). Muslims in general were also very active in volunteer associations.) Moreover, in February 2014, Swiss voters approved a referendum—by a tiny margin, 50.34 percent—that established immigration quotas and also "introduced hiring preferences for Swiss nationals" (*Encyclopaedia Britannica* Online 2019). However, it is essential to note that all of the *Suisse romande* cantons except one voted against it: Geneva, by 60.9 percent, and Vaud, by 61.07 percent, for instance. In contrast, of the German-speaking cantons, only Zurich, Basel-City, and Zug refused the text.

On the topic of discrimination, Gianni, Guigni, and Michel (2015) asked respondents if they had felt discriminated against within the preceding twelve months. Nearly a third of Turks and residents from the Maghreb felt they had experienced discrimination based on their skin color or race (53). This kind of discrimination was directed more often at men than at women, whereas religious discrimination was more frequently directed at women (35 percent of females with North African origins) (53–4). A third of Muslims from each group and also a third of non-naturalized non-Muslims had felt discriminated against on the basis of their nationality or origin, demonstrating that one in three foreigners in Switzerland are likely to experience this form of prejudice, regardless of their religion (54). In addition, it affects a significant portion of residents who were born in Switzerland or have spent most of their lives in the country (55; 60 percent of Maghreb-origin "immigrants" were born in Switzerland!). The high proportion of discrimination experienced in the context of employment is probably part of the explanation for the high unemployment rate the researchers documented among Maghreb immigrants, and shows that discrimination affects Muslims' access to the job market, thereby hindering their economic integration.

Furthermore, "the Swiss respondents distanced themselves more from Muslims in general than from the three nationalities," declaring, for instance, that "they would not want to have Muslims as in-laws, co-citizens, friends, neighbors or colleagues" (Gianni, Guigni, and Michel 2015: 57). That said, they wanted much more distance with Maghreb immigrants than those of the other two nationalities, in line with the fact that "people from North Africa are more frequently associated with the stereotypical image of the Muslim 'Islamist' or 'terrorist' than the two other groups" (57). This is despite the fact that immigrants from the Maghreb proved to be the best integrated of the three main groups of Muslims—even though they are the group with the least stable residence status.

As already discussed, the cantons of Switzerland have a high level of autonomy, which means that different cantons may address a given issue in different ways. Therefore, in relation to religion, religious accommodation, and religious and cultural diversity, as in other aspects of society, "different solutions ... co-exist under a common roof" (D'Amato 2015: 285). For instance, as we have seen, in the *Suisse romande* cantons of Geneva and Neuchatel, there is clear separation of church and state, while other cantons "have chosen one of the Christian religions as their state religion" (285). While this arrangement allowed the accommodation of both the dominant Catholic and Protestant religions in Switzerland's history, it was much less successful in incorporating "new, recently arrived religious minorities" (286), including Muslims. According to the author, this co-existence of "different forms of recognition" often proves inequitable for minority religious groups or may at least be seen as inequitable by the groups themselves, depending on how these forms of recognition resolve "crucial questions affecting those minorities" such as, to give just one example, "the construction of cemeteries" (289). Finally, the EURISLAM project found that "the tendency to generalise and turn Muslims into one category is more visible in the Netherlands and Switzerland" (Hoksbergen and Tillie 2012) than in the other four countries studied.

Cembrero's (2016) text is a very useful resource for understanding the specific nature of Spain's Muslim population. For example, he distinguishes between the UK and France, on the one hand, and Spain, on the other:

In the United Kingdom and in France, Muslim immigration is in part a result of the colonial past of these powers, a past in which [national] history does not directly overlap with the history of Islam. In Spain, on the other hand, these

immigrants are not entirely a foreign body. They are connected to a Muslim past
which included a period of absolute splendor. (Cembrero 2016: 337)

That said, immigration to Spain is both more recent and less abundant,
proportionally speaking, than that of many other European countries (Cembrero
2016: 17). The vast majority of Spain's Muslim immigrants are from Morocco
(19), making for a very different Muslim population than that of, for instance,
the UK. In addition, as Astor (2015: 247) notes, "[a]lthough Islam had a deep
presence in the Iberian Peninsula between the eighth and fifteenth centuries,
Muslims have only recently emerged as a substantial religious minority in
contemporary Spain" (247).

The response to this minority at the end of the last century was very different
than that seen recently in Switzerland, for instance. Consider the attitude toward
mosques:

> During the 1980s and 1990s, municipal governments in several Spanish cities
> actively promoted the establishment of highly visible "cathedral mosques,"
> generally by ceding land to mosque developers. In contrast to France, where the
> promotion of cathedral mosques was connected to the objective of fostering the
> development of a distinctively "French Islam" (Maussen 2009), the proliferation
> of cathedral mosques in Spain was driven by the interest of urban planners
> and politicians in enhancing the global and cosmopolitan image of their cities.
> (Astor 2015: 253)

Perhaps in part for this reason, Astor maintains that Spain achieved a "rather
seamless incorporation of Islam, institutionally and socially, during the last two
decades of the twentieth century" (Astor 2015: 254). This period also saw an
economic boom that brought many migrants to the country, including Muslims.
At the same time, they tended to settle in poorer neighborhoods, and as time
went on, in some towns and cities "mosques came to be perceived as symbolic of
the 'colonization' of neighborhood life by Muslim immigrants" (Astor 2015: 255).
Such attitudes fed into a new shift: "[d]uring the late 1990s and early 2000s …,
significant socio-demographic and political transformations … introduced new
challenges and contributed to a hardening of the general climate surrounding
Islam" (254). Piquer Martí attributes this to a shift in how the country saw itself
in relation to immigration and the rise in numbers of immigrants: for a long time
a "país de emigrantes" (country of emigrants), it became in the 1990s "un país
receptor de inmigrantes" (country that takes in immigrants) (Piquer Martí 2015:
139). Moreover, the way that media reported on the phenomenon of migration
had a significant and negative impact on the public's perception of immigrants
and in particular those arriving from the Maghreb:

The coverage the media gave to this new phenomenon … would have a decisive impact on public opinion about non-EU citizens. For example, the press began to develop a pattern of journalistic discourse on dinghies/migrant boats based upon opinion pieces and a constant trickle of short articles about the capture, arrival and deaths of immigrants who were crossing the Strait [of Gibraltar] in these precarious vessels in order to enter Spain illegally (Nash 2005: 37). In general, journalistic discourse focused on the massive presence of these migrant boats and gave little attention to the motivations behind immigration to Spain. In this way, the cultural representation of the African from the Maghreb took form through a conceptual homogenization of immigration which excluded the possibility of considering each case of immigration as a concrete and specific one. (Piquer Martí 2015: 139)

Piquer Martí also chastises the Spanish population for its Islamophobia and "historical amnesia," which allow it to forget how closely intertwined the country and Muslims are—not only historically, but geographically, politically, socially, and culturally.

Islamophobia in Spain is real. According to data gathered by SOS Racism (AA. VV., 2012: 33), 37 percent of the Spanish population believes it is acceptable to expel a student for wearing the hijab and opposes the construction of mosques. Arab immigrants are the main targets of racism and xenophobia. (Piquer Martí 2015: 140)

That said, in 2014, Spain ranked eleventh out of thirty-eight countries on the Migrant Integration Policy Index.

With respect to accepting more refugees, Cembrero (2016) reproduces various examples of political discourse linking them to the risk of terrorism, just like in the UK and especially with respect to Syrian refugees, from 2013 to 2015:

"We must urgently take in refugees, but this has to be done in a way that is compatible with security" because among them there could be "terrorists trying to infiltrate the country," warned Fernández Díaz [former minister of the interior, including at the time of the Nice event] from Paris. "A while ago, Daesh threatened exactly this," he added. Javier Maroto, Deputy Secretary-General of the *Partido Popular*, added more fuel to the fire: among Syrians, he claimed, "there are a lot of jihadists" who will one day "bomb our cities." Of the hundreds of thousands of refugees who have entered Europe, only two Syrians … have raised suspicions, at the end of 2015. The Swiss police arrested them in Geneva. (Cembrero 2016: 50–1)

Barbero (2016: 370; his translation) includes another statement by Fernández Díaz in November 2014: "Jihadist terrorists are trying to sneak among the flood [note the water metaphor] of illegal immigrants who enter Spain jumping over the fences in Ceuta and Melilla."

How is the Muslim population distributed across Spain? Interestingly, the nationality most represented within the Muslim population is Spanish (779,080)—Cembrero maintains they are converts and immigrants who have acquired citizenship—followed by Moroccan (749,274) (Cembrero 2016: 45). Islam is more omnipresent in the autonomous cities of Ceuta and Melilla than anywhere else in Europe. In terms of Muslim populations by *comunidad autónoma*, Catalonia comes first, with 510,481 Muslims; Andalusia second, with 300,460. That said, Spain has not had the same level of influx as other countries in the region (48).

One of the major points on which the Muslim and non-Muslim populations differ is the importance of religion in their lives; this applies across Europe more generally but is particularly pronounced in Spain: "Religion has more power to bring Moroccan immigrants together in Spain than in other European countries. Fifty-five percent go to the Mosque assiduously, six percent more than the European average" (Cembrero 2016: 189). In stark contrast, in a 2015 worldwide Gallup poll, "[f]ifty-five percent of Spanish people declare[d] themselves non-religious or atheist" (364), and it was estimated that "half of the Spanish population even consider[ed] that religion plays a negative role" in people's lives (365). In a similar vein, according to Abad Liñán's (2018) article, while 92 percent of people in Spain had a Christian upbringing, only 66 percent consider themselves Christian now. Spain is third in numbers of people abandoning the faith. Asked how important religion was for national identity, 38 percent of Spaniards said "very or fairly," while 59 percent indicated it had no or very little importance. Compare with three other European countries relevant here, France, the UK, and Switzerland:

Switzerland　Very or fairly important: 42%
　　　　　　Of no or little importance: 58%
UK　　　　　Very or fairly important: 34%
　　　　　　Of no or little importance: 65%
France　　　Very or fairly important: 32%
　　　　　　Of no or little importance: 65% (Abad Liñan 2018).

Both the decreasing importance attributed to religion by non-Muslim European populations and the political bias toward Christianity nevertheless present in policies of countries that claim to be secular may explain the following tendency of Islam: "Islam needs to modernize, but it is also a religion that has often felt itself to be under attack by the West and by the governments of Muslim nations, who try to manipulate it. Therefore, instead of opening up, it turns inward to defend itself, and sometimes, it takes a step backward" (Cembrero 2016: 287–8).

Finally, as we have already seen, lack of economic and educational opportunities is also a barrier to effective integration. According to Eurostat,[27] in 2016, 32.7 percent of youth aged fifteen to twenty-nine in Spain were unemployed. Among European countries, only North Macedonia and Greece had higher unemployment. In contrast, the figure for France was 17.7 percent; for the UK, 9.4 percent; and for Switzerland, 6.2 percent. Cembrero (2016: 257–8) highlights the fact that the Spanish figures were in fact significantly higher in Ceuta and Melilla, where the population is also young, many of the youth are irregular immigrants, and the school dropout rate, as we have seen, is 25.2 percent. On the question of religious education in particular (also see section "Politics, Law, and Religion"), the eminent

> imam [Riay] Tatary and many other Muslim officials believe that, in addition to being a right, classes about Islam would be useful in the current climate. "A unified curriculum—with appropriate text books—can *prevent terrorism,*" Tatary declared in 2015. "If [young people] learn about it in school they may be less tempted to seek out answers to their questions on certain internet sites, many of which are not appropriate," said the *ulema* (Muslim sage) Rachid Boutarbouch. (Cembrero 2016: 371; my emphasis)

Moreover, if Islam were taught in schools, children would "see it as something that belongs within the social environment in which they live, whereas if they only hear about Islam in a makeshift garage-mosque from an imam who speaks to them in Arabic, they will see it as something foreign' ..., maintains Zoila Cambalía Solís, Professor of Ecclesiastical Law at the University of Zaragoza" (Cembrero 2016: 371).

That said, in all of Spain, there are only forty-seven high school teachers of Islam. Ninety-five percent of Muslim students do not take religion classes (again, despite the fact that it is their legal right), and 90 percent of Islamic religion teachers are unemployed (369). It follows that where there are teachers, their numbers are insufficient to meet the high demand (370). "Theoretically, if just ten parents demanded Islamic religion classes for their children, the high school would have to provide them." And yet, at the time Cembrero was writing (2016), no Muslim group had gone to the courts to obtain them (370).

This section has provided various kinds of information. For example, the national origins of Muslims in the three countries in question diverge, again showing that "Muslims" across Europe are not a monolithic group. That said, the *Suisse romande* and Spain both have a lot of Muslims from the Maghreb; this subgroup often experiences discrimination and gets equated with terrorism and security risks due to physical appearance and provenance. Muslims may have difficulty obtaining certain cultural and religious rights due not only to various barriers (legal; economic; educational) to their integration and to discrimination, but also due to a bias toward Christianity even in countries that claim to be resolutely secular.

History/Experience of Terrorism

In considering the associations often made between Muslims and terrorism in UK, Swiss, and Spanish online news, it is important to consider the role terrorism has played in these countries. In the UK, terrorism has had two main "faces," in recent times: "nationalist," and "religious." The ideology and the violent acts of the Irish Republican Army (IRA) throughout most of the twentieth century "encompassed both" (Warsi [2017] 2018: 82). Switzerland, in contrast, has experienced just a tiny handful of "terrorist incidents." Why? The population is small; it is not a member of the EU or NATO and is not involved in any fighting in the Middle East, hence it is not a target for reprisals; and it is one of the most repressive among (geographically) European countries.

Compared to the UK and France, Spain has seen little terrorist activity in the past few years. Different actors propose different reasons for this. Cembrero (2016: 165) states that according to various "experts" "who study the phenomenon," including academics and the police, "the infrequent nature of terrorist activity" in contemporary Spain is attributable to a number of factors, and in particular, the type of immigration that predominates in Spain: "first-generation immigration." He juxtaposes this with the identity crisis that later generations will (supposedly) experience. A member of Rajoy's government attributed it to a higher level of integration of immigrants than in other European countries (165–6) (again, one always wonders how integration is defined, operationalized, and measured), while a migration expert (166) attributes it to the fact that migration was structured purely by the labor market rather than by the imposition of ideologies that would grate on Muslims, unlike in other countries. For Cembrero (167), it is above all down to security and resources (and, importantly, their reattribution after Spain's long experience combating ETA).

What of the prevalence of extremism in Catalonia? Again according to Cembrero (2016: 179), it is explained by a whole host of factors, including various kinds of barriers to integration and, in turn, identity issues, or systemic problems related to security: "carelessness on the part of the Generalitat (regional government), issues of identity, especially of young people, coupled with obstacles to developing the Muslim religion, marginalization and precarity, ghettos (almost non-existent in other regions of Spain)," or the fact that the economic crisis was particularly hard on Muslim residents of the region (179). Furthermore, the "main forces involved in counterterrorist efforts in Barcelona"—the *Mossos*, the *Cuerpo Nacional de Policía* (CNP), and the *Guardia Civil*—"have a terrible relationship," which negatively affects security (179). Nevertheless, "the Paris attacks of November 2015" led to a rapprochement between the Ministry of the Interior and the Catalan and Basque Interior advisors (183).

As we have seen, Ceuta and Melilla are, with Catalonia, hubs of extremism that also have significant Muslim populations. That said, while 2015 saw a rise in extremism in Ceuta and Melilla, 66 percent of those detained were Spanish, and their activities basically consisted of "developing propaganda and recruiting with the intention of sending recruits to the Middle East. Only in one case" (Cembrero 2016: 261) was there the intention to commit an attack, but the four men involved only possessed a pistol. Nevertheless, "[t]he Minister of the Interior, Jorge Fernández Díaz, went so far as to compare them to the Kouachi brothers, who had just riddled with bullets the editorial team of the weekly magazine *Charlie Hebdo* in Paris" (261). Cembrero (263) does point out, however, that not only the marginalization and poverty prevalent in Ceuta and Melilla, but also the proximity of Morocco play a role in the radicalization of young Muslims in these cities. "A third of the Moroccan jihadists in the Middle East are from the northeast of Morocco" (264). In addition, radical imams are not allowed to preach in Morocco but can do so in Ceuta and Melilla (263–4).

Given recent terrorist events and national responses to them, particularly in terms of counterterrorism laws and policies, as well as prevailing public opinion about Muslims and Islam that is only reinforced after such events, it is reasonable to believe that measures will become more, not less, restrictive of Islam and Muslims. At the same time, the real or believed threat will continue to be taken as a justification to use "extraordinary measures in the name of security" (Gianni, Giugni, and Michel 2015: 107) which have been proven to disproportionately affect Muslims or those perceived to be Muslim. All of these trends are likely to have "a profound social and cultural impact" and to "affect policies related to the integration of Muslims" (107). The danger of this series of processes is that it goes well beyond the more restricted question of countering terror and keeping citizens safe, to encompass what is believed to be possible or impossible in the areas of integration; national, political, or social identity; freedom of expression; equality; and coexistence (107).

Characteristics of the News Landscapes

According to Rodríguez-Martínez, Mauri-De los Ríos, and Fedele (2017), the media system of each country studied here corresponds to a different media systems model, as defined by Hallin and Mancini (2004). According to the authors, the UK news fits the liberal model, characterized by a low degree of "state intervention in the media sector," "a high degree of deregulation [and] a well-developed journalistic professional culture" (Rodríguez-Martínez, Mauri-De los Ríos, and Fedele 2017: 60). Switzerland corresponds to the democratic corporatist model, defined by "a high level of professionalization among journalists" (60), a key role for public media, and a clear separation between media and political power. Finally, Spain comes under the polarized pluralist[28] model, "characterized by a relatively weak professional culture"; "while public media systems are present, there is a high degree of political influence in both public and private media" (60).

Regarding the UK, Hallin and Mancini (2004: 246–7) highlight "the persistence of party-press parallelism"[29] in the press and the fact that this disproves "the common assumption that commercialization automatically leads to the development of politically neutral media." Importantly, they also point out that "[t]here is a tension between the fact of private ownership and the expectation that the media will serve the public good" (247). They go further in highlighting disadvantages of the nevertheless-popular liberal model: this type of press sees lower circulation than that of the Democratic Corporatist countries and is "characterized by partisan imbalance and a fairly high degree of instrumentalization" (247). Furthermore, while the authors highlight the "lack of diversity in US newsrooms," this is patently true of the UK as well. While "[i]nformation-oriented journalism predominates in news systems that fit under this model, there is "a bit stronger commentary tradition in Britain" (75).

According to Hallin and Mancini (2004), the Democratic Corporatist countries among which they classify Switzerland show a high degree of political parallelism. (This is also true of the other two countries studied here even though the authors classified them under two other models.) Democratic Corporatist countries exhibit a "high level of journalistic professionalization," "including a high degree of consensus on professional standards of conduct, a notion of commitment to the public interest, and a high level of autonomy from other social powers" (145). "Traditions of self-government" but also of a "welfare state" mean there is emphasis on press freedom but also on various forms of "public sector involvement in the media sphere" (145), as "the media are seen as a social institution and not as purely private enterprises" (196). Nevertheless, it would be flawed to uncritically accept that the *Suisse romande* fits their model, as they associate Switzerland with Northern Europe and in particular Germany and Austria, and not with France. Indeed, in the French-speaking part of Switzerland, the two largest Swiss media companies, private enterprises Tamedia and Ringier, control 88 percent of the market (compared to 71 percent in the German-speaking region). This translates into significant homogeneity of information (ATS/B. O. I. 2017). With respect to my corpus, Tamedia owns *La Tribune de Genève* and Ringier owns *Le Temps. Le Courrier*, in contrast, is owned by the non-profit organization *Nouvelle Association du Courrier* (NAC), itself composed of twenty-six different associations (also see section "Le Courrier" of Chapter 2).

Feddersen's (2013) study of the Swiss press, cited by Gianni, Giugni, and Michel (2015), shows that between 2001 and 2009, the religious designation "Muslim" gradually replaced identity markers based on the nationalities of groups whose members are often also Muslim. This shows that if identity descriptors for minority groups change, this may go in the direction of the kind of essentialism which is more and more common "in the public debates about Islam in Europe, and this has significant implications for public perception of Muslims" (Gianni, Giugni, and Michel 2015: 81). Indeed, because Islam is presented as, and, in turn, comes to be considered as, "incompatible with the values of democracy, Muslims are represented as undemocratic 'by nature' (Cesari 2004)." Gianni, Giugni, and Michel's own study proves that in Switzerland, at least, this is a blatant misrepresentation of Muslims.

The starting date of Feddersen's (2013) corpus, of course, is linked to 9/11. Yet Gianni, Giugni, and Michel point out that representations of Islam and Muslims in the Swiss media have a certain continuity and should not be simplistically linked to that "watershed moment," as they are emblematic of the "problematic relationship that Swiss society has always maintained with immigrants and, more generally, with the figure of the Foreigner" (2015: 108). The fact that the spike in news articles about Islam and Muslims was in 2004, "when the Swiss population voted on a federal popular initiative on facilitating naturalizations" (108), and not in 2001, supports this claim.

We saw above that although only a minute percentage of Muslims in Switzerland actually practice Islam, many non-Muslims have come to fear a Muslim takeover of the country. D'Amato (2015) attributes responsibility for this to politicians and the media. News outlets in Switzerland have tended to disregard non-practicing Muslims—the vast majority—and focused instead on a small minority of ultra-orthodox or extremist groups:

> In the regular media coverage and in political debates, those secular Muslims who do not practice or who see practice as a private affair are invisible and go unnoticed. Thus, the public image is dominated by orthodox and conservative, even violent and extremist religious groups, which presents problems for many Muslims in Switzerland. (D'Amato 2015: 295)

Swiss media is far from alone in disseminating such essentialist representations, of course. Weller and Cheruvallil-Contractor (2015) observe a similar phenomenon in the UK:

> In the 1990s, and especially in and around institutions of further and higher education, groups such as Hizb-ut-Tahrir attracted a certain following among young Muslims radicalized by the *Satanic Verses* controversy, the killing of Muslims in Bosnia, and the invasions of Afghanistan and Iraq (Hussain 2007). In many ways this and other similar groups attracted media and other attention that was disproportionate to their overall size and influence. (318–19)

Miqdaad Versi monitors media organizations in the UK for inaccurate reporting on Islam and Muslims. Writing about his research, Ponsford (2017) observes that while "Muslims comprise five percent of the UK population," news about them appears "to account for the majority of newspaper mistakes which disparage a particular religion." In addition, this directly affects attitudes toward Muslims: a study by Cambridge University published in 2016[30] found that the prevalence of "negative narratives" in media reporting about Muslims in the UK was fueling a rise in anti-Muslim hostility.

Spain's history of dictatorship has also shaped its press. Hallin and Mancini (2004: 61) observe that in countries like Spain, Italy, and Portugal where there have been "sharp political conflicts often involving changes of regime," "[t]he media typically have been used as instruments of struggle …, sometimes by dictatorships and by movements struggling against them, but also by contending parties in periods of democratic politics." Arnold (2019: 190; also see section

"Regulation of News Outlets" of Chapter 2) highlights the influence of "an authoritarian past" on the development of and preferences in regulation in Spain:

> The end of dictatorships and the collapse of the communist systems have shaped the development of media structures and media regulation. For instance, social upheaval was followed by major reservations about any kind of state regulation and intervention. The media were anxious to secure their autonomy from the state. At the same time, the media often were privatised in a frantic and disorderly manner. This development resulted in the emergence of media enterprises that owned a large proportion of the media and were able to exert political pressure themselves.

Spain supposedly falls under the Polarized Pluralist Model (Hallin and Mancini 2004) but is said to show, like Britain, a high level of political parallelism. Suárez-Villegas et al.'s (2017) ongoing study of Spanish media "is based on the hypothesis that journalistic culture in Spain does not respond to a unique media system or model (like the Mediterranean or polarized pluralist models)" as proposed by Hallin and Mancini in *Comparing Media Systems*. While they do not go far enough, Hallin and Mancini not only point out a lot of exceptions within their models (so that one wonders about their utility) but also recognize the heterogeneity that can exist within a country: "the media in Quebec and Catalonia are distinct in a number of ways from the media in the rest of Canada or Spain" (2004: 71); "[r]egional media reflect the often special political alignments of the autonomous regions" (105). The authors also claim that in Spain, "journalists will express allegiance to the Liberal Model of neutrality and objectivity, while the actual practice of journalism is deeply rooted in partisan advocacy traditions" (14).

The *Observatorio de la islamophobia en los medios* studies the presence of Islamophobia in Spanish news online, including the two newspapers in my corpus. The observatory selects articles which address Islam and Muslims by searching for the terms *islam, musulmán/a/s, yihad, yihadismo, yihadista/s, islamismo, islamista/s,* and *islamophobia*. During August and September 2017 (the first time the observatory measured such statistics and, notably, a period during which data were undoubtedly affected by the Barcelona attacks of August 17 and 18, 2017), 25 percent of the news articles in the corpus which addressed Islam were undeniably Islamophobic,[31] 31 percent encouraged Islamophobic interpretations, and 44 percent did not show Islamophobic tendencies. The vast majority of the articles surveyed were news articles. Moreover, 451 articles had a negative tone while just 37 had a positive tone. Nineteen percent of informational articles were Islamophobic whereas 46 percent of opinion or blog articles were. A significant shift has occurred since, however. Indeed, in the final trimester of 2018, 25 percent of informational news articles were openly Islamophobic while only about 8 percent of opinion/blog articles showed this tendency. In addition, 23 percent were blatantly Islamophobic, 20 percent favored Islamophobic interpretations, and 57 percent showed no Islamophobic tendencies. During this more recent period, there was more positive coverage, too: 139 articles or about 33 percent addressed a positive theme. Trends were similar in the two preceding trimesters of 2018. The shifts suggest strong influence from the Barcelona attacks during 2017; they also demonstrate the ideological underpinnings of news articles which are supposedly just there to provide information about events.

Now that we have a wealth of background information on the three countries that provided the news articles for our corpus, we can proceed to the stylistic analysis of the texts.

Analysis of Stylistic Features in British, Swiss, and Spanish News

In this chapter, I present a detailed analysis of stylistic features of online news texts from the UK, French-speaking Switzerland, and Spain. I examine their treatment of the notion of "jihad" and of Muslims; their references to French society, government, and politics; and their use of modality (a grammatical feature which communicates degrees of possibility, certainty, or other such contingencies), alliteration/assonance, and metaphor. I draw conclusions about the tendencies of news from each context, in particular related to the interpretations of events and of French society that seem to be favored or endorsed; how Muslims are portrayed; and how a "discourse of fear" is fueled or, on the contrary, attenuated.

UK

Statistics for the UK corpus are presented in Table 3. This subcorpus is very "balanced" in the sense that articles from each newspaper represent about half of the total subcorpus.

Table 3 Statistics for the UK Corpus

News source	Number of articles	Number of words	Percentage of corpus
The *Guardian* (TG)	13	13,558	**49%**
The *Telegraph* (DT)	14	14,294	**51%**
Total	**27**	**27,852**	

"Jihad"

Table 4 indicates the frequency with which the term "jihad" or derivatives of it appeared in *Guardian* and *Telegraph* articles, occurrences which clearly did not correspond to *Guardian* guidelines, and the articles in which the terms appear. The *Telegraph* articles were examined in terms of the *Guardian* guidelines as well because the *Telegraph* provides no instructions regarding use of the term. Table 4 shows that non-corresponding instances only appeared in the *Guardian*, and frequently across articles from that subcorpus (in eight out of the thirteen articles), despite the detailed definitions and distinctions provided by the self-same news source. Table 5 presents the textual segments containing these occurrences.

Table 4 Occurrences of the Term "Jihad" or Its Derivatives in the UK Corpus

News source	Number of occurrences	Instances clearly not corresponding to guidelines	Where such instances appear
TG	12	9	TG1, 2, 3, 4, 9, 14, 15, 17
DT	15	0	-

Table 5 Textual Segments in the *Guardian* Containing the Term "Jihad" or Its Derivatives

Case	Term	Relevant textual segment	Fits Code
TG1	Jihadi	**jihadi** strategic thinking, which encourages extremists to use violence to destabilise states or nations to allow their eventual conquest.	No
TG2	Jihadi operation	The use of a vehicle, the target, and the fact that the attack took place on the highly symbolic Bastille Day all suggest a **jihadi operation**.	No
TG3	Jihadi	Now, even without any link to Isis yet evident, **jihadi** terrorism has taken on a new face: the wild rampage of a truck on a touristy, festive Mediterranean shoreline.	No
TG4	Jihadis	More than 230 people have been killed in attacks claimed by **jihadis** in France since the start of 2015 [...]	No
TG9	Jihadi	Initial details suggested a tactic that **jihadi** propaganda has suggested for several years, with a vehicle ploughing into a crowd.	No

Case	Term	Relevant textual segment	Fits Code
TG14	Jihadi	In recent months France was already seen by its head of internal intelligence as the country most under threat from **jihadi** terrorism.	No
TG15	Jihadi	Father of truck driver who committed atrocity said he was violent as a boy but showed no **jihadi** tendencies.	No
TG15	Jihadi	But he insisted the teenager had shown no **jihadi** tendencies [...]	No
TG17	Jihadis	[...] the Côte d'Azur has earned itself a new, unwelcome reputation: as a breeding ground for **jihadis**.	No

The term "jihad" and its derivatives are used so frequently in contemporary discourse that they have become "buzzwords." Employed without definitions in news texts, they are apparently assumed to be "understood." Yet my results suggest that they are sometimes both misunderstood and misused by journalists. In particular, the press often capitalizes on them in order to feed a discourse of fear. The result is three-fold:

1. "The press has converted 'jihad'" and related notions "into a synonym of Islamic terrorist" (Piquer Martí 2015: 149).
2. This is one way the press contributes to negative views about Islam, Muslims, and even those believed wrongly to be Muslim.
3. Muslim communities, not only on the receiving end of the prejudice but also witnessing, in the press, aspects of their religion being instrumentalized, conflated with violence or, at the least, over-simplified or otherwise misrepresented, are more likely to distance themselves from what is clearly a hostile environment.

The following section looks in detail at how both Muslims and France, two potential "Others" for the readership, are depicted in the *Guardian*.

Portrayal of France; of Muslims

Multiple *Guardian* articles celebrate various aspects of Nice; not only its glamor, sun, sea (TG17), and "festive ... shoreline" (TG3), but its "cosmopolitan" character, enhanced by the diverse mix of people who visit and live there (TG3), including "40,000 Tunisians" (TG15). In other words, "France's proud cultural heritage" (TG3) is emphasized. The city's cultural standing is also underscored through a number of artistic and literary references, for instance to Chekhov (TG3), F. Scott Fitzgerald (TG3 and 17), Picasso, or Oscar Wilde (TG17). Yet the *Guardian* also recognizes that there is a darker side to "the France of wine and charcuterie, chateaux and cheese" (TG1; note the alliteration). Indeed, the newspaper historicizes the "impact of western colonialism" (TG2) in France, the enduring societal tensions that have resulted, and their consequences for "[d]isaffected youths in the region" (TG17).

At the same time, also considered "representative of French life" are the "concert hall[s], bars and a football stadium" (TG1) that were targeted during the 2015 terror attacks. This does not sound much different from English life and may create a feeling of proximity, and in turn sympathy, with the other culture which has come under attack. These emblems of social and cultural activity are evoked to drive home the idea that what has been targeted is the core of French, and indeed Western, culture and values. This message is meaningfully reinforced through metaphor: Daesh's target is "the standard bearer of western secular liberalism" (TG1). France is the noble democratic society, victimized by violent and malevolent non-Western forces.

In contrast to the *Guardian*, the *Telegraph* focuses on negative aspects of Nice. For instance, it emphasizes the terrorist threat that the city and the *Côte d'Azur* region represent: in DT25, the sentence "Nice is considered a town under particular terrorist threat" appears twice. DT7 informs us that "Nice has the dubious distinction (note the alliteration) of being the French city that sent the most volunteers to fight in Syria and Iraq." What has happened there has ramifications for the entire Western world, and to make the point, the right-leaning news source gives credence to Trump: "Images of terrorism in Nice confirm Trump's narrative that the West has lost its way and new management is needed" (DT27).

In addition, the *Telegraph* rarely historicizes. One telling exception, however, is the assertion that "in the Fifties and Sixties, Portuguese and Spanish immigrants moved into social housing and integrated into French society without complaint" (DT7), unlike Muslim immigrants, who are clearly seen by the journalist as difficult, problematic, incontrovertibly "other." This aligns with Gianni, Giugni, and Michel's (2015) observation that even though people living in a democratic society have the right to question the system, to complain, when the Muslim "Other" does so, it is proof that he or she is not integrable. According to the journalist, Muslim immigrants should "blend in" (DT7). In addition, the *Telegraph* focuses on present results rather than past historical dynamics, in particular the "failings" of integration (such failings are emphatically referenced twice in DT7 and twice in DT26. As we have seen, such evaluations depend upon how the thorny term "integration" is defined. Security services and authorities are also described as "struggling" in DT18 or "overwhelmed" in DT21). The *Guardian* refers to such shortcomings as well, but particularly security failings, and they are more objectively presented and/or contextualized. For instance, TG1 recognizes France's reliance, in intelligence and counterterrorism matters, on "structures at a European level – which have been repeatedly found wanting." The *Telegraph*, however, tends to blame the socialist government. A *Telegraph* excerpt—DT21, "Unlike Britain, … France can do little to prevent the flow of suspected terrorists or weapons into its territory"—also attributes France's problems with terrorism to open borders; the journalist believes that Britain is better off remaining outside the Schengen Area. Britain and the conservative policies in place there are portrayed as superior.

References to the Muslim countries that are major sources of immigration to France also play into the presence or absence of a historicizing perspective. Algeria is mentioned five times across the *Guardian* articles in relation to colonial history and immigrants. In contrast, it is mentioned just once in one *Telegraph* article, DT7. This article also attenuates the "bitter" nature of the colonial legacy in favor of a discussion of radicalization, which is portrayed as being visited upon France from abroad. References to Tunisia either appear in conjunction with the perpetrator's profile, or contribute to contextualization: the country is mentioned in relation to the perpetrator eleven times in the *Guardian* and seventeen times in the *Telegraph* (see the excerpt from DT23 about the attack at Sousse, p. 95). It is mentioned for purposes of contextualization four times in the *Guardian* but just once in the *Telegraph*.

In her study of news dispatches, Davier (2015) observed that these texts often introduced "so-called 'background' paragraphs" (541) which contextualize the place(s) and event(s) being discussed. The ways in which this material is selected and incorporated "can shed a new light on" (541) the topic and story that precede it. As will be clear from the examples presented above, in my corpus, such paragraphs predominantly appear in the *Guardian* articles; DT7 is a notable exception (see further discussion of that article below).

While criticism of French policies is frequent throughout the corpus, the messages of the *Guardian* and the *Telegraph* are different; this difference, I argue, stems mainly from the newspapers' diverging treatment of the notions of "integration" and of "Muslim." The two terms appear most in TG1, DT7, and DT26, with "Muslim" occurring significantly more often in DT7 and DT26 than anywhere else in the corpus. TG1, having stated early in the commentary on French society that "France has a history of Islamic extremism reaching back decades," gives more space to "grave problems within France itself," also referenced in TG4 as "society's ills … and what was termed France's 'social and ethnic apartheid'" (unattributed quote). Among the internal problems of France, TG1 highlights the marginalization of certain groups which can, it is suggested, make them more prone to becoming involved in terrorism. DT7 and DT26, both of which would qualify as "news analysis" texts but read like editorials, treat the issues very differently than the *Guardian* does. In DT26, while the journalist ostensibly presents two sides by discussing the positions of two "experts," a strong net message of his text is that religion is behind terrorist attacks. The headline could not put it more clearly: "How religion can drive someone to slaughter his fellow citizens – and believe they deserve it."

DT7 is written by a French foreign correspondent who emphasizes her French identity in the text through such indexicals as "here," "we French," and so on. The text lashes out at the kind of rhetoric employed in TG1. Indeed, while failings in "integration" efforts and the bitterness left by the Algerian war are mentioned, albeit much more briefly than in TG1, blame is laid squarely at the door of (1) Daesh and other extremist groups who work to radicalize Muslims in France, (2) "imams" operating within the country and in particular in "jails," which are predominantly occupied by "Muslim men" and, more or less indirectly, (3) all Muslim men. Through use of thematization (syntactic positioning of an element that gives it emphasis) and an active construction, the message is that France was overwhelmed, not responsible: "Radicalisation came to France in waves."

In that statement, a metaphorical reference to water is also used. (For more on metaphor in the UK corpus, see section "Metaphor" below.) The water metaphor is one of two types identified by Piquer Martí (2015) which are employed in the news to qualify Muslims as a threat: "natural disaster" metaphors evoking chaos or the uncontrollable through the use of wave- and water-related imagery. Moreover, the French journalist explicitly links Muslim identity and violence, informing readers that Nice is "the French city that sent the most volunteers to fight in Syria and Iraq: more than 120 young Muslim men."

The journalist also employs an argument frequently used against specifically Muslim immigrants. First, vehemently criticizing those who intimate that "we [the French] 'parked' [their term, not hers] Muslim immigrants into banlieue 'ghettoes' and treated them appallingly," she claims, as we saw with her reference to Portuguese and Spanish immigrants, that the problem must lie with the Muslims themselves. When she does make concessions, it is to emphasize her point all the more: "If many do integrate, Muslim men still disproportionately people

French prisons." This aligns with Amiraux and Fetiu's (2017: 71) observation that "Muslim communities – and the young male segment of them in particular – are identified as being *failed citizens*" (emphasis in the original). In DT7, negativity is highlighted through alliteration; the verbal use of "people" also suggests the journalist is writing in L2. In addition, in a move reminiscent of a would-be feminist perspective that criticizes Islam and Muslims on the basis of the belief that they subjugate women, she distinguishes between the successes of *female* Muslims in French society—which she celebrates but also attributes to a desire "to escape the overbearing domination of their fathers and brothers"—and the failures of Muslim men. Furthermore, "overbearing domination" is presupposed by the definite article "the," insinuating that it is always present in these family relationships and that all Muslim men subjugate women. This is a frequent argument against the faith, employed, for example, in support of the burqa ban in France (the garment had already been mentioned earlier in the article).

Given who is to blame—extremists from elsewhere, imams and Muslims—there is blatant reliance here on the "us/them" dichotomy. In contrast, the TG1 article subtly observes that a (misguided? obsessive?) focus on secularity is perhaps part of France's problem, and the journalist interrogates the notion of "integration" *à la française*: "the French policy of 'assimilation' rather than multi-cultural integration into the supposedly secular republique' [*sic*] has, critics say, created fertile ground for polarization." (The modal "supposedly" creates critical distance.) In line with a left/center-left political agenda, the British journalist thus positions an approach to "integration" which values multiculturalism[1] as superior to the French insistence on assimilation to a resolutely French identity which, whatever else it might mean, is supposed to be *laïque*. (As we have seen, states that claim this status very often remain steeped in Christian tradition, or at least favor Christianity over most other faiths.)

These findings also raise the important question of the role of journalists' identity in shaping news content. Therefore, I end this section by highlighting an interesting choice made by another French journalist, this time in the *Guardian* (TG3). She ends her article with a quotation from Albert Camus, not only a renowned French author but one who wrote on the Algerian war and its implications for France. A translation of Camus's phrase from *Actuelles III: Chroniques algériennes (1939–1958)* (1958) evoking "les noces sanglantes du terrorisme et de la répression" features in the final sentence: "Voices of reason and moderation will be drowned out – *the bloody wedding of repression and terrorism*, as Albert Camus once called it" (my emphasis).[2] The journalist includes the kind of water metaphor ("drowned out") discussed elsewhere in this volume, while Camus's original phrase contains another metaphor whose rhetorical effect is achieved through a surprising juxtaposition. Some British readers might not see the highly relevant link made with Algeria, especially since Camus is not contextualized for them. This could contribute to creating a distance between the reader and the culture in question. On the other hand, the choice could also reflect the confidence the journalist has in her readership's literary and cultural awareness and/or intellectual curiosity.

"Bringing the Story Home"

In both sources, references to Britain and Britons work to "bring the story home" (recall Cottle ([2011] 2012) and Freedman (2017)) and in ways that are likely to heighten the sense of crisis, although these effects seem even more pronounced in the *Telegraph* articles. Where the *Guardian* includes such references, France often still remains the central focus:

> France also suffered in August 2015 when a gunman opened fire on a high-speed train that was carrying more than 500 people, before he was overpowered by three Americans – two of whom were soldiers – and a British passenger. (TG9)

A *Telegraph* article instead talks about "suffering" from a resolutely domestic perspective:

> In Britain we suffered our own lone wolf attack when two Islamist extremists hacked to death Fusilier Lee Rigby on a south London street with machetes in 2013. (DT18)

The relevance of the Nice attack for Britons is nonetheless an important aspect of *Guardian* reporting:

> The UK Foreign Office called on all Britons in France to exercise caution and follow the instructions of local law enforcement officials. (TG9)

> A number of Britons were also caught up in the attack. (TG16)

(The heading of DT25, "Britons caught up in *terror*" (my emphasis), while similar, is more dramatic.)

> The extension will see a visible security presence, both in Nice and across France, continued for another three months. This will entail more police and soldiers on the streets, a graphic reminder to Britons, who make 17 million visits to France each year, that the country, according to the Foreign Office, faces a "high threat from terrorism". (TGObs17)

The *Telegraph* employs the particularly insidious strategy of linking Lahouaiej-Bouhlel to an attack in Tunisia and to threats to Britons because the attack occurred near his home town:

> According to Tunisian security sources, he hailed from the Tunisian town of Msaken, which is close to the seaside city of Sousse, where 38 people, including 30 Britons, were gunned down by terrorists in June 2015. (DT23)

Finally, as already alluded to above, the *Telegraph* even suggests that Britain is safer than France:

> Unlike Britain – which has always retained its frontier controls and has the natural advantage of being an island – France can do little to prevent the flow of suspected terrorists or weapons into its territory. (DT21)

> Even if the plot avoids detection, the terrorists still face the problem of actually executing the attack. Here, everything depends on the quality of their training – and, in Britain at least, this has often been found wanting. (DT20)

> In the United Kingdom, the Security Service (MI5) and the police have together disrupted seven terrorist attacks in the last 18 months. (DT22)

The home country is more central than in the *Guardian* and is portrayed as superior.

Modality

Modality (defined in the Introduction) is often carried by verbs but can also be conveyed by other categories of words (e.g., "apparently," "maybe," "likelihood," and "certain"). In Davier's comparative news study of an English-language and a French-language corpus (2009: 78), which also examined modality, she pointed out that the law governing English media was stricter than that in France, Switzerland, or the United States. This, coupled with recent laws protecting intelligence bodies and a slate of anti-terror laws, suggests that when reporting on terrorist attacks, English journalists "may take more precautions" (Davier 2009: 79) in divulging information and in the language used. Indeed, Davier found that journalists writing for the *Guardian* on the terror-related event in question in her study used considerably more markers of modality than their French counterparts (79). But this does not tell us a lot, given that modality can express aspects as divergent as certainty and doubt. Table 6 presents data on modality from the UK subcorpus.

Table 6 Statistics for Modality in the UK Corpus

Modality	TG	DT
Total	106	129
Percentage of all occurrences in UK corpus	45% of all occurrences	55% of all occurrences

The *Telegraph* employs modality more frequently than the *Guardian*. This is all the more true since it has a greater tendency to employ multiple modal markers within the same phrase. What kinds of modality prevail here?

Both sets of news articles use markers of uncertainty about twice as frequently as markers of certainty. There are two tendencies in particular, however, that are worthy of note. First, with regard to particular examples of uncertainty, "reportedly" and "alleged(ly)," which allow the user to distance her- or himself from the information or avoid asserting it is factual, there are just two instances of "reportedly" and no instances of "alleged(ly)" across all the *Guardian* articles, whereas one or both appear, and often multiple times, in five different *Telegraph* articles, as shown in Table 7. Nevertheless, neither newspaper has numerous occurrences.

Table 7 Occurrences of "Reportedly" and "Alleged(ly)" in the UK Corpus

Modality	TG1	TG17	DT5	DT6	DT7	DT8	DT23
Reportedly	1	1	1	2	0	1	3
Alleged(ly)	0	0	0	1	1	1	0

The second and more interesting tendency is related to the ways in which the news sources combine modal words, including by merging uncertainty with certainty. The following paragraph from the *Guardian* is a particularly telling example of this. By closely aligning "if" constructions and modal elements, such passages come to frame the hypothetical as fact. Let us examine the way this phenomenon plays out in TG2. First, note the words in bold below:

> There are various **possibilities**. Lahouaiej-Bouhlel **may** be a genuine loner and suffering serious mental illness. His act **may** have no ideological element at all. This, however[,] **seems unlikely**. A second **possibility** is that, already angry and violent, he was inspired, **if not** directed, to commit his attack by Isis or extremist Islamic militancy more generally. ... this **would** indicate the continuing power of the group's ideology. In this case it is **almost certain** he **will** have some contacts with others involved in hardline Islamic activism in Nice ... This scenario is more alarming, **suggesting the possibility** of more attacks to come. (TG2)

The modal phrase "seems unlikely" discounts the conjectures preceding it. It is doubtful that Bouhlel was mentally ill and it is likely that ideology was behind his actions. The second possibility, on the contrary, is given a patina of factuality through the lasting focus upon it and through an accumulation of journalistic choices largely relying on modality. The phrase "if not directed" insinuates that it is actually very likely the perpetrator was directed by ISIS, although this has not been proven. (The same type of construction occurs in TG1, written by the same journalist.) With "this would indicate," we are momentarily back in the realm of the hypothetical; however, the text quickly shifts from "this case" to "it is almost certain" as well as "will," moving us back toward the realm of certainty and fact. Despite the return to the notions of "scenario" and "possibility," the final message is that more attacks will come.

There are numerous instances of both conjecture in the absence of fact, and this kind of portrayal of the hypothetical as fact, in both sets of articles. That said, the *Telegraph* appears to portray hypothetical as fact within more concise segments, that is, phrases or sentences rather than paragraphs; this does not necessarily make the effects less pervasive, however. One example from DT21 is "**If so** [if Bouhlel acted 'on the incitement' of Daesh], this event provides further **proof** of France's acute vulnerability to Islamist terrorism."

This "patina of factuality" trend is also present in the *Telegraph* articles in the very early moments of reporting, and it is more insidious. Consider this sentence from DT18 (July 15):

> the **fact** that the key suspect in last night's attack was, **as far as we understand**, a French-Tunisian petty criminal known to the police **indicates** the French authorities **need to** improve their methods of monitoring **potential** Islamist terrorists.

"Fact," albeit tempered via a non-essential subordinate clause that introduces some doubt, carries the weight; furthermore, what is *also* presented as fact is the idea that (a) the perpetrator was an Islamist terrorist, (b) petty criminals are highly likely to become terrorists, and (c) therefore, petty criminals should be put under surveillance. This reflects support for conservative policies of greater surveillance to enhance security. It also raises the thorny issue of who is to determine who constitutes a "potential Islamist terrorist." Similarly, the next day in DT6, the phrase "no **known** links to terrorism" is followed by "[t]he **fact** that the killer was known to the authorities **will be** of grave concern to those trying to prevent terrorist attacks in France." The message: this was a terrorist attack.

Observing instances of modality suggests that the two sources diverge in the way they address the claim by Daesh that Lahouaiej-Bouhlel acted on the terrorist organization's behalf. Both sources observe that the perpetrator had "no **known** links" to Daesh or extremists (the exact phrase appeared in DT6 on July 16; TG2 on July 17; DT23 and DT24 on July 18). Even more important, they do so *after* Daesh claims responsibility on July 16. However, through modal use in discussions of the claim, what is insinuated is that if the links are not (yet) known, they exist nonetheless. TG2, for instance, compares Lahouaiej-Bouhlel to other attackers proven to be terrorists. The argument turns around a "lack of piety among militants" which the perpetrator also demonstrated. "Lahouaiej-Bouhlel **certainly** matches the classic profile of [the] French violent Islamic extremist in many ways," the journalist asserts, adding that the perpetrator's apparent disregard for religious precepts

> was **true** of the dozen or so French and Belgian young men involved in bombings and shootings earlier this year, and of Mohammed Merah, who committed the first major attack in France in 2012. (TG2)

By extension, it is insinuated, whereas the role of religion is debatable, Lahouaiej-Bouhlel is clearly an extremist. In addition, "**If true** [if Lahouaiej-Bouhlel is involved with Daesh], this **would indicate** that Isis has continuing capacity for ambitious terrorist operations in Europe despite the pressure the group is under. And that **would be** a highly concerning prospect" (TG2). Here we see a blurring of supposition and fact (another instance of "true"; the indicative "has") which means that even though there is a shift back to supposition ("would be"), the idea that the information is factual—and now, extremely serious—is firmly in place.

What happens earlier on, before Daesh even claims responsibility? TG9 (July 15) evokes a "**possible** affiliation." More interestingly, it maintains that there was more than one perpetrator (never proven), already suggesting a coordinated attack: "**it is difficult to conclude** that *their* assault was not intended to be directed at the heart of France's national identity"; "[i]nitial details **suggested** a tactic that jihadi propaganda has suggested for several years" (my emphasis). TG12 (also July 15) makes a concession but gives credence to an authority figure's (French President Hollande's) early conclusion that this was terrorism, while also quickly turning a possibility into a quasi-certainty:

> François Hollande, the French president, has called the killing of 84 people watching a Bastille Day fireworks display a terrorist act, even though there has been no claim of responsibility for the atrocity in Nice and no **confirmed** identification of the attacker.

These **may** come shortly, and are **likely to confirm** suspicions of the involvement – direct or indirect – of either Islamic State or al-Qaida.

Even though the tone changes the next day, paradoxically, in conjunction with the claim by Daesh (TG15 observes that "[i]t is still **unclear** whether he had any involvement in a terrorist organization," while TG16 refers to the "claim" seven times and uses the phrase "no evidence" twice), the seed has been planted—this was a terrorist attack connected to an extremist group—and at a time when, in reality, there was still much uncertainty.

Like the *Guardian*'s texts, those of the *Telegraph* refer to Daesh's claim often. However, whereas later in its cycle, the *Guardian* indicates multiple times that the "claim" of responsibility by Daesh has not been substantiated, when the *Telegraph* indicates this, which is only once out of the eight times it refers to the claim, it emphasizes the "failure" of French authorities to establish the link, simultaneously discrediting them and giving credence to the claim: "investigators have failed to establish links between the Bastille Day killer and Isil" "despite the terror group claiming him as a 'soldier of Islam'" (DT8, July 18). Furthermore, four news analysis articles, either emphatically (DT7, DT18, DT26) or subtly (DT27), blame Muslims or Islam.

Finally, in an interesting departure from the messages we have seen conveyed so far, DT25 gives credence to an alternative hypothesis, that the perpetrator was suicidal, rather than violently—and religiously—motivated:

A police source has told *The Telegraph* that Bouhel **might** have been motivated more by a desire to commit suicide than by an Islamist ideology. (DT25)

This possibility is not given much attention, however, which is discussed in the conclusions to this chapter.

Alliteration

The *Telegraph* articles include significantly more instances of alliteration than the *Guardian* articles. As Table 8 shows, by far the greatest percentage of occurrences of alliterated content is negative. In addition, there are 8 percent more of these in the *Telegraph*, which also has 10 percent fewer positive instances.

How does alliteration contribute to representing France, Muslims, and the events in question? Both sources emphasize the trauma resulting from the Nice attack through the use of alliteration (for instance: "**t**ry **t**o come to **t**erms with the **t**errible events" (TG11), "**s**tunned and **s**ickened" (TG13), or "**sh**ell-**sh**ocked" (DT7)). However, the *Telegraph* uses it more frequently in conjunction with the

Table 8 Alliteration and Connotation in the UK Corpus

Alliteration	Guardian	Telegraph
Negative	61%	69%
Positive	20%	10%
Neutral	19%	21%

violent aspects of the event itself ("**r**am **r**aid," twice (DT5), "killing and **m**ai**m**ing the **m**axi**m**um number" (TG18), "**m**urder on a **m**assive scale," "**s**meared with dried blood while **s**mashed children's buggies and other debris were **s**trewn across the **s**easide promenade" (DT19), or "**m**ethod of **m**urder," twice (DT20)). Particularly telling are the findings on alliteration related to government or politics, on the one hand, and to religion, on the other. Examples of these are presented in Tables 9 and 10.

TG1 acknowledges, and emphasizes through alliteration, not only the French authorities' "failings" in response to terrorist attacks (also contextualized as part of a complex set of problems), but also improvements achieved thanks to measures introduced in 2014 but only now (2016) being demonstrated due to the "time" needed to "find and train" the requisite personnel. TG4, 13, and 14 highlight the difficulties President François Hollande is facing due to the attacks that have taken place on his watch. TG4 also reports criticism by the socialist Prime Minister Manuel Valls of the opposition's proposals, and the journalist opts to include a critical reference by Valls to the right-wing Trump. Conversely, in DT27, devoted to Trump's chances in the upcoming election, while Trump is not portrayed as perfect (his "proposed ban on Muslim immigration" is probably unconstitutional), he is seen as a viable response to the danger of terrorism (and the journalist claims that Hillary Clinton, Obama, and the Democrats are worse than Trump). The first sentence from DT7 included in Table 9 highlights the tensions in France's political sphere; in addition, unlike the *Guardian* articles, DT7, 18, 19, and 26 alliteratively underline the authorities' weakness or ineffectiveness, with DT18 even including a jibe: that officials were surely "quietly congratulating themselves" after France hosted the Euro 2016 football tournament without incident, only to face this attack soon after. The political leanings of the sources come through in these examples, in part because they are reinforced via alliteration. While Richard Barrett (DT22) speaks out against "a dramatic increase in the securitisation of French society" and calls for inclusive dialogue between communities and officials, his

Table 9 Alliterated Content Related to Government and Politics in the UK Corpus

Government/Politics	
News source	Textual segment with alliteration/assonance
TG	
1	"failings of the fragmented bureaucratic and still under-resourced security services"
1	"time taken to find and then train"
3	"play out politically in France"
4	"president is under pressure"
4	"anger and accusations"
4	"pleading for the preservation"
4	"what he deemed divisive Donald Trump-style proposals"
13	"pressure to take more decisive action to defend France"
14	"constitutes a crisis for Hollande's premiership"
DT	
7	"France finds itself caught in a fatal loop of fear and recrimination, where each side's grievances fed [*sic*] from the existence of the other"
7	"mismanagement of security measures"
18	"suggests that the French security authorities are still struggling to come to terms with the sheer scale of the threat"
18	"their methods of monitoring"
18	"quietly congratulating themselves"
19	"unprepared and unable"
20	"success of the security forces. Suicide attacks have become so difficult that the terrorists have been forced to switch tactics."
22	[no one is] "complacent about continued success"
22	"government policy or public perception"
22	"development of a dialogue"
26	"state of security"
26	"increased police presence"
27	"the race to the Right"
27	"proposed ban on Muslim immigration contradicts that much misread document"
27	"responding to crises in a cool way" [actually criticism of Obama as only "reactive"; Trump is different]

position unfortunately appears to be an anomalous one in the *Telegraph* articles analyzed, despite the fact that he is the "former director of global counter-terrorism operations for MI6." Finally, while DT20 praises "the success of the security forces," this refers to any forces facing the new "lone-wolf" truck attack tactic, not French efforts specifically.

Let us now turn to the interplay between alliteration and the treatment of religion by the news sources. Table 10 presents the relevant textual segments.

Table 10 Alliterated Content Related to Religion in the UK Corpus

Religion	
News source	Textual segment with alliteration/assonance
TG	
1	"supposedly secular"
17	"accused of antagonising Muslims"
DT	
7	"Money for mosques followed; then the imams to preach in them"
7	"Muslim men still disproportionately people French prisons"
7	"strive at school" [Muslim women–in part to "escape" the "domination" of Muslim men]
20	"contact with a charismatic preacher"
21	"Muslim minority"
26	"drive someone to slaughter his fellow citizens"
26	"a minority of French Muslims"
26	"the role of religion"
26	"the central role of religion"
26	"while it could be argued follows a flawed reading of the religion"
27	"stop Muslims from migrating to America"

I have discussed DT7 in detail elsewhere (Riggs 2018); among other issues was the question of journalist identity. The above results on alliteration show that while the kinds of positions taken in DT7 are more typical of *Telegraph* "news analysis" articles, the case is not an isolated one. The results also confirm a more general trend: the *Telegraph* emphasizes religion much more than the *Guardian* does. TG1's reference to the "supposedly secular" France is a criticism of the country's policy favoring assimilation over multiculturalism, while TG17 observes that Nice's former mayor has been "accused of antagonising Muslims" and refers to an aggression against soldiers by "a man," no religion indicated, "outside a Jewish community center." Thus, examples of "tensions in Nice" are provided without blaming a specific religious group.

The situation is quite different in the *Telegraph* "news analysis" articles. As clearly seen in the examples of alliteration above, DT26 points the finger at Islam while for DT7, Muslims are a central "problem." Whereas in DT27, reference to the Nice attack is mainly a pretext to talk about Trump and US politics, the link is clearly made between Muslims and terrorism, and credence is given to the implicit prediction that the American public, having observed international events such as this attack, will elect the man who promises to "stop Muslims from migrating to America." Interestingly, DT26's attention-grabbing headline about "slaughtering fellow citizens" contradicts the idea, dear to conservatives including the DT7 journalist, that terrorists are "others" who "flow" in from abroad.[3] It would be easy enough for UK readers to recall the London 7/7 attacks, in which the perpetrators were UK citizens. In addition, the multiple attacks that have taken place in the UK *since* the Nice event, that *have* occurred despite border controls, also refute this position. The perpetrator in Nice was not a suspected terrorist and, while originally from Tunisia, had already lived in France for a number of years. It is true that the profile of terrorists in France has often been one of French sons of immigrant parents, as TG2 explicitly states: "the classic profile of [the] French violent Islamic extremist" is that he was "born in the country of immigrant parents." Yet much debate surrounds the easy equating of such individuals' violence with being Muslim. Nevertheless, Islam is often a central focus of news coverage and, in this corpus, strongly emphasized through alliteration in the *Telegraph* articles. Indeed, DT26, published on July 15 before much was known about the attack, centers on the debate between France's "two most recognized experts on Islam in the West." This kind of reporting choice immediately and unequivocally *makes it about Islam.*

Metaphor

The pervasiveness of the "war on terror" trope in the media ever since 9/11 is attested in the literature; this and my own cursory observation that the kind of texts studied here incorporated violence even when terrorism was not the topic led me to formulate the hypothesis that metaphors would most often be negative, and that a significant number would evoke war and violence specifically. For this reason, I begin the discussion of metaphor in the corpus with a review of the findings related to war/violent metaphor.

War/Violent Metaphor

The present subcorpus confirms that the "war on terror" trope, made a household name by the George W. Bush administration after 9/11, is alive and well. According to Titley (2017: 7), "[t]he attacks in Paris of January and November 2015 positioned France as a key site in an amorphous war that spills across territories and boundaries." In the aftermath of those attacks and the Nice event, such positioning, performed by the authorities and by the press, prevails: use of the trope in official discourse is reproduced by both the *Guardian* and the *Telegraph* (albeit more frequently by the former). TG4 reminds readers that "Hollande had already declared that France was 'at war' following November's Paris attacks," while TG14 recalls his "war-like stance" at that time. In relation to the Nice attack, DT6 quotes then interior socialist minister Bernard Cazeneuve as saying "We are at war with terrorists who want to strike us at any cost and who are extremely violent," while TG13 reproduces far-right *Front National* leader Marine Le Pen's "call [] for a 'war on Islamic fundamentalism'" and her accusation that "all that had happened so far was a 'war on words.'" TG14 and TG16 repeat part of Le Pen's statement as well; TG15 includes part of the statement by Cazeneuve quoted in DT6 and also cites right-wing former president Nicolas Sarkozy's use of a war metaphor.

Official discourse and the decision by journalists to quote it thus clearly situate Nice within the "war on terror" event chain. In doing so, they also clearly qualify the violent act as an act of terror. What is more interesting, though, is that war- and violence-related metaphors crop up in these articles in relation to content and themes that are *not* directly related to terrorist violence. Table 11 shows the results of the coding of metaphors in terms of connotation and whether they describe terrorist violence (TV), do not describe terrorist violence (NTV) and, within the latter category, are nonetheless related to violence (V):

Table 11 Quantitative Data on Violence and Connotation of Metaphors in the UK Corpus

Metaphor		Negative			Positive			Neutral				
Source	Total	TV	NV	V	TV	NV	V	TV	NV	V		% violent
TG	51	17	11	6	0	3	0	2	10	2	Violent: 27*	53%
DT	49	15	6	4	3	5	1	10	10	3	Violent: 36	73%

TV=Terrorist violence

NTV=Not terrorist violence

V=Violent nonetheless

*The figures in this column were determined by adding up those from the "TV" and "V" columns.

Two sets of results in particular stand out: one related to negative connotation, the other to violence. Violent metaphors constitute over half of the occurrences of the stylistic feature in both sets of articles. The *Guardian* tends more toward negative metaphors than the *Telegraph*, notably even when the content described is not terrorist violence. In contrast, across connotations, the *Telegraph* includes more violent metaphors than the *Guardian*. However, we have just seen a number of instances in the *Guardian* of violence introduced through direct quoting, which was purposely left out of the quantitative data analysis in order to ensure the focus was on the journalists' own style.

Let us now look at war- and violence-related metaphors in detail. By using the imaged phrase "standard bearer," which carries naval or military associations, twice, TG1 emphasizes its assertion that France is seen, including by Daesh, as the symbol *par excellence* of "western secular liberalism." According to the journalist, this makes the country a target. Moreover, in line with what Lakoff and Johnson (1980) label the "countries as persons" conceptual metaphor, France is often personified in both sets of articles through discussion of the emotions and reactions of the country. TG9 uses violent metaphor to explain why Daesh has targeted France and, in particular, why the organization chose the symbolic Bastille Day: it "represents a significant blow by French people to a tyrannical regime and, as such, the spirit of the French republic itself." Thus, Daesh has struck France when it will hurt most. TG1 continues with the battle-related imagery further on:

> And this may be a final reason why Isis has focused on France. The group has been heavily influenced by both millennial thinking, which stresses the imminent final battle between the forces of belief and unbelief...

The *Guardian* article emphasizes the idea that Daesh is on a religious crusade, and the presence of alliteration makes the phrase even more salient. Similar imagery appears elsewhere in the *Guardian* articles, in addition to Hollande's aforementioned "war-like stance" (TG15). France, too, must take a war-like position: "Terrorism has upended politics in France since 2015, and now that is about to get worse. It has put the nation on a war footing." "Sparring" appears twice in TG4 to highlight the political disunity which reigns following the Nice attack:

> After last year's attacks there were brief pauses in political sparring, but this time the accusations began sooner. (TG4)

> After the attacks last year ... there was a short pause in political sparring. But this time the anger and accusations began even before families could bury their dead. (TG4)

Also note the assonance with "a" in the second example. The same article uses the term "martial" to further emphasize this contrast between political positions after the "Charlie Hebdo" and Bataclan events, on the one hand, and after Nice, on the other:

> After the Charlie Hebdo attacks, the tone of the government's approach was to try to understand society's ills and act on what was termed France's "social and ethnic apartheid." After November's attacks, the tone was more martial. ... This time Hollande is pleading for the preservation of national cohesion and unity.

Here as elsewhere there is strong emphasis on national political disarray (again reinforced through alliteration). Coupled with the violent act itself, this may heighten the impression that events are out of control, that there is a crisis situation, an impression which is also encouraged by many other stylistic choices throughout the corpus.

In terms of war-related metaphor and in particular how it is associated with politics, the *Telegraph* corpus shows similar patterns, but it attributes more blame to the socialist government through a combination of metaphor and other choices. As in the *Guardian*, there is concern about how these violent attacks may fuel the cause of France's far-right *Front National*. In DT7, the attacks are associated with Muslims and it is assumed that the electorate will do the same:

> Nice, together with the regional capital, Marseille, and countless smaller towns with large Muslim populations in south-east France, is the Front's prime battlefield. (DT7)

Moutet, the French journalist who wrote DT7, goes on to assert that the attack on Bastille Day revellers in Nice was, in fact, "a major coup for Isil"—for her, Daesh is clearly behind it—"because it will exacerbate the racial tensions upon which it [Daesh] thrives." It would have been fair to admit that the *Front National* also thrives on racial tensions.

One of Moutet's metaphors may give the initial impression that she faults all politicians equally:

> Meanwhile, France's politicians, unlike after previous terrorist attacks, have left their shell-shocked constituents bereft. (DT7)

Note the alliteration, emphasizing the striking equation of the ramifications of the attack with the ramifications of political turmoil. Moutet's use of violent metaphor continues:

> With next year's presidential and general elections in their sights, they have given up on national unity to denounce mismanagement of security measures. (DT7)

(DT24 makes a similar observation using metaphor: "political unity ... has shattered"; see discussion of the full sentence below). In reality, rather than faulting all politicians, both DT7's and DT24's authors actually favor a conservative position; DT7, through Moutet's negative stance on Muslims, reinforced through alliteration (Riggs 2019b) and what she terms the "failings of integration," and DT24, through incorporation of direct quotations from right-wing figures, not both sides, so that it is criticism of the then socialist government and its "failures" that come to the fore:

> Nice has long been a bastion of the Right. Christian Estrosi, a security hardliner and ex-minister under Mr Sarkozy who is now president of the wider Riviera region, accused the government of failing completely in Nice. (DT24)

Furthermore, while both news sources refer to the claim made by Daesh that Bouhlel was a "soldier" of Islam, the *Telegraph* both uses the metaphor more often and tends to take the claim at face value, while the *Guardian* emphasizes the lack of evidence for the claim. Finally, DT7's author concludes via a violent metaphor that the Nice attack is decisive. She also intimates that France was unified before the spate of attacks of which Nice is the most recent, in line with her blame of Muslims and radicalization which, according to her, came from outside, and with her failure to acknowledge longstanding social problems (contrary to the *Guardian*):

> Nice, I am sad to say, may prove the most divisive blow against the France of liberté, égalité and fraternité. (DT7)

Let us now consider metaphor usage related to plants/growth, disease and water.

Plants/Growth

This rubric reveals a key difference between the two news sources. TG1 uses plant- or growth-related metaphor to evoke the underlying, longstanding social and economic causes of the violence France is experiencing: "Other reasons for the violence are rooted in grave problems within France itself." The article goes on to discuss security problems and failings, recognizing that they are not just down to France, but also the result of shortcomings at the European level; some "grave problems" emphasized by this and other TG articles are social and create "fertile ground for polarization." TG3 takes a similar position:

> Hollande has announced more airstrikes in Iraq and Syria against Islamic State, as well as the calling up of reservists and a three-month extension of France's state of emergency – none of which is likely to address the roots of the problem.

The instance of "root" found in the *Telegraph* subcorpus plays a very different role, emphasizing instead the presence and threat of Salafism:

> Salafism, a form of conservative Islam which rejects liberal French values and provides the theological underpinnings of global jihadism, has taken root. (DT26)

In sum, the two news sources appear to employ plant/growth metaphors in conjunction with distinct phenomena, but all are negative.

Disease/illness

We have seen that certain *Telegraph* articles that actually resemble editorials emphasize the terrorism narrative and the connections between Muslims and terrorism. This happens in part through the journalists' use of disease-related metaphor. In DT26, on July 15, British journalist Meleagrou-Hitchens asserts that

> [t]he person who drove that lorry believed he was part of an altruistic and utopianist global project intended to save humanity, not destroy it. The people he killed were, in his eyes, a cancerous obstacle to this vision, and having chosen to reject it had to be removed from the equation. (DT26)

Despite having zero familiarity with Bouhlel, he unequivocally makes Bouhlel a religious extremist and makes religion, and in particular Islam's supposed abhorrence of the Western "Us," the issue. Use of a disease metaphor serves his purpose.

Now, consider Moutet's choices in the following excerpt from DT7:

> Bouhlel's alleged associates have now been arrested and held by the French police, looking for the connections that have escaped them until now. … Meanwhile, a divided country is once again questioning the motivations of the enemy within. Isil's deadly ideas are airborne, like a virus. … The more they separate seemingly ordinary Muslims from the national community, the better, they believe – especially if activists and the commentariat's useful idiots reinforce the notion that the perpetrators were "driven to it". (DT7)

Her strong metaphorical language emphasizes the threat, and the possibility of contagion, represented by Daesh, and denigrates a position more typical of the left—and, indeed, of the *Guardian*.

Water-Related Metaphor

Both Baker et al. (2013) and Piquer Marti (2015) have highlighted the role of water-related metaphor in negative discourse about Muslim immigrants and refugees. The results of my study suggest that their use is more nuanced. In TG1, the wave metaphor is fairly standard and uses 9/11 as a benchmark, and the cause of the violence is interrogated:

> There will also be the question: why is France suffering a wave of extremist violence that is more intense – certainly more lethal – than any other seen in the west since the 9/11 attacks almost 15 years ago? (TG1)

However, such metaphor contributes to contextualizing and historicizing the events as well:

> France has a history of Islamic extremism reaching back decades. The 1990s saw two waves of attacks. One was linked to the bloody civil war between authorities and extremist groups in the former colony of Algeria. A second involved homegrown militants in the north of France who evolved a particular brand of terrorism mixing armed robbery and jihadism. (TG1)

While the article does bring up terrorism early on (July 15), it in various ways refutes the narrative that recent terrorist attacks constitute a "crisis." This is also supported by the *Guardian*'s greater general focus on underlying and longstanding social causes of extremism, which we see here with "history … reaching back decades," reference to the civil war with Algeria, and the "homegrown" (another growth metaphor) nature of certain violent activists. The metaphorical "brand" also suggests that there are various types of extremism, with different types of actors, motivations, and *modi operandi*.

Next, we find a very different kind of criticism through metaphor ("drowned out") from that which we saw in the *Telegraph* articles just discussed, and the water-related metaphor of "pouring" is used to describe compassion, rather than immigration (recall Baker et al. 2013):

> Beyond the terrible loss of families for ever [*sic*] torn apart and traumatized just because they wanted to watch fireworks on a warm summer evening, the wider result [note the alliterative effects with "t" and "w"] of this tragedy is that extremes, political and religious, will continue to feed off each other. Voices of reason and moderation will be drowned out (TG3).

> [C]ondolences poured in [for those families and the deceased]. (TG13)

Moreover, TG16, which was written by a journalist who visited M'saken, Tunisia, actually uses water imagery and a related reference to a natural phenomenon to depict the history of Bouhlel's psychological state. He had a "stormy adolescence"; "[i]n France his violent temperament resurfaced." These and other images also contextualize by helping the reader to picture the setting, which is portrayed in a neutral-to-positive light aided by use of metaphor (as is Nice, in the *Guardian* but not in the *Telegraph* (Riggs 2019b)):

> Once a small town, M'saken has in recent years been swallowed up by the expanding Sousse coastal conurbation, its wealth fuelled by miles of hotels along glittering beaches. The town has handsome cafes and wide boulevards, its prosperity underlined by a shiny Renault dealership on the main street. (TG15)

In contrast, as already mentioned, according to Moutet in DT7, "Radicalisation came to France ... in waves"; that is, external forces, not France, are responsible for it (also see Riggs 2018). Similarly, DT21's water-related metaphor is a dig at what are, to a conservative observer, the downsides of being in the European Union and the Schengen zone:

> France can do little to prevent the flow of suspected weapons or terrorists into its territory. (DT21)

Terrorists and their tools come from outside.

Finally, the phrase "in the wake of," used a total of three times in DT18, emphasizes both political turmoil and the terror event chain:

> Political unity that stood firm in the wake of the Charlie Hebdo and Paris November terror attacks has shattered in the wake of this latest massacre.

To summarize, the findings on metaphor point to its ubiquity in language, demonstrate that the "war on terror" trope is still widely used by both politicians and the media, and suggest that the *Guardian* and the *Telegraph* use certain types of metaphor in divergent ways. For example, while both news sources use war and battle metaphors to emphasize political disarray in France, the *Telegraph*, in line with its political leanings, more roundly blames the then socialist government. In the *Guardian*, plant- and growth-related metaphors point to longstanding societal problems that underlie radicalization and terrorism, while in the *Telegraph*, these and disease-oriented metaphors tend to emphasize the threat that Islam and Muslims represent. Finally, violent and negative metaphors abound in both news sources, even in textual segments where terrorist violence is not the topic, which may contribute to fomenting fear and a sense of threat.

French-Speaking Switzerland (the *Suisse romande*)

Table 12 recapitulates the data for the subcorpus from French-speaking Switzerland.

Table 12 Statistics for the Swiss Corpus

News source	Number of articles	Number of words	Percentage of corpus
Le Temps (LT)	12	9,342	29%
La Tribune de Genève (TDG)	26	16,730	52%
Le Courrier (LC)	10	5,992	19%
Total	48	32,064	

Few relevant *Courrier* articles came up in my search. Those that did are remarkably short, and most come from the *Agence Télégraphique Suisse* (ATS). All but one of the articles in the *Temps* subcorpus either come from *Agence France Presse* (AFP) or were written by Richard Werly, a correspondent working in Paris. The remaining article was written by Etienne Dubuis. The *Tribune de Genève* subcorpus is by far the largest, and the majority of the articles taken from that newspaper come from the AFP or ATS in combination with "nxp" (Newsexpress, a section of Tamedia that prepares press releases for the Web).

"Jihad"

The morphology of the French language means there is just one word for "jihadist" (with two possible spellings: *jihadiste, djihadiste*) and therefore there is no such issue as that we saw with the term "jihadi" in the *Guardian*. Nevertheless, occurrences of the French equivalents of "jihad" and its derivatives are relatively common, particularly in *La Tribune de Genève* (TDG): it has thirty-three occurrences, while *Le Temps* (LT) has eleven and *Le Courrier* (LC), ten. TDG1 uses "jihad" or related terms in presenting a timeline of violent attacks that had occurred in France since January 2015. TDG2 mentions two previous attacks abroad, in Canada, and in London—the killing of British soldier Lee Rigby—while TDG6 reminds us that in March 2004, Madrid had experienced "the most deadly jihadist attacks ever to hit Europe." These and other articles from all three Swiss sources place the Nice attack squarely in an event chain of "jihadist" attacks in France and abroad, and the move is often accompanied by quotes from various "specialists." TDG12 indicates that there is no link between this attack and Switzerland but warns that "the jihadist threat remains high," while TDG23 is mainly about then Head of the Department of Justice and Police Pierre Maudet's call for Swiss police to be trained to deal with jihadist violence. Domestic considerations in the wake of the attack are thus also a key focus of the *Suisse romande* news texts. TDG26 explains that Nice is a "breeding ground for jihadists" and TDG7 discusses a "jihadist recruiter" who has lived—and, we are to assume, recruited—there for a number of years.

Various segments in *Le Temps* that use the term evoke the perpetrators of the "jihadist attacks" of 2015 and the shift in the behavior of French political leaders since: namely, that the unity they showed in that period is already absent immediately after the Nice attack. Political disunity was also highlighted in the UK subcorpus. In *Le Temps*, certain positive measures taken by Hollande's government are pointed out (LT3), and the "fractures" in society that divide the population and make some young people more vulnerable to jihadist propaganda (LT7, LT12), discussed. According to LT12, the "jihadist threat" is admittedly higher since January 2015 (LT12). In the "Related Links" section accompanying the same article, *djihadistes* appears three times.

Thus, the two sources discussed, while they use "jihad" in different ways, make the concept fairly central and position the Nice attack in an event chain of "jihadist" violence. *Le Courrier* shows a similar pattern. LC2 also evokes the killing of Lee Rigby in London and the attack in Canada, but this time to link the Nice attack with other attacks with *vehicles* in the past, perpetrated "for the jihadist cause." LC2 and LC4 inform us that Nice is the city that has seen the most "jihadists go to Syria and Iraq," despite the fact that in LC4, the paragraph containing this information begins with the phrase "No proven link with radical Islam." The same paragraph also talks about the infamous recruiter. LC4 observes that Lahouaiej-Bouhlel "has not traveled to the countries of jihad." The same article also asks whether the claim by the "jihadist group" Daesh is an attempt at distortion, but this element comes very late in the text (last phrase of paragraph eight). The lead of LT6, too, observes that Daesh's claim was "perhaps opportunistic." All three newspapers nevertheless consider that information about jihadists and their violence is highly relevant when reporting on the attack in Nice.

Portrayal of France; of Muslims

In segments related to French society, the *Tribune de Genève* strongly emphasizes Nice's history; architecture; and, along with the other two Swiss newspapers, the city's world renown, beauty, and popularity with tourists from all over the world. This allows the *Tribune* to reinforce what it maintains in multiple articles, that the attributes of the city make it a "symbolic," "emblematic" target for terrorist violence. The *Tribune* also devotes one article to the French fund used to provide compensation to victims of terrorism, which is not seen in any other news source studied here. The newspaper briefly highlights the above-average unemployment rate of the city, whereas *Le Temps* emphasizes the problem of unemployment in disadvantaged neighborhoods across France as one of the significant "problems" or "fractures" plaguing the country. Like all of the newspapers in the corpus, the Swiss sources indicate that Nice is a hub of Islamist radicalization. The *Tribune* also explicitly connects France and Geneva: "in Geneva, where many French people live and work" (TDG12). In addition, the *Tribune* is the Swiss news source that focuses most on the ramifications of the attack for Switzerland (tourism; the Swiss casualties of the attack; calls for more police training). That said, it also devotes an article to the decision by Spain to reinforce security in tourist areas in the wake of the attack. It is at such moments, or when reporting on the details of the event and of Bouhlel's background, rather than on the topic of French society, that TDG contextualizes; this distinguishes it from the other two Swiss newspapers.

The term "Muslim" (*musulman*) appears just twice in the *Courrier* corpus, nine times in that of *Le Temps*, and six times in the *Tribune de Genève*, but in the latter, all six instances are within direct quotes. The most marked expressions of attitudes toward Muslims all come from LT6, written by Richard Werly, and all encourage negative interpretations (although the third excerpt is slightly more nuanced):

> the other hypothesis: that a man who had never been registered as radicalized by the intelligence services simply managed to remain "off their radar screen," which explains the concern of many neighborhoods in France that have a significant Muslim population.

> A latent civil war: in a country with a population of between five and six million Muslims, how can acts of violence by disturbed people who want to take action "like soldiers of ISIS" be avoided?

> If, however, the connection between the man and Daesh proves to be a lot less clear, the debate will be above all a societal one, and risks reviving concerns about a latent civil war on the part of numerous police officials and experts: in a country with a population of between five and six million Muslims—a dozen victims of the Nice attack were Muslim—how can acts of violence by disturbed people who want to take action "like soldiers of ISIS" be avoided?

The first two excerpts, a segment of text and a heading, equate being Muslim with becoming radicalized or with being more susceptible to becoming unbalanced and, in turn, radicalized. Moreover, the first excerpt is an example of conjecture in the absence of information, also seen in the UK corpus, while the last excerpt, in addition to building upon the preceding heading, is introduced by an "if" construction which, as we saw in TG2 (UK subcorpus) above, builds from the hypothetical to a strong likelihood or even inevitability ("comment éviter": how can it be avoided). In an article published the following day (July 18), however, Werly recognizes the vulnerability of Muslim youth as an underlying factor in the fracturing of society by "Daesh":

> The first fracture is the effective abandonment of many neighborhoods where a section of the Muslim youth is preyed upon by Islamist recruiters. This is not to say that Daesh rules the roost in these peripheral areas afflicted by unemployment and drug trafficking. On the contrary: many residents, Muslim or not, successfully overcome the challenges and avoid the worst. But six months of exceptional measures are not enough to resolve problems that have built up over years. (LT7)

Here we find a historicizing tendency also seen in the center-left *Guardian*. Furthermore, it is similar in tone to the attitudes expressed toward Muslims in

Le Courrier: these two sources (but not *La Tribune*) emphasize the efforts of "Daesh" to create division between Muslims and non-Muslims in French society and the terrorist organization's hope that some Muslims will feel so marginalized and persecuted that they will turn to violence. Indeed, *Le Courrier* criticizes the way right-wing rhetoric plays into the hands of ISIS, aiding the organization to deepen divisions in European countries in order to weaken them and intensify the cycle of violence. After demonstrating that the French right wing is adopting the extreme and anti-Muslim discourse of the far-right, LC5 observes:

> These declarations will only delight ISIS, whose goal is to provoke conflicts around questions of identity in Western societies in order to push a certain number of Muslims who have been discriminated against to adopt the rhetoric of persecution and to encourage terrorist activities. (LC5)

This recognition of the complexity and danger of the responses to such discourse is not present across the entire corpus. Finally, the occurrences of "Muslim" and the related content reveal a lesser focus on religion in these Swiss newspapers than, for example, in the UK *Telegraph*.

Modality

Table 13 presents the data on modality in the subcorpus from French-speaking Switzerland. *Le Temps* shows remarkably frequent use of *peut-être* (perhaps, maybe) and *risquer/risque* ((to) risk). It also vacillates between questioning the validity of the terrorism label and suggesting this was the evident conclusion to draw, in part using modality. For instance:

> The **perhaps** opportunistic claim by Daesh (LT6, July 17)

> A man ... who **perhaps** simply succeeded in staying "off the radar" (LT6)

> It took less than two hours for police to confirm what **seemed self-evident**, after having first evoked a "criminal attack". The characteristics of this massacre are indeed those of a terrorist attack, **perhaps** not directly commissioned by Daesh, but **probably** inspired by the extremist Islamist organization. (LT8, July 18)

> According to the same source, among the hundreds of witnesses already interviewed by investigators, several have alluded to the religiosity of the killer.[4] The perpetrator of the attack, claimed by Daesh, **seemed** up to now to have more of a profile of a disturbed person and was unknown to French intelligence services. (LT5)

Table 13 Statistics for Modality in the Swiss Corpus

Modality	LT	TDG	LC
Total	66	70	25
Percentage of all occurrences in Swiss corpus	41% of all occurrences	43.5% of all occurrences	15.5% of all occurrences

At the same time, *Le Temps* relays the opinions of experts who believe Daesh's claim of responsibility is vague and that nothing proves the organization was behind the attack. The newspaper places the issue elsewhere: "the possibility that a disturbed person can be radicalised rapidly speaks volumes" (LT7). Indeed, it concerns itself more with political maneuvering and with the "inevitable social consequences" (LT12) of the attack. Moreover, it highlights France's weakness:

> By claiming responsibility, and given the personality of the *Promenade des Anglais* killer, ISIS is showing more than ever just how helpless France is when faced with one of the greatest evils of this century: the nebulous but bloody scourge of terrorism. (LT6)

According to the journalist, Nice belongs in the terror event chain.

We saw that in LT6, Werly uses the term "hypothesis" and an "if" construction in ways which equate a large Muslim population with an accrued risk of radicalization, violence, and even "civil war." The journalist also evokes growing doubts (the notion abounds) about "the effectiveness of the state of emergency" (LT3) and implicitly echoes the sentiment in LT7: France is, "after six months with a state of emergency in place, also to blame for its own divisions and blindness." The conclusion is drawn that France's own internal issues and shortcomings have made it vulnerable to such attacks. In addition, the notion of risk is predominant in the Swiss subcorpus and in particular in *Le Temps*; it appears in the multiple instances in which the possibility of a civil war is evoked, and it is linked to a lack of confidence in the government's anti-terrorist strategy. In addition, *Le Temps* reports rumors involving torture and hostage-taking that were never corroborated or were proven to be false, as well as rumors claiming that the police hid information about the mass attacks that took place in 2015. This is despite newspaper guidelines typically stipulating that unverified information should not be reported. It also discusses the risk of denial and the risk that the truth will be sacrificed or doctored by the government. Put otherwise, through modality and related notions, *Le Temps* highlights the potential for opportunistic dishonesty on the part of the government, since Hollande is planning to run for re-election in 2017.

On the question of whether or not Bouhlel was a terrorist, *Le Courrier* vacillates in even more pronounced ways than *Le Temps*, and this vacillation is marked by modality. In LC4 (July 18; headline: "A Terrorist Who Came Out of Nowhere"), one paragraph begins with the presupposed "the terrorist" while the following paragraph opens with the sentence fragment "No proven link with radical Islamism." Two paragraphs later, the journalist states,

> Nothing makes it **possible** to confirm that the perpetrator of the massacre acted in the name of ISIS. The terrorist organisation claimed responsibility for the attack on Saturday [July 16]. (LC4)

On the previous day (July 17), LC5 had observed,

> The late claim of responsibility for this attack by ISIS at this stage, **should** be taken with caution, as **should** the last-minute "radicalisation" of the killer.

However, while an agency (ATS) text observed on July 15 that "the driver of the lorry showed no apparent religiosity" (LC1), another article by Thierry Jacolet from the same day makes the link with terrorism: the attack "has just plunged France into terrorist horror again" (LC2). Moreover, Jacolet, unlike the other two Swiss news sources, makes the following strong assertion which raises the question of what definition of terror he is basing himself upon (see section "History/Experience of Terrorism" of Chapter 3):

> Premeditation, which makes this attack a terrorist act. (LC2)

And yet, as we have seen, Switzerland does not have a law specific to terrorism; and under the French penal code, premeditation is what makes it possible to define a murder as assassination. LC4 clearly labels Bouhlel a terrorist while also using a modal construction particularly common in this news source, a verb in the conditional tense (*aurait*, a French equivalent of "allegedly"):

> The terrorist **allegedly** even cut ties with his family in Tunisia.

The same modal marker is used quite frequently in this small corpus, and to avoid unequivocally confirming various kinds of information: Bouhlel "was allegedly radicalized rapidly," is "allegedly in the process of getting divorced," "allegedly never set foot in a prayer hall," "nevertheless allegedly had links with the recruiter of jihadists based in Nice"; or the "alleged" details about one of the Swiss victims of the attack.

The shifting positions of the news source do not mean it refrains from criticizing Bouhlel, who is guilty of domestic violence, including through use of modality:

> Body building and MMA (Mixed Martial Arts), a combat sport in which virtually all forms of attack are allowed, **apparently** didn't suffice for him to get his aggression out. (LC4)

In part through modality, *Le Courrier*, like *Le Temps*, also criticizes Hollande and the state of emergency, which it considers ineffective. Having just questioned the supposed rapid radicalization of the killer, LC5 is particularly scathing about the media and politicians and, first and foremost, about Hollande:

> Many of the political and media reactions that immediately followed this ignoble act in France now **prove** to have been particularly opportunistic and irresponsible. Starting with the reaction of French President François Hollande who, just a few hours after the tragedy and without any solid evidence, labeled it Islamist terrorism. (LC5)

Finally, in relation to the prevalence of the theme of war, *Le Courrier* combines it with modality in a strong statement: "a *certainty*: France has definitely entered a state of war" (LC2; my emphasis).

The *Tribune de Genève* employs modality in various ways, including to make the story relevant for Switzerland ("there is no apparent link between Switzerland and the attack in Nice") and in reporting on authorities' calls for better training of police and a "national reflection on terrorism." Interestingly, however, the *Tribune* also reflects on the ramifications of the attack for Spain, and resulting policy there. Thus, we find consideration of what the attack means for France's neighbors (and not just Switzerland). The *Tribune* is also the Swiss news source that speaks most often of *revendiquer/revendication* (to claim (responsibility)/a claim (of responsibility)) on the part of Daesh. In addition, when the *Tribune* evokes the claim of "rapid radicalization" made by the authorities, it typically does so with the conditional tense, and the claim is in quotation marks in six out of the seven occurrences of the phrase, which is another way of establishing distance from the statement. Bouhlel's visit to the *Promenade* before the attack (which would prove premeditation) is also reported using a verb in the conditional tense. However, later on in the news cycle, the *Tribune* observes multiple times that the opinions of experts, some of whom are quoted, tend toward Islamist involvement. That said, in other statements accompanied by modals, the *Tribune* indicates that Bouhlel showed no signs of religiosity or links with terrorist groups and observes that he instead seems to fit the profile of a disturbed person. It nevertheless also reports a statement by a police official criticizing the media for putting forward this hypothesis.

In sum, there are similarities and differences in the ways the three Swiss newspapers use modality. *Le Temps* emphasizes risk and doubt, especially related to the possibility of more violence and civil war, and to the government's competence and honesty. Both *Le Temps* and *Le Courrier* employ it to criticize the government, and they vacillate on whether or not the attack was a terrorist act, whereas *La Tribune de Genève* more often uses modality to keep a critical distance from that possibility.

Alliteration

Table 14 shows the percentages of instances of alliteration accompanying negative, positive, or neutral content in the three Swiss news sources. It is noteworthy that there are almost exactly as many neutral occurrences as negative ones in *La Tribune*. This is partly explained by the numerous instances of alliteration in texts addressing travel-related issues, very relevant for *Suisse romande* readers, as a number of them would have been traveling to Nice or contemplating doing so during the summer, given the city's relative proximity and the plethora of cheap flights from Geneva.

All three Swiss sources use the phrase describing Bouhlel's attack with the truck "foncé sur la foule" (plowed into the crowd), and the *Tribune* (TDG) combines it on eight occasions with various other terms starting with "f." For example:

> Quelques minutes après la fin du feu d'artifices, le camion blanc a foncé dans la foule sur la Promenade des Anglais fermée à la circulation [A few minutes after the fireworks ended, the white truck plowed into the crowd on the Promenade des Anglais, which was closed to traffic]. (TDG3)

> La Promenade des Anglais, où un camion a foncé dans une foule venue admirer un feu d'artifice, est une destination **ph**are [The Promenade des Anglais, where a truck plowed into the crowd that had come to enjoy the fireworks, is a leading [tourist] destination]. (TDG22)

> un Tunisien a fauché la foule après les feux [A Tunisian plowed into/mowed down the crowd after the fireworks]. (TDG14)

Table 14 Alliteration and Connotation in the Swiss Corpus

Alliteration	*Le Temps*	*La Tribune*	*Le Courrier*
Negative	64%	50%	60%
Positive	9%	2%	7%
Neutral	27%	48%	33%

These choices have the effect of emphasizing the violence and deadliness of the attack.

In relation to violence, both *La Tribune* and *Le Temps* use the alliterated phrase "tués par un Tunisien" [killed by a Tunisian], thereby highlighting the killer's nationality; *Le Courrier* does not. Another point at which the *Tribune* combines violence and alliteration is in a list of the violent attacks that had taken place in France since the beginning of 2015, thereby drawing attention to the event chain to which the Nice attack is portrayed as belonging. There are six instances of alliteration in the list alone, of which two examples are "des militaires américains maîtrisent un homme lourdement armé" (American soldiers overpower a heavily armed man) and "avec pour la première fois dans ce pays des actions kamikazes" (with, for the first time in the country, kamikaze actions) (TDG1). Here are examples from the other two newspapers:

> produire un maximum d'effets avec un minimum de moyens [three occurrences of this phrase]. Minimum de moyens matériels: un camion frigorifique loué deux jours avant le massacre dans une commune voisine. Minimum de moyens humains [produce maximal effects with minimal means. Minimal material means: a refrigeration truck rented two days before the massacre in a neighboring town. Minimal human means]. (LT2)

> Comme pour mieux frapper la France en son cœur, lacérer ce qu'elle incarne: la démocratie, les libertés, la laïcité, l'esprit épicurien. Autant de valeurs vomies par le terrorisme islamiste. [As if to better strike France in its heart, to lacerate what France embodies: democracy, freedom, secularism, the epicurean lifestyle. The kinds of values vomited by Islamist terrorism.] (LC2)

What is more, the second excerpt sets up a strong contrast featuring a simplistic, idealized image of France.

Like the Spanish *El País* (see below), both *Le Temps* and *Le Courrier* also use alliteration to accompany their discussion of societal and political issues, thereby emphasizing topics that they also address more frequently than *La Tribune* does. For example, le débat sera surtout sociétal [the debate will be above all a societal one]. (LT6)

les inévitables séquelles sociales [the inevitable social consequences] [including the risk of civil war, attacks on mosques, etc., following the government's failures]. (LT12)

En janvier 2015, une première série d'attaques sur trois jours (17 morts au total) avait suscité une certaine unité de la classe politique, sidérée comme le reste de la société par ces attentats [In January 2015, a first series of attacks over three days (17 deaths in all) had created a certain unity on the part of political leaders, who were shocked, like the rest of society, by the attacks]. (LT3)

Le Temps highlights the fact that on this occasion unity is nowhere to be found. In addition, current government policy is not convincing:

derrière cette démonstration de force, le doute est énorme [behind/despite this demonstration of force [the French government's counterterrorist measures], the doubt is enormous]. (LT6)

Le Courrier's treatment of political and societal issues is in fact even more linked to measures taken by the government. In LC3, Thierry Jacolet underscores through alliteration their ineffectiveness and their failure to reassure the public. For instance:

L'attentat a révélé les limites de la lutte antiterroriste en France. François Hollande a renforcé des mesures qui peinent à convaincre. [The attack revealed the limits of the fight against terrorism in France. François Hollande has reinforced measures that are struggling to convince [the country]]. (LC3)

Having just discussed the abundance of security cameras in Nice, the journalist asks:

Comment un poids lourd peut-il pénétrer un 14 juillet sur un axe bondé, fermé à la circulation et ceinturé par la police en plein état d'urgence? [How can a heavy truck get onto a crowded road, closed to traffic and surrounded by police, on Bastille Day, in the midst of a state of emergency?]. (LC3)

The alliteration highlights further evidence that the measures in place are insufficient.

In *La Tribune*, the idea that Bouhlel's act was premeditated is accompanied by alliteration and modality:

la piste d'un acte prémédité semble [modality] se préciser trois jours après l'attentat perpétré par Mohamed Lahouaiej-Bouhlel, dont le profil suscite toujours des interrogations [The theory of a premeditated act seems to be confirmed, three days after the attack perpetrated by Mohamed Lahouaiej-Bouhlel, whose profile is still provoking questions] [there is also a second, briefer occurrence]. (TDG26)

In *Le Courrier*, acknowledgment of Bouhlel's mental issues is accompanied by alliteration, which makes it more salient. For example:

a **p**ermis de dessiner le **p**ortrait d'un homme instable, **p**lus **p**réoccupé **p**ar son corps que **p**ar la religion [made it possible to establish the portrait of an unstable man, more preoccupied by his body than by religion]. (LC4)

Mohamed Lahouaiej-Bouhlel **p**résente un **p**rofil de **p**ersonnage instable, **p**erturbé, inédit pour les **p**oliciers chargés de la lutte antiterroriste [The profile of Mohamed Lahouaiej-Bouhlel is that of an unstable and disturbed individual, a new situation for the police in charge of counter-terrorism]. (LC4)

Finally, the strong tendency in the *Telegraph* to use alliteration with content about religion is absent from the Swiss corpus, which gives religion much less attention generally.

Metaphor

As with metaphor in the UK corpus, a table is used to indicate connotation and the presence/absence of violence in the metaphors found in each of the three Swiss newspapers. However, because there is such a difference in the number of articles in each of the three news sources, it is more informative to express violent metaphors as a percentage of the total number of metaphors in each set of articles. The corresponding percentages are presented in Table 15. It is important to keep in mind that the LC corpus is very small.

War/Violent Metaphor

As Table 15 shows, this type of metaphor is prevalent in the Swiss subcorpus. Moreover, when such metaphors are not related to terrorist violence itself, they are most often connected to criticism of the French government or of the country's upcoming presidential campaign. For instance:

Political leaders on the left and on the right have been **tearing each other apart** via the media since the deadly attack in Nice. (TDG24)

The numerous presidential hopefuls [on the right] have been **launching verbal attacks** on each other, each one more **violent** than the last. (TDG25)

On Sunday, former Prime Minister Alain Juppé, who is also a candidate in the conservative party's presidential primary, again lambasted [literally: **shot red bullets at**] the government. (TDG26; the same metaphor is used in TDG16)

Exploitation of fear is sure to be an **arm of mass electoral conquest** in May 2017. (LT10)

Table 15 Quantitative Data on Violence and Connotation of Metaphors in the Swiss Corpus

Metaphor		Negative			Positive			Neutral				
Source	Total	TV	NV	V	TV	NV	V	TV	NV	V		
LT	98	13	30	40	0	0	0	0	12	3	Violent:	57%
TDG	83	22	15	9	0	4	1	0	29	3	Violent:	42%
LC	40	17	6	8	0	1	0	1	6	1	Violent:	67.5%

TV=Terrorist violence

NV=Not violence

V=Other violence

In addition, *Le Temps*'s previously mentioned focus on the possibility of a civil war is sometimes accompanied by the metaphorical term *larvée* (not violent in itself; it is related to "larva" and is the equivalent of "latent"). In a heading we saw in the previous section, *larvée* is used in a way which also conveys a negative message about France's significant Muslim population:

A latent [literally: at **larva** stage] civil war: in a country with a population of between five and six million Muslims, how can acts of violence by disturbed people who want to take action "like soldiers of ISIS" be avoided? (LT6)

Discussion of war is particularly prevalent in *Le Temps*, for example, in the metaphorical "the internal 'war' demonstrated by the attack in Nice is now **the first front** … A war, but on which **front**?" (LT10) or the air-/fire-related one (also see below), "a 'risk of civil war' increasing due to [literally: whose **flames are being fanned by**] the terrorist threat" (LT6).

Finally, in *Le Courrier*, in contrast to most of the examples in this section, violent metaphor mainly relates to terrorism itself.

Plants/Animals/Growth

The key metaphor in the Swiss subcorpus that fits under this heading is the same one that we encounter across the corpus: the image of a "breeding ground" or an almost identical phenomenon (i.e., "fishing ground"). It appears three times in *La Tribune* and once in *Le Temps* but is absent from *Le Courrier*. Every occurrence describes Nice as a "breeding ground" for jihadists. In addition, the verb *semer*—"to spread" or, literally, "to sow the seeds of"—is used in negative ways in all three sources: "to spread death" (twice in TDG, once in LT and LC), to spread terror (once in LC), and to spread horror (once in LT). That said, this type of metaphor is not prevalent in the Swiss news articles examined.

Disease/Illness

Disease/illness metaphors, on the other hand, are relatively common in the Swiss subcorpus. In relation to this type of metaphor, let us first return to an excerpt from *Le Courrier*, which includes both metaphor and alliteration, the sole instance of this kind of metaphor in *Le Courrier*. The excerpt maintains that Bouhlel attacked France during the highly symbolic Bastille Day celebrations, as if to

> **lacerate** what France embodies: democracy, freedom, secularism, the epicurean lifestyle. The kinds of values **vomited** by Islamist terrorism. (LC2)

The excerpt employs both violent- (ripping, slashing, tearing apart) and sickness-related metaphors. As discussed above, they contribute to emphasizing the great and acrimonious divide between a monolithic "them" and an also-monolithic "us" (and as we are talking of terrorism in conjunction with this particular event, we are meant to associate Bouhlel with terrorism), while painting French—and by extension, Western—values as uniformly positive. The alliteration in "values vomited" [*valeurs vomies*] gives even greater force to the negative image.

Le Temps includes a whole host of disease/illness metaphors; what is most interesting is *how* they are used, which certainly contrasts with *Le Courrier* above.

> How do you counter the **epidemic** of deadly ripostes by petty criminals who are violent and lost, and who have been **intoxicated** by radical Islamic propaganda or are simply fascinated by the death instinct that it disseminates? (LT6)

> The hypothesis of a disturbed "**lone wolf**", overcome by a deadly madness fed by the anti-Western hate that is disseminated by radical Islamic propaganda, represents the worst kind of challenge in a country where the high unemployment rate **plagues** neighborhoods [literally: is turning them **gangrenous**] and where the justice system lacks the resources needed to lock up many of the offenders detained by the security forces. (LT6)

The first **fracture** ... is the de facto abandoning [by the state] of many neighbourhoods [...] suburbs **plagued** [literally: **eaten away at**] by unemployment and drug trafficking. (LT7)

While the journalist takes into account the influence of Islamist propaganda, those who act violently are not qualified as terrorists (one might say they come closer to sounding like victims), and unemployment, and the poverty and exclusion that result, are identified as underlying causes of the kind of violence described. These are not simply cases of "us" versus "them," but rather of societal and political problems that France as a whole is facing. Nevertheless, we saw above that LT6 did also link the Muslim population, and problems with violence.

The following excerpt also employs "gangrene," this time highlighting through metaphor what we have seen emphasized via other stylistic choices, namely, the criticism and distrust of Hollande's government that abounds in this source:

At this stage, and to avoid the **gangrening** effect of generalized suspicion, the government absolutely must prove itself to be irreproachably transparent. (LT7)

Let us now briefly turn to instances of metaphor connected with water.

Water-Related Metaphor

These are common but represent a heterogeneous mix of phenomena, sometimes related to violence and sometimes not, covering anything from plunging to distilling to the raining down of tears. In addition, the metaphor of the wave is particularly common, but is never used in the way that Piquer Martí (2015) observed and criticized, that is, to describe a mass arrival of migrants. Where its use is most consistent is in *La Tribune*, where it appears four times, to describe a wave of attacks, terrorist actions, preventive arrests, and departures to Syria. Thus, in this source, this type of metaphor is more closely associated with terrorist violence than in the other two Swiss newspapers.

Fire- or Heat-Related Metaphor

Finally, it is logical that news in one language might show a greater preponderance of, or affinity for, a given instance of figurative language than news in another language. This is the case of fire-related metaphors in the Swiss subcorpus, although their use, as with water-related metaphor above, is heterogeneous. For example, an excerpt from *Le Courrier* that contains a fire metaphor is characteristically critical of Hollande and his government:

François Hollande who, just a few hours after the attack, qualified the killing, without any clear evidence, as Islamist terrorism. And announced immediately afterwards that he would intensify bombing in Iraq and Syria which, unfortunately, will only **add fuel to the fire** (LC5).

Another fire-related metaphor from the same source portrays something very different:

These soldiers who are exhausted [literally: **burnt to a cinder**] after months of surveillance (LC3).

In contrast, fire-related metaphors in LT are quite consistent: out of nine, six depict political turmoil, in the form of criticisms of Hollande's administration and/or lack of unity among politicians. The one metaphorical phrase related to fire/heat in TDG (TDG20; it is repeated twice), literally "to fizzle out" but also related to the misfiring of a gun, also describes the prevailing lack of political unity following the attack. As with other stylistic features, political issues seem to be what are most consistently highlighted by various kinds of metaphor in the Swiss corpus.

Spain

As the statistics in Table 16 indicate, articles from *El Mundo* tend to be longer than those published in *El País*, whereas the articles from each newspaper account for about half of the total subcorpus. Therefore, like the UK subcorpus, this one is fairly balanced.

I do not include a separate section on "jihad" here because use of the term follows the pattern we have seen: it is omnipresent. Interestingly, "jihadism" features as one of the "related themes" listed in eleven of the articles in *El País* (EP), and just three in *El Mundo* (EM). "Terrorism" is a "related theme" in

Table 16 Statistics for the Spanish Corpus

News source	Number of articles	Number of words	Percentage of corpus
El País (EP)	36	27,342	51%
El Mundo (EM)	31	26,343	49%
Total	67	53,685	

twenty-eight EP articles and in six from EM; "Islamist," in eleven EP articles and in zero EM articles. That said, in the texts themselves, *El País* gives less space than *El Mundo* to Nice's "jihadism problem," although it does acknowledge it; one blatant example is the headline "Niza, el caladero yihadista de Francia" (EP34) (literally, Nice: France's jihadist fishing ground). All things considered, regardless of the nuances brought by stylistic features and other choices discussed below, the Nice attack is placed squarely in an event chain of jihadist activities at the earliest stages of reporting, just like in the other subcorpora.

Portrayal of France; of Muslims

Like most of the sources, the Spanish newspapers paint Nice in a positive light. In *El Mundo*, it is described as a beautiful, glamorous, and historic city, associated with luxury and the *Belle Époque* and highly popular with tourists, who are extremely important for the city's economy. *El País* celebrates these attributes in a similar fashion while also highlighting the importance and popularity of the *Tour de France*, which takes place in July and is the main topic of EP2.

That said, *El País* also highlights the "dangerous tension" (EP21) between Muslim and non-Muslim communities in Nice as well as the distrust and suspicion of Muslims (EP12, EP21) that was already widespread there before the attack. While both *El País* and *El Mundo* discuss the difficulties and prejudices that Muslims in France face, *El Mundo* also emphasizes Muslims' problems integrating in the country, treating the group as a monolith and the problem as a generalized one. In contrast, *El País* is particularly critical of "French populists and extremists" using the attack for political gain, and quotes then Prime Minister Valls' position that such groups are "irresponsible" for calling for harsher measures against immigrants and Muslims in the wake of the attack (EP26), while *El Mundo* gives less attention to this aspect. Finally, the two newspapers are the only ones in the full corpus that explicitly cite condemnation of the attack by Muslim authorities in Nice. For instance:

> the Imam and his secretary general are saddened by Friday's attack. The discourse is the same as always: Islam preaches peace and solidarity. (EP34)

However, the phrase "the same as always" conveys some doubt about their position, especially in the light of information presented immediately afterwards: that the "alleged terrorist" Bouhlel lived in the same neighborhood as the mosque and that the "jihadist" recruiter also mentioned in the other subcorpora operated there.

El Mundo tends less toward criticizing politicians and populists and more toward highlighting problems and shortcomings related to integration and security. The very first line of EM15 emphasizes France's security issues and its supposed difficulties integrating Muslims, themes which are often preoccupations of the right. Furthermore, according to the same article, it is because of these problems that massive attacks have continued to occur in France and not in Spain or the UK (even though all three, it notes, are part of the international coalition fighting Daesh). Indirectly, then, the "home" country is depicted as more effective than France in the areas of security and integration. Moreover, a metaphor is used which indirectly highlights the supposed danger Muslims represent (see section "Metaphor" below).

The *El País* article EP27 actually provides a response to such criticisms of security, with concrete figures and other details demonstrating the plethora of security measures put in place in Nice, described as a "security laboratory," from its 1,260 security cameras (1+ for every 300 inhabitants) to its "400 municipal police officers, almost one per thousand residents." The problem, it is subtly suggested in *El País*, lies elsewhere: in divisive politics, a complex and polarized population, economic problems such as "an unemployment rate of 15%, higher than the national average" (EP12), or even the fact that proper mosques are forbidden in Nice. It is noteworthy that *El País* is the only newspaper in the corpus that informs readers about this rule:

> a poor neighbourhood where there are various prayer halls and a mosque (officially, it is only an association, as Nice has not allowed any official mosques) (EP34)

> this association—which is how Muslim places of worship must establish themselves in Nice. (EP36)

In conjunction with its focus on security and integration, EM15 does take a very novel, reflective, and balanced approach at one point, by adopting a Muslim perspective to explain how certain Muslims could come to find "Western values" perverse:

> For a Baghdadi who, after 13 years of war, with some 170,000 civilians killed in violent attacks according to Iraq Body Count, just saw, on July 3rd, more than 250 people die in a shopping center in the district of Karrada when a van full of explosives blew up—an attack claimed by Daesh which virtually nobody in the West even heard about—the logic of democratic Western values will appear as perverse and hypocritical to him as that of Daesh seems to most Westerners. (EM15)

EM19 also takes Muslims' perspective into account, this time by acknowledging the suffering that Muslim communities in France must be experiencing, not only because of the attacks—the journalist reminds us that a Muslim mother of seven was killed by Bouhlel—but because of "painful accusations" against them. The same text also highlights the statement condemning the attack, at the earliest hour, by the Conference of Imams of France: at five o'clock on the Friday morning, just hours after the attack, the organization expressed its pain and qualified the attack as "cowardly and odious." The article goes on to cite a line from the Qur'an that coincides with the claim that Islam is a religion of peace and solidarity (EP34) and was to be included in the forthcoming Friday prayers, but without the doubt potentially conveyed by the *El País* article (see above).

In addition, EM23 works in a similar vein to EP26 but more explicitly, by highlighting "the rise in Islamophobia in Europe, particularly in France" and the widespread tendency to reject Muslim refugees and immigrants who arrive on European shores after fleeing zones of conflict. Finally, however, one must also note a very different message, which is reminiscent of the article by Méléagrou-Hitchens (DT26) in the *Telegraph*: that despite emphasis by some on the lack of in-depth religious knowledge of many perpetrators of these kinds of attacks, the influence of religion on their violent actions, the role of Islam, is "evident" (EM21):

> The superficiality of the theological knowledge of some extremists and their limited religious practice are used to deny the evident role of religion. Also ignored thus is the Islamization of the fanaticism and extremism that induces people to assassinate human beings in cold blood and which is developed according to/relies on a particular interpretation of Islam.

Given that the religion is rarely reported upon except in conjunction with extreme violence, it is easy to see how public opinion comes to equate Islam with terrorist violence.

That said, *El Mundo* (EM17, EM18)—unlike the *Telegraph*, for example—does situate terrorism in France historically; this means that while it puts a lot of emphasis on the presence of jihadists/jihadism in Nice, it also recognizes that terrorist violence is far from being simply a current "crisis." At the same time, with regard to the current situation, it attributes blame to problems with integration in France, and gives particular attention to both France's and the EU's shortcomings in responding to "jihadism." In addition, EM14 subtly but insidiously—in part through a misleading use of statistics—associates the presence of jihadists in Nice with the city's large Tunisian population, the city where Bouhlel was born, and foreigners (recall that the *Guardian* instead used figures about the Tunisian population to celebrate Nice's cultural diversity):

> In addition to being one of the French cities most affected by the jihadist phenomenon, given that more than a hundred of its residents have allegedly gone to Syria, Nice is also known among Tunisians as "M'saken 2". Almost 40% of Tunisians from this town of about 80,000 inhabitants go to the French Riviera city to find work and send money to their families. (EM14)

The article that includes the excerpt below also discusses the foreign population of Nice (including via a graph) and immediately goes on to provide the history of the terrorist attacks that have happened there:

> Of the inhabitants of Nice, almost 60,000 are foreigners. 37.6% are European, mainly Italian (11.2%) and Portuguese (4.9%), and 50.9% are from African countries, especially Tunisia (17.7%) and Morocco (11.4%). (EM18)

I would point out that at the beginning of 2016, Nice had a population of 346,000 people, meaning that *all* foreigners represented just 17 percent of the population, and Tunisians—as far as I understand it; the breakdown of the percentages is not clear—just 3 percent. As Bugnot (2012: 983–4) observes, numbers which "themselves become facts can reflect an intentional angle of approach," while "an accumulation of numbers" can create a kind of "crescendo that is vaguely menacing in its demonstration of difference." The sequencing of information in the articles clearly links Tunisians and terrorism.

Compare the above with EP, in which an inflammatory statement by the then president of the *Provence Alpes Côte d'Azur* (PACA) region and current mayor of Nice, Christian Estrosi, is criticized:

> Estrosi is not satisfied with any response [by the socialist government] and, in a country with a population of between five and six million Muslims, he is feeding the dangerous tensions between communities. (EP21)

In addition, EP provides an explanation of Nice's "cosmopolitan population" (EP12) and complex cultural make-up, including the history surrounding *pieds noirs*, French-on-French prejudice, and immigration, and how all of these, coupled with high unemployment, have fed into support for the far-right *Front National* in the region. Indeed, EP emphasizes societal tensions, the suspicion and distrust of Muslims that have taken root (the metaphor is used in the Spanish) in the region of Nice, the rampant xenophobia and Islamophobia in France, in particular on the part of the political right, who also use it for political gain, and then Prime Minister Valls' criticism of this strategy as "irresponsible." *El País* criticizes the far-right and in particular the way that Jean-Marie Le Pen capitalized upon the prejudice that *pieds noirs* experienced, as well as the fact that his successors continue to apply this strategy today:

> The *Front National* is the second municipal force in Nice and disseminates in the southeast of France a multifaceted identitarian discourse. It attracts not only conservative voters suspicious of the explosion in migration, but old French-labor-movement communists, frustrated at the changes wrought with the arrival of North African laborers and the unexpected competition they represented. (EP12)

In contrast, in an *El Mundo* article whose opening image is of the emblematic Marianne[5] brandishing the French flag in one raised hand and cradling a cubist (are we to think of Picasso?), childlike, dead or dying figure in the other, the "Us"/"Them," "Islam"/"West" binary is evoked, specifically Islam versus Western philosophy, along with characteristics—or clichés—of France:

> Many commentators were drawing connections yesterday between this philosophy [Western philosophy, epitomized by France] and each target of the principal attacks in France in the last year and a half: freedom of expression in "Charlie Hebdo," national unity in a soccer stadium, love of life, leisure and music in the Bataclan, bars and restaurants, and two days ago, Nice, one of the top tourist destinations in France, celebrating its national holiday with fireworks and music by the sea. (EM15)

While EP6 also has recourse to such characteristics/clichés, it is not to set up the same opposition but instead to acknowledge the risk of terrorist attacks at Bastille Day events in Europe, and the resulting need for security measures:

> Along with the signs of national identity (Francophone music, champagne and French wine, and even a large placard criticizing the trade agreement that the EU is negotiating with the United States), the inevitable security measures accompanied the celebrations. (EP6)

Let us now turn to the discussion of results on modality from the Spanish subcorpus.

Modality

Table 17 presents the statistics for modality in the *El País* and *El Mundo* articles.

Table 17 Statistics for Modality in the Spanish Corpus

Modality	EP	EM
Total	75	81
Percentage of all occurrences in Spanish corpus	48% of all occurrences	52% of all occurrences

Both Spanish online newspapers often attribute opinions about whether Bouhlel was or was not affiliated with terrorism to other sources in ways that are accompanied by modality, and in particular "alleged(ly)," "supposed," or "suspected." Both sources also give a fair amount of space to Bouhlel's personal/mental problems. However, this does not stop them from referring to him as "the terrorist" at other points, nor from focusing on Daesh and jihadism. EP also states that the risk of an attack on July 14, Bastille Day, was known to European security forces and speaks of their "apparent inaction" (EP6), while EM emphasizes the European Union's loss of credibility in France. In addition, EP states that the French police

> know that the massive police and military deployment across the country—more than 100,000 during the month of the World Cup alone—is of little use; the same is true of the government's bombing of Syria and Iraq, which it is again planning to intensify. (EP25)

EM instead speaks positively (albeit not often) of the state of emergency, of which such wide deployment is a part. Here, it is *necessary*:

> The enemy is not only external, but also internal, as among the terrorists there are French nationals. This dual dimension has reinforced the **belief that it is necessary** to act both internally – hence the extension of the state of emergency – and externally, where close collaboration with another power such as the United States is considered essential. (EM21)

The newspaper does also acknowledge "alleged problems with security measures [in Nice]," however. EP instead highlights France's difficulties in the face of constantly evolving terrorist tactics and either remains neutral on the state of emergency, or criticizes it, as in EP3 and EP25.

In terms of "bringing the story home" (Cottle [2011] 2012; Freedman 2017), *El País* discusses the risk of attacks in Spain, security measures taken in the home country, including by the Interior Ministry, which "sees signs of Islamist involvement," and official meetings about both security and counterterrorism issues and decisions. A lot of space is given by both sources to possible Spanish victims in Nice. Moreover, in a formulation almost identical to a statement we saw in the *Tribune de Genève*, *El País* observes:

> the **alleged** perpetrator of the attack, identified as Mohamed Lahouaiej Bouhlel, does not **appear** to have links with Spain. (EP18)

Again, we see a focus on the home country and the possible ramifications of the attack for Spain, not surprising since it is France's neighbor. That said, the risk of a terrorist attack at the Olympic Games in Brazil, which were three weeks away at the time of the attack, is the subject of early articles in both newspapers as well. (EP's message is that a terrorist act there is unlikely, while EM focuses on the extreme lack of resources available to police in Rio and the resulting concern about a possible attack.) Home country and proximity are not the only determiners of newsworthiness.

Finally, in terms of the labeling of the event as terrorism, on 18 July, well after a number of other sources have accepted the thesis that the attack constituted an act of terrorism, EP emphasizes the lack of clear proof. For example:

> There is still a lot of **doubt** [both metaphor and alliteration are used] after Friday's attack about whether he [Bouhlel] **truly** had connections with ISIS and religious extremism, especially given the scarcity of evidence found during the investigation. (EP34)

And yet, as we have seen, the article's headline is "Nice: France's Jihadist Fishing Ground"; it gives a lot of space to Nice's links with terrorism; and the above excerpt comes in the very last paragraph. That said, on the same day, EP also published "Sufría un principio de psicosis y alteración de la realidad" (He was experiencing the beginnings of psychosis and an altered sense of reality), which in itself gives some credence to the idea that he was mentally ill and disturbed. The article also includes the following:

> Bernard Cazeneuve, although he still hasn't provided any clear **proof** that confirms this line of thinking and although the intelligence services didn't have any evidence to make them **suspect** that [Bouhlel] had links with Islamism, indicated yesterday that the attacker had **apparently** been "radicalized very rapidly". (EP36)

Despite the final emphasis in the sentence, this excerpt places the former interior minister's position in doubt, in large part through use of modality.

Table 18 Alliteration and Connotation in the Spanish Corpus

Alliteration	*El País*	*El Mundo*
Negative	44%	57%
Positive	10%	13%
Neutral	46%	30%

Alliteration

As Table 18 shows, alliteration accompanies negative content much less frequently and neutral content much more frequently in the Spanish subcorpus than it did in the English one (see p. 100). In relation to the Swiss subcorpus, the percentage for *El País* is on a par with *La Tribune*; of *El Mundo*, with *Le Courrier*.

El País also has significantly fewer instances of alliteration than *El Mundo*: 41 versus 61. In *El País*, neutral alliterated content often involves procedural information about the Spanish government's response to the attack, such as efforts to establish whether Spanish citizens were affected; more general administrative procedures (e.g., a budget meeting); information about the attacker; or facts about the attack and the police investigation. Interestingly, in strong contrast to the English corpus, alliterated content related to government and policy is also often neutral in *El País* (recall that alliteration stood out in the English corpus in relation to the government, and to religion). Take, for instance, an article highlighting the political divisions in the aftermath of the attack, whose headline begins "Unity among Political Parties Is Cracking" (EP7). It begins by highlighting the "inhabitual criticisms" of the government by politicians of other persuasions, including former president and conservative Nicolas Sarkozy, but ends by informing the reader that Sarkozy had previously supported the government in its aim to extend the state of emergency. This information is accompanied by alliteration:

> Sarkozy había dicho anteriormente que apoya al Gobierno en la primera y principal medida adoptada: prorrogar el estado de excepción tres meses más, hasta el 26 de octubre. [Sarkozy had said previously that he supported the government in its adoption of the first and principal measure: extending the state of emergency three more months, until October 26.] (EP7)

This and various other texts do nevertheless focus on political divisions in France.

Interestingly, where *Spanish* government is concerned, on the other hand, various alliterated segments instead emphasize its unity, effectiveness, empathy, and engagement (positive connotation):

> Las instituciones **m**adrileñas **m**ostraron esta **m**añana su apoyo a Francia. [The institutions in Madrid showed their support for France this morning.] (EP9)

> Rajoy destacó el **c**ompromiso y la **c**ooperación leal de España frente a la "amenaza global del terrorismo, que requiere una respuesta global e integral". [Rajoy emphasized the commitment and loyal cooperation of Spain in the face of "the global threat of terrorism, which requires a global and comprehensive response".] (EP13)

Non-alliterated segments reinforce this tendency:

> All of the representatives of the rest of the political parties lamented the brutal attack and expressed their condolences to the victims and their families. At the same time, they joined in praising the utility of the antiterrorism pact, projecting an image of political unity. (EP5)

> In a series of messages in the early hours of this Friday morning, Mariano Rajoy, Pedro Sánchez, Albert Rivera and Pablo Iglesias expressed their shock at the attack in Nice and condemned the terrorist act. The leaders of the PP, PSOE, Podemos and Ciudadanos referred to the attack (EP14).

El Mundo also celebrates the unity of the Spanish political parties, but in particular where security and the "fight against jihadism" are concerned:

> Los partidos que han asistido a esta reunión salieron con un **m**ismo **m**ensaje: aunque la situación política sea inestable y España continúe con un Gobierno en funciones, no afecta a la seguridad del Estado. [The parties that attended this meeting came out with the same message: although the political situation is unstable and Spain is being led by a caretaker government, this does not affect the security of the country.] (EM7)

> All of the parties gave their support to the Ministry of the Interior, the government and the State Security Forces in their fight against jihadist terrorism. (EM7)

Both sources subtly portray Spain as superior where unity and security are concerned. One small distinction, however, is that this article highlights the refusal of the political party Podemos to sign the *Pacto Antiyihadista*. This may be because the party is far-left and therefore not in line with the political leanings of the newspaper. *El País*, on the other hand, simply notes the observer status of Podemos without making the reason explicit:

On behalf of Podemos, Rafa Mayoral attended [the meeting]. As on other occasions, he attended as an observer. (EP5)

Recall that the *Guardian* and the *Telegraph* differed in how much they combined content about religion with alliteration. The *El País* articles rarely focus on religion, and therefore there is little alliterated content related to religion. Nevertheless, an instance related to religion that was already mentioned in the section "Portrayal of France; of Muslims" (p. 127) does carry alliteration:

El discurso es el de siempre: el Islam **p**reconiza la **p**az y la solidaridad. (EP34)

As we saw previously, the tone of the sentence ("the discourse is the same as always") as well as the surrounding content can be read as questioning Muslim officials' claim that "Islam is a religion of peace and solidarity"; in any case, the text does not simply take the claim at face value. At the same time, several instances of alliteration in *El País*, coupled with modality, also highlight the lack of clarity about whether Bouhlel really had any connections with terrorist groups or religion:

Estaba fichado **p**or delitos comunes y violencia doméstica **p**ero no **p**or **p**osibles vínculos con el terrorismo. [[Bouhlel] had a record for petty crimes and domestic violence but not for possible links with terrorism.] (EP19)

El episodio del viernes todavía **d**espierta **d**udas sobre su vinculación real con el Estado Islámico y el fanatismo religioso [Friday's episode is still raising doubts about his actual connection to the Islamic State and religious fanaticism]. (EP34)

The second excerpt also comes from July 18th, by which time a number of the sources analyzed here had basically accepted the idea that Daesh was directly or indirectly behind the attack. Yet the text goes on to cite a woman who has experience working with radicalized youth who *does* believe Bouhlel was radicalized. There is a balancing of positions; opposing opinions are presented.

In a pattern we also saw in the UK subcorpus, there are more alliterated elements related to religion in the center-right *El Mundo* than in the left-leaning *El País*. One such instance is related to the threat of Salafism:

De Ceuta, una ciudad en la que **s**e ha **s**ido permisiva con el **s**alafismo, en la que hay barrios en los que domina una especie de neomachismo **m**usulmán y en la que se ha detectado un **in**cremento alarmante de **in**tentos de captación en los **c**olegios han salido, según las estadísticas, la mayor parte de islamistas nacidos en España. [Ceuta—a city that has been permissive with Salafism, with neighborhoods where a kind of Muslim neo-machismo dominates and where an alarming increase in recruiting attempts in high schools has been detected—has been, according to the statistics, the point of departure for most of the Spanish-born Islamists [going to Syria and Iraq]]. (EM10)

The only cause mentioned is extreme religion; there is no reference to other specificities of Ceuta's context that we saw in Chapter 2. Nevertheless, the same text, headlined "Analfabetos del Corán" ("Illiterates" of the Qur'an), emphasizes the fact that the typical jihadist really has little or no knowledge of Islam, including via very large and visible graphs and a paragraph about women who have gone to Iraq and Syria. Together, these visual and textual elements challenge some common stereotypes about who becomes radicalized and how. Furthermore, in EM20, author Jesús Ferrero refers to "Arabist and novelist" Felipe Maíllo Salgado's demonstration of how terrorist groups subvert the messages of the Qur'an for their violent ends, and illegitimately so since the sacred book is not intrinsically violent. The reference is accompanied by alliteration and metaphor (on the latter, see section "Metaphor" below):

el arabista y novelista Felipe Maíllo Salgado explica que está muy **l**ejos de ser **l**ícito **c**itar de forma fraudulenta y oportunista fragmentos del Corán que **p**ueden **p**arecer violentos, sin tener en cuenta otros fragmentos del libro que complementan y relativizan esa violencia, amans**ándola** y ubic**ándola** dentro de un contexto más general y fundamentalmente pacificador. Algo que nunca van a hacer las voces que guiaban al asesino de Niza porque su intención es **des**componer y **des**hilvanar el mensaje del Corán de forma maniquea y populista, a fin de instaurar una gramática tan simplista como brutal, presidida por la dialéctica de las **v**íctimas y los **v**erdugos. [The Arabist and novelist Felipe Maíllo Salgado explains that it is very far from being licit to cite, in fraudulent and opportunistic ways, fragments of the Qur'an that can seem violent, without taking into account other fragments of the book which complement and downplay that violence, softening it and situating it within a context that is both more general and fundamentally pacifying. This is something that the voices that were guiding the assassin of Nice will never do because their aim is to unstitch and break down the message of the Qur'an in a Manichean and populist manner in order to establish a system [literally: a grammar] as simplistic as it is brutal, based on the dialectic of the victims *versus* the tormentors.] (EM20)

The message: the Qur'an has been manipulated by extremists. Still, the role of Daesh in the Nice attack is not in doubt. Finally, despite the nuanced view presented in that article, we must not forget that *El Mundo*'s EM21 insists vociferously on "the evident importance of religion" (see p. 129) in radicalism and terrorist actions. Clearly, religion is more of a preoccupation for *El Mundo* than for *El País*, and its importance is in part emphasized through alliteration. Alliteration also accompanies other content related to radicalization:

> Niza es conocida como una de las cunas del yihadismo [Nice is known as one of the cradles of jihadism]. (EM17)

> que se radicalizó muy rápidamente y sin dejar rastro. [who was radicalized very rapidly and without leaving a trace.] (EM25)

An interesting instance of alliteration in *El País*, ostensibly neutral, focuses on facts and numbers related to immigrants in Europe in order to refute the popular perception that they constitute a threat and to question the heavy-handed measures being considered to control them which have just been discussed in the article:

> Porque, más allá de las percepciones personales, el peso de la población extranjera en Europa es muy limitado: representa un 4% sobre el total. [Because, beyond personal perceptions, Europe's foreign population is actually very small (literally: of limited weight): 4% of the total population.] (EP8)

Importantly, given the previous discussion of integration and texts' differing approaches to it, this article emphasizes that improving integration efforts is the only viable means of stopping this kind of attack:

> The second type of measure is the only lasting one, but it offers only small returns in the short-term. It involves prevention: taking measures to integrate not only foreigners but also citizens who, despite holding a European passport, feel connected to another culture. (EP6)

However, there is nothing to suggest that the journalist supports the model of integration based upon reciprocity that was put forward in Chapter 2 above as the most viable one.

Another instance of alliteration in *El País*, while coded as negative, accompanies content which contextualizes, as it conveys the idea that poverty is a factor in radicalization. It also includes a metaphor that we have seen before:

> [La pobreza,] aunque no es causa directa del terrorismo, sí crea el caldo de cultivo para el reclutamiento de los yihadistas [[Poverty,] although it is not a direct cause of terrorism, does create a breeding ground for the recruitment of jihadists]. (EP17)

Similarly to what we saw in the *Guardian*'s coverage, the purpose of the paragraph that includes this excerpt is to emphasize underlying socioeconomic problems that can lead vulnerable populations to become radicalized, and the alliteration reinforces that emphasis further. Finally, in an article whose headline holds the far-right responsible for deepening France's political divisions, another instance of alliteration with "c" sounds also uses metaphor to discuss the opportunistic way "the most radical leaders" are benefiting from "public indignation" in the wake of recent terror attacks:

> cabalgan [ride] sobre la creciente corriente de indignación popular [they are riding the rising tide of popular indignation]. (EP21)

Otherwise, alliteration in EP accompanies quite administrative/procedural content.

As we have already seen, there is a greater focus on security concerns in *El Mundo* than in *El País*; this is reminiscent of the UK *Telegraph* to some degree, and the emphasis is reinforced by instances of alliteration. Nevertheless, such instances appear more balanced than alliteration accompanying content about security in the UK newspaper. Interestingly, *El Mundo* manages to incorporate a focus on security while also emphasizing the role of the then socialist government in it, simultaneously also giving credence to then Prime Minister Valls (whose name even features in two headlines). The second such article (EM29) evokes a link between the government's success in apparently thwarting a terrorist attack before the World Cup, and the state of emergency that was in place and that the government sought to extend after the Nice attack. Valls' insistence on the efficacy of the state of emergency and other occurrences of the term "state of emergency" are accompanied by both alliteration and assonance. This position distinguishes *El Mundo* from the *Telegraph*, which tended to find fault with the socialist government that was in power in summer 2016. That said, whereas texts in *El País* questioned former Nice mayor Estrosi's emphasis on security, *El Mundo* compliments the man for his sincerity when he angrily demanded how such an attack could happen within a security perimeter:

> Christian Estrosi, se desmarcó ayer del discurso oficial ... con una sinceridad rara vez vista por nuestros lares. [Christian Estrosi distanced himself from the official discourse/rhetoric ... with a sincerity rarely seen on our shores.] (EM15)

Moreover, EM21 criticizes European shortcomings in the counterterrorism response, and the criticisms are accompanied by alliteration. *El País*'s EP6, on the other hand, blames the unpredictable and constantly changing nature of attacks, rather than European states themselves, for these shortcomings. Security on the *home* front, in contrast, is portrayed by both news sources as functioning well when they highlight meetings that took place in the aftermath of the attack to strategize Spain's protection and response within the framework of the *Pacto Antiterrorista* (Anti-Terrorist Agreement) and the *Plan de Prevención y Protección Antiterrorista.*

Metaphor

Table 19 presents the statistics regarding metaphor, connotation, and violence in the Spanish subcorpus. Compared to *El Mundo*, *El País* uses more metaphors, a higher percentage of metaphors related to violence (inferior only to the *Telegraph*; on a par with *Le Courrier*, but that is a much smaller subcorpus), and more metaphors related to terrorist violence specifically. Metaphor usage in the Spanish subcorpus is discussed below. There are no sections for plants/growth metaphor or disease metaphor because these types were extremely rare in the Spanish corpus. Two exceptions are:

1. "to spread/sow the seeds of terror" (EM19), identical to a phrase seen in the Swiss corpus;
2. the city where distrust/suspicion of Muslims is most deeply rooted (EP12).

War/Violent Metaphor

Two categories of imagery related to war and violence are particularly salient in this subcorpus: the proverbial war/war on terror vocabulary, including bullets/targets, and heart metaphors combined with violence. *El Mundo* uses the precise phrase "war on terror," along with a metaphorical reference to an arsenal:

> Valls points out ... that since 2012, the French government has been working on building an arsenal [of measures] for the war on terror (EM27)

El País also evokes war, and uses "arsenal" twice. With the Nice attack,

> [t]he war has changed this time, and the government was not expecting it (EP25)

In addition, the perspective is quite different from the EM excerpt above:

> The third jihadist massacre in 18 months in France is the one that has triggered the fewest measures, [as] the counterterrorist arsenal was already empty (EP26)

> The government is calling for unity and has also gone on the defensive, highlighting the arsenal of counterterrorism measures already put in place, and their successful outcomes (EP38)

Table 19 Quantitative Data on Violence and Connotation of Metaphors in the Swiss Corpus

Metaphor Source	Total	Negative			Positive			Neutral			Total violent	% Violent
		TV	NV	V	TV	NV	V	TV	NV	V		
EP	117	41	15	23	1	5	2	0	18	12	79	68%
EM	81	25	13	10	3	6	1	1	19	3	43	53%

TV=Terrorist violence

NV=Not violence

V=Other violence

El País also observes that France, although it has been "practically bulletproofed" (EP3), is fighting a war "against jihadism on three fronts" but is "unable to cover all flanks" (EP6) and is also "losing the virtual battle [of ideology]" (EP33).

The above violent metaphors do not directly describe terrorist violence itself. Target or bullet metaphors sometimes (but not always) do:

Terror has France in its sights/line of fire (EP30)

[for jihadists,] France thus loomed as a gigantic target of hate (EP3)

there is no "magic bullet" that makes it possible to eradicate the jihadist threat completely (EM21)

El País also combines a target and a heart metaphor:

assassinating more than 80 defenseless people in the heart of a large country that has been living with the threat of jihadism since the Armed Islamist Group (GIA), which included Algerian Salafists, made France its bullseye in the 1980s. (EP33)

Regarding heart metaphors, all except one of the occurrences in the Spanish corpus are violent and negative. They make the vulnerability, fear, and suffering of France powerfully tangible:

the first jihadist strike in the heart of the country (EP3)

The massacre [literally: butchery] of July 14 on its pavements thus also struck, symbolically, the heart of the Tour de France (EP2)

The fear of terrorism, which since the attack on *Charlie Hebdo* had demonstrated its ability to reach the heart of France (EP3)

It would be impossible to choose a more apt day to strike [literally: wound] the French in the very depths of their hearts (EM20)

[Reporting] from the heart of the suffering in Nice (EM25).

It is important to notice how very frequently "jihad" and terrorism are the topic of all of the content cited so far.

Finally, as we have seen across the corpus, French politics is often described via war/violent metaphor, albeit somewhat less pervasively. It is interesting that both Spanish newspapers focus a lot on the *Front National*. For example, EP12 does so in conjunction with the newspaper's efforts to historicize and contextualize, and uses war/defense metaphors:

The touristic city is a stronghold of the *Front National* and also characterized by problems of coexistence, both historically and more recently (EP12).

It is noteworthy/surprising that the Le Pen family built the fortress of the *Front National* in the least French city in France. (EP12)

The right and far-right are also portrayed as playing a key—and opportunistic— role in political upheaval:

After the attacks by the far right and with nine months until the election, the French right is keeping its swords raised against the Government. (EP38)

The *Front National* shrewdly waited until Daesh claimed responsibility before joining the fray (EM24).

Similar types of metaphor are used to convey the fact that the population is losing faith in the government and feeling generally fed up with the political infighting:

The political skirmish is provoking a very different reaction [than after the 2015 attacks, when Hollande's popularity soared]. (EP38)

Others take the opportunity to criticize the government and the opposition for "continuing the internal battles" while the country bleeds out (EM19)

The fact that there is a greater proportion of EP articles among all of the above excerpts aligns with the statistics in Table 19 on violence and negativity.

Water-Related Metaphor

The first excerpt from *El País* below fits the type of metaphor usage that Piquer Martí (2015) highlighted, but its purpose in this particular instance is to highlight the responsibility of European countries to solve geopolitical conflicts that cause the mass movement of people:

the need to put an end to the conflicts that are creating a wave of refugees not seen since World War II. (EP17)

Perhaps surprisingly, *El País* also uses the "flow" metaphor to describe a tactic supposedly used by Daesh to get jihadists into European countries: their

opportunistic use of migratory flows (EP30),

a phenomenon which is typically invoked by the right wing (recall Fernández-Díaz in Spain) as an anti-immigration argument but has been proven to occur only extremely rarely. Less surprisingly, a wave metaphor is used to describe the violent events of 2015 and 2016:

after the wave of attacks that the country has been through (EM24)

a wave of attacks in different leisure establishments in Paris (EP4)

We have already seen that across the corpus, stylistic features shape descriptions of political conflict and disunity. In EP21, commentary on the *Front National* and on politics is accompanied by water-related metaphor:

> Marine Le Pen brought her vehemence to bear in the first wave of disagreements among the parties (EP21)

> On Saturday, Le Pen launched a destructive/divisive message that falls on sympathetic ears [literally: seeps into fertile ground]. (EP21)

El Mundo also uses multiple water metaphors, but instead to describe criticism of the socialist government in power:

> Following the wave [literally: rain] of criticism received (EM28)

> The criticisms of the French government that rained down [literally: poured in] after the attack in Nice on July 14 (EM27).

Use of water metaphor is heterogeneous and not particularly pervasive in this corpus, but it is employed differently in each Spanish newspaper in relation to politics.

Animal-Related Metaphor

Use of animal-related metaphor is more salient in the Spanish subcorpus than in the others, in particular because it involves extended metaphor. As discussed above, EM15 attributes to security failures the fact that France has had massive attacks in the recent past while its partners in the international coalition fighting Daesh have not; *El País* instead gives more space to societal factors. As we saw above, *El País* emphasizes the connection between poverty and mass violence with the "breeding ground" metaphor, which is ubiquitous across the full corpus: in order to address terrorism, it is necessary to

> attack poverty, as even though it is not a direct cause of terrorism, it does create breeding grounds for the recruitment of jihadists. (EP17)

All of the other animal-related metaphors in *El País* and most in *El Mundo* refer to "lone wolves." The metaphor is ubiquitous across the languages in question here, which is why I have not given it much attention before now; but interestingly, both Spanish newspapers develop an extended metaphor around the trope, with the "most extended" one appearing in EP33, whose headline is "Nice and Mustafa's Wolves." Mustafa was an Al-Qaeda leader, and, significantly, the opening image of the article is a photograph of the man sitting with Osama bin Laden. The article discusses the so-called "frustrated jihadists" who have not been able to travel to Syria or Iraq, describing them as "vermin" who "deliberate in their lairs about where and how to do the most harm to their potential victims"; one terrorist is described as having "died cornered in the bathroom of his house." Moreover, rhyme is used in the text to underscore the ideologies and influences of terrorist groups that turn these individuals into "lone wolves." The Spanish also carries rhythm and alliteration, making the content particularly salient:

> Los lobos de la yihad no nacen, casi siempre se hacen. [The wolves of jihad are not born jihadists, they are almost always made jihadists.]

This particular statement aligns with *El País*'s position that jihadists become so in part due to their (adverse) life experiences. *El Mundo*, on the other hand, connects jihadism to Muslims: France has

> a much larger breeding ground of potential terrorists among the five million French Muslims who have problems integrating. (EM15)

This claim is not only reminiscent of LT6 and journalist Richard Werly's insistence on the size of the population; it also makes the shocking claim, through the presupposition carried by the definite article *the* five million, that the entirety—or almost the entirety—of France's Muslim population is not well-integrated (without, of course, defining what integration means).

In addition, in a shorter extended metaphor, EM12 instead asserts that Spanish Islamists—a predominant focus of the newspaper's discussion of terrorism and a way of "bringing the story home"—are *not* "lone wolves," but "travel in a pack" (the phrase appears twice). Moreover, in a combination that is similar to that of EP33, EM30 explains that Daesh's official spokesman Abu Mohamed al Adnani recorded a video exhorting his "cubs" in the West to perpetrate "ram raids" during the holy month of Ramadan; the article includes three different still shots, presumably from the video in question, of young, intense-looking men carrying rifles and wearing combat gear and headscarves or balaclavas. Given the association between the content and accompanying images in the articles just discussed, both newspapers place Nice in an event chain whose protagonists are archetypal jihadists of a similar ilk to the most notorious one, Osama bin Laden. Finally, we also see *El Mundo*'s characteristic defense of security and intelligence measures bolstered by an animal-related metaphor, as it warns against "the error of making intelligence services the scapegoat when terrorism strikes" (EM21).

Other Metaphor

In this section, I would like to return briefly to the interesting metaphorical use of *hilo* [thread] and *deshilvanar* [to unstitch, untack] in this corpus. It is another stylistic element which reflects a certain balancing of perspectives in *El Mundo*:

> In relation to the effects that this crime could have, it is noteworthy that there has been an increase in Islamophobia in Europe and particularly in France, as well as more and more rejection of Muslim refugees and immigrants who come to Europe from conflict zones. Both effects can have disastrous ramifications for coexistence by polarizing societies, thereby playing even further into the hands of those who are holding the reins [literally: maneuvering the threads] of such terrorism, and who are pursuing precisely this aim: the division and breakdown of the countries they attack (EM23).

> their intention is to unstitch and break down the message of the Qur'an in a Manichean and populist manner in order to establish a system [literally: a grammar] based on the dialectic of the victims *versus* the tormentors. (EM20)

The excerpts are a useful reminder that different languages often favor different metaphors when dealing with a given theme, but also of how one metaphor may be—and sometimes must be—translated with another in the target language. This would be an interesting area for further research on stylistic characteristics of news texts.

Comparative Conclusions

In this chapter, I draw from the findings presented in the previous chapter in order to compare and contrast the news from the three contexts in terms of their portrayal of France and of Muslims, and their use of the stylistic features of modality, alliteration, and metaphor. I had thought that French-language Swiss news would be more fact-based and homogenous than news from the other two countries, and that it would convey less prejudice and engage in less stereotyping of Muslims. While these expectations do not align with what we learned about Swiss society in Chapter 3, they were linked to both the way Swiss news is produced, and the supposedly center-left political position of news outlets from the French-speaking region, which does not reflect that of the rest of the country. I expected British and Spanish news to divide along political lines on all of the variables studied except alliteration, which I thought would be far more common in British news. Similarities and differences in how each country's news articles encourage prejudice and the conflation of terrorism with Islam, and contribute to a discourse of fear, will be the central focus here. Finally, connections will be drawn between these similarities and differences, and the comparative discussions of the three societies earlier in this book.

The novel approach I applied in this study, which considers news about events, countries, and people abroad as an instance of cultural translation and consisted of examining stylistic features of news about a violent attack abroad, yielded interesting results which mostly confirmed my hypotheses. The attack in Nice was certainly an extremely violent, shocking, and reprehensible act. It was also seen as a justifiable reason to report frequently and at length on the "significant" Muslim population of France, terrorism, radical Islam, jihadism, and Daesh, and to link these themes closely together, regardless of the political leanings of the newspapers (where identifiable) and the countries where they are published. All of the news sources focus on Islamic extremism, despite the uncertainty that surrounded Bouhlel's religious and extremist links at the time of the attack and the reporting in question, and despite occasional acknowledgment that he was probably psychologically unstable or perhaps even suicidal. Indeed, all of the online newspapers refer to terrorism and/or "the terrorist," even though they acknowledge, at other points, that such links have not been proven. Moreover, indications that the crime was premeditated are generally seen (without proof of political/religious motive; recall the differing definitions of terrorism presented in the section "History/Experience of Terrorism" of Chapter 3) as sufficient reason for using the terror label as soon as reporting on the event begins, whereas this has not been the case with other perpetrators of violent attacks causing massive casualties (recall that of Andreas Lubitz and Germanwings, discussed in the Introduction). The *Guardian, El País, Le Courrier,* and to a lesser extent *Le Temps* are nevertheless more likely to recognize difficulties and discrimination faced by Muslims and the way that discourse surrounding this kind of attack deepens social divisions, thus aiding Daesh in its efforts to destabilize societies. Except for *Le Temps,* whose political leanings remain unclear, the list corresponds to center-left-leaning news sources.

How do the different newspapers report on these themes? In relation to portrayals of France and Nice, the country is depicted across the corpus as emblematic of Western democracy and values, which are uniformly positive. Nice is celebrated for its beauty, culture, history, and attractiveness for tourists, but also portrayed as a breeding ground for jihadists. These moves are also part of a tendency to set up an opposition between the victim—the monolithic Western "Us"—and the violent, threatening "Them." That said, the *Guardian, Le Courrier, Le Temps,* and *El País* all historicize and contextualize more than the *Telegraph, La Tribune,* or *El Mundo,* by discussing the history and complexity of immigration in France or the connections between poverty, unemployment, and violence, for instance. The *Telegraph* and *El Mundo* tend to focus more on the threat of radical Islam to the home country and portray that country as superior, although *El Mundo* is more balanced than the *Telegraph* in these areas as well as in its treatment of religion (see the metaphors connected to discussion of the Qur'an in *El Mundo,* for example). The *Telegraph* truly conveys the most extreme and prejudiced views in the corpus. It is telling that two striking examples of such views, DT7 and DT26, are also the articles that most employ the term "Muslim" out of all the texts in the corpus. That said, a journalist from *Le Temps* twice links France's Muslim population with an accrued risk of violence, and *El Mundo* misuses statistics in a way that links foreigners, and in particular North Africans, with violence. The right side of the political spectrum more frequently supports strong and enhanced anti-terror measures, and this is seen in the *Telegraph* and *El Mundo*; they also depict the home country as tougher on security than France. The left instead emphasizes the ineffectualness of such measures, and this tendency is reflected in *Le Courrier* and *El País* in particular.

The positions described above are conveyed or reinforced in large part through stylistic choices. Regarding modality, according to the statistics, all of the newspapers examined except *Le Courrier* use it in about equal measure. That said, the type of modality that is employed varies. The trends were indeed different in the Swiss and Spanish subcorpora, on the one hand, and in the UK subcorpus, on the other: rather than tending to give unproven content a patina of factuality, as in the UK corpus (although this did happen; see discussion of LT6 by Werly), modal use in the other two corpora more often established distance from such content or allowed vacillation (e.g., on whether Daesh was involved and whether its claim of responsibility was valid; whether Bouhlel was religious; whether he was radicalized; whether he had accomplices; whether there were any Spanish victims) as well as emphasizing Bouhlel's personal and mental problems, although these trends were stronger in left-leaning sources. *La Tribune* put particular emphasis, through modality, on the questionable nature of claims about Bouhlel's religiosity and extremism. That said, it also established the link "premeditation=terrorism" using modality; moreover, the equation was made more salient through use of alliteration. *Le Temps* was the only newspaper to report rumors that had proven to be unfounded, and it also used modality to emphasize risk and doubt more than the other sources, including to roundly criticize the then socialist French government. In *Le Temps*, the notion of risk also accompanied violence, and civil war specifically, which is likely to contribute to feelings of fear, a sense of threat, or the impression that France's problems are not under control, all of which we also saw in the UK corpus.

The statistics on alliteration show that most sources associated the stylistic device with negative content much more frequently (well over 50 percent of occurrences of alliteration) than with positive or neutral content. The exceptions are *Le Temps* (50 percent negative, 48 percent neutral) and *El País* (44 percent negative, 46 percent neutral). In general, alliteration often accompanied descriptions of extremists' tactics and penchant for violence, thereby making them all the more salient and perhaps also heightening fear and the sense of threat. Two Swiss sources also used the stylistic device to emphasize the nationality of the attacker ("tués par un Tunisien"—killed by a Tunisian). In the Swiss texts, and in particular in *La Tribune*, alliteration often accompanied information about Nice's status as a major tourist destination and information related to Swiss tourists, their options for changing their travel to Nice, and so on. In the Spanish texts, it often accompanied administrative or procedural information about the case or about governmental or institutional meetings or processes, which could explain the lesser number of negative instances. That said, across the corpus, alliteration did often accompany information (and judgments) about politics and policy, as was the case in the UK subcorpus. On the other hand, unlike in the UK *Telegraph*, it rarely accompanied religion-related content in the other two subcorpora; the exception is the right-leaning *El Mundo*. Here, though, the role and power of Salafism in Spain were emphasized (perhaps excessively), extremists' "fraudulent and opportunistic" misuse of the Qur'an was also criticized, and the criticism was rendered salient through alliteration. Religion is therefore a theme that *El Mundo* appears to treat in a more balanced way than the *Telegraph* does.

There was also not as clear a divide in use of alliteration within the Swiss and Spanish subcorpora as appeared to exist in the UK subcorpus (recall the way DT7 depicted Muslim men, which contrasts with the *Guardian*'s criticism, accompanied by alliteration, of France's integration model, or the much greater emphasis on religion through alliteration in the *Telegraph*), and while alliteration did often accompany negative content, the result was not always the creation or intensification of threat. Nevertheless, various instances of alliteration, even by seemingly quite-balanced sources, demonstrate that emphasis on the "Us" versus "Them" dichotomy is still omnipresent in reporting about violent attacks seen (rightfully or not) to be linked to radical Islam. Bugnot (2012: 986) asks, "What are, in reality, these two worlds that are in conflict? A minority religion and/or race, on the one hand," European countries, on the other. Reliance on this simplistic dichotomy not only hinders the integration of those seen as "Them"; it also makes impossible an eventual cosmopolitan approach to news, effective intercultural mediation, successful cultural translation.

In terms of metaphor, according to the statistics, the two UK newspapers used it with similar frequency. In the Swiss corpus, metaphor was employed 98 times in *Le Temps*, 83 times in *La Tribune*, and 40 times in *Le Courrier* (which is not negligible, given the small number of articles). Finally, *El País* used the stylistic device much more than *El Mundo* (117 occurrences vs. 81). Metaphor was frequently negative (only the *Telegraph* and *La Tribune* go somewhat against this tendency), and very often war-related or otherwise evocative of violence (percentages of violent metaphor: TG, 53 percent; DT, 73 percent; LT, 57 percent; TDG, 42 percent; LC, 67.5 percent; EP, 68 percent; EM, 53 percent).

The longstanding "war on terror" trope is still in play, in particular through the quoting of authorities who use it. What is of particular note, though, is that violent metaphor was very often used *even when the violent attack itself was not the topic*. This particular trend confirms Bugnot's finding that when content in the press is linked to Islam, it is accompanied by a whole "semantic network that revolves around violence" (2012: 989). Moreover, as war imagery colors much of the content, and in particular descriptions of the political situation (it is the UK newspapers, TDG, LT, and EP which most often employ violent, negative metaphors to qualify the political and societal situation, and specifically to evoke the conflict among France's top politicians), and as violence and negativity pervade the texts, an impression of chaos, crisis, threat, and danger, already present due to the nature of the event in question and use of other stylistic devices, is likely to be heightened and, in turn, to foment fear and distrust of certain groups. On this parameter too, then, most of the sources in the corpus are guilty—the word is appropriate—of evoking a war between cultures, between Islam and "the West," even though the perpetrator's links to extremists acting in the name of Islam and in particular to Daesh were never, to my knowledge, clearly established.

In relation to illness/violence metaphor in particular, recall the discussions above of how terrorism and the related terms of "extremism" and "radicalization" have been "made to mean" over time; criticisms of the Prevent strategy; or opposition to multiculturalism. Moutet's use of the virus metaphor could not illustrate more precisely Kundnani's (2017: 148) description of how the terminology, which also underpins antiterrorism policies, has evolved:

> The concept of "extremism" underwent a transformation following 7/7. … It now emphasised attitudes, mindsets and dispositions. Above all, it referred to a free-floating ideology that did not work through recruitment but through radicalisation. "Radicalisation" referred to the process by which extremist ideology captured the minds of the young and made them into potential terrorists. Extremism was pictured as a virus, flowing from radicaliser to radicalised, infecting, spreading, infiltrating (Bettison 2009: 130–1). Naively allowing Muslims too much separation and autonomy, in the name of multicultural tolerance, had encouraged the spread of the virus.

As we saw with the virus metaphor and other disease/illness metaphors discussed in Chapter 4, the right may be more prone to using them to demonize extremists and, by extension, Muslims, while this kind of metaphor may instead contribute to contextualization in left-leaning sources. The results suggest that more work should be done on disease-related metaphor in news about violent events,

Muslims, and Islam, in particular how it may tie in with particular political positions (as the quote from Kundnani suggests). The findings also show that in this kind of study, quantitative data do not tell the whole story: even infrequent occurrences of a stylistic feature can be salient and influential.

There are nevertheless differences within and across subcorpora in how articles address the themes of Islam and terrorism and how they convey violence and negativity, and these are also partly explained by metaphor usage. Therefore, let us now consider the other types of metaphor identified and examined throughout the corpus. With respect to the UK newspapers, while both emphasize the political disarray which followed the Nice attack, the right-leaning *Telegraph* blames the socialist government that was in power, emphasizes the fact that the Nice attack falls within a violent event chain, and tends to fault Muslims/Islam and extremism, which are also portrayed as external forces, through the use of water-related and plant/growth metaphors. The *Guardian*'s use of such metaphors instead emphasizes the underlying social and economic (and therefore also partly internal) causes of violence in France, and historicizes and contextualizes both the event and the perpetrator's identity and background. Put otherwise, both newspapers use water-related metaphors in the ways identified (and criticized) by Baker et al. (2013) and Piquer Martí (2015) (for instance, using "wave" to convey the uncontrollable nature of a phenomenon such as immigration or terrorist attacks), but only the *Guardian* uses them in other ways as well. Regarding the use of water-related metaphor in the other subcorpora, it is very heterogeneous in the Swiss corpus, except for its accompaniment of violent themes in the *Tribune*. In the Spanish corpus, its use in *El País*—perhaps surprisingly—very much corresponds to the aforementioned authors' descriptions, whereas in *El Mundo* it tends instead to be used to criticize the then socialist government in France.

Regarding plant/growth metaphor—and, I shall add, animal metaphor, as it is more relevant in the Swiss and Spanish subcorpora—the former type stands out much less in newspapers from these two countries. In contrast, as already mentioned, all of the sources employ equivalents of "breeding ground" (Nice as a breeding ground for jihadists/terrorists). This gives the impression that violent "jihadists" are proliferating there. Moreover, in contrast to *El País* but very much like the Swiss *Temps*, *El Mundo* links the risk of jihadism to a significant Muslim population when it indicates that France has

a much larger breeding ground of potential terrorists among the five million French Muslims who have problems integrating. (EM15)

Perhaps more interestingly, the animal metaphor "lone wolf," which has practically become lexicalized in relation to terrorist attacks, becomes an extended metaphor in both Spanish newspapers. It is thus in a sense "reactivated" in this subcorpus in a way that is totally absent from the other sources, and embellishes the writing and the imagery— as well as the sense of threat.

Finally, while the corpus is relatively small and focuses on a very specific event, meaning that one cannot generalize about differences in different cultures' choice of metaphor, it is worthwhile here to comment on three particular types of metaphor identified: that related to fire, in the Swiss corpus, and those related to heart and thread, in the Spanish corpus. While certain types of metaphor were found across languages, these were much more language-specific, at least where the particular event and themes reported upon were concerned.

This corpus supports Lakoff and Johnson's (1980) assertion that conceptual metaphor is omnipresent in our discourse and shapes the way we take in and interpret information. We are accustomed to metaphor; do we also take its power for granted? We need to be aware of the prevalence and weight of metaphor in others' and our own discourse, in our own and others' interpretations of ideas and situations. This goes for journalists, too, as Rice-Oxley (2016), incorporating a lovely water metaphor, convincingly asserts: "Suffice [it] to say that it is vital to measure every word in our news stories carefully to navigate these precarious waters of meaning."

It is true that by virtue of the sequencing of this study, with news from the UK being analyzed first, the UK findings became a kind of measuring stick according to which the other news sources were compared and contrasted. It is possible that simply by changing the order of the analyses, results would have been at least somewhat different. However, one has to choose a starting point, and I would argue that the very fact that the Anglo-Saxon model for news is often described as the foundation for news models across the world justifies the chronology of the study.

There was a strong and very early focus on terrorism and terrorist motivations in the news sources studied, despite the perpetrator's background, psychological problems, and lifestyle. The latter characteristics were in fact part of counter interpretations (recall Titley 2017) which did not "stick." The terrorism narrative instead came to overshadow more measured, balanced approaches by other authorities because of the interpretations that had already been developed and reinforced around prior links in the violent event chain. Given these observations and given the selective use of the "terrorist" label in conjunction with recent violent events around the world, one can ask, and journalists should ask, whether the early presumption of terrorism was justified, and whether the presumption was made because of France's recent history or, instead, because the perpetrator was a Tunisian living in Nice (point of departure for a significant number of men who left to fight in Syria, as the news sources indicate).

Examining the impact of journalist identity on style and content was beyond the scope of this study; however, when one consults the full list of articles (see Appendix), one can see that it is an important question. Consider, for instance, the fact that R. Werly wrote almost all of the *Temps* articles that did not come from agencies; that N. Nougayrède, A. Chrisalis, and A.-E. Moutet are all French; that the texts by Moutet and Méléagrou-Hitchens were the most virulent in their blame of Muslims and Islam. I talk about journalist identity to some degree in my 2018 article, and Bielsa's (2016a) discussion of foreign correspondents in her work on cosmopolitanism provides some useful considerations about the topic. It certainly warrants further research.

Finally, I would like to briefly discuss two articles that came up in my search when I was selecting news texts for the corpus, articles which I was unable to include in the analysis precisely because they were not published under "News" sections of the website. Interestingly, both were from *El País*. "From María to Myriam" is a personal story of conversion and has nothing to do with jihadism, nor does it say one word about it. It is the kind of article that gives Islam a face, makes it individual and local, and thereby represents a small effort to counter the depiction of the "Muslim world" as a monolithic "Other." The other article presented Cembrero's text and could encourage readers to educate themselves about the history, presence, and role of Islam in Spain. Given the way I selected articles for my corpus, it cannot be concluded that this kind of article never appears in the other online newspapers searched. Nevertheless, their appearance here was a timely reminder that another kind of news about Muslims can be disseminated, but that such stories remain relatively rare.

Stylistic Features of News as a Catalyst for Change? Lessons for Journalism, Translation Studies, and "Europe"

In this chapter, I will briefly explain why the findings presented in this volume are important for journalism, Translation Studies, and "European" societies in general. The results of the study will hopefully remind journalists to reflect more upon their stylistic choices and make readers more aware of the far-reaching influence of stylistic choices in the creation of a narrative, which is what news texts really are. Furthermore, the findings nuance, I argue, the assertion by many scholars that the news outlets of European countries are moving toward a standardized, "European" form of news, and I consider this a strength. The study also builds bridges between literary and non-literary analysis, which is rare, and supports the current trend, in Translation Studies, of broadening the definition of "translation." The concept of "cultural translation" contributes to this trend while also providing a paradigm for those who inform the public to consider their role, writing and choices: every form of communication is translation; journalistic communication is a civic responsibility, performed in the service of intercultural mediation and the optimizing of communication and understanding across borders, groups, and societies. I conclude with ideas for improving journalistic practice, including ensuring the independence of members of regulatory bodies; doing more to guarantee journalists' conformity to editorial guidelines; or recruiting, training, and hiring more minority journalists. Such initiatives are perhaps small steps in addressing societal trends and attitudes such as Islamophobia, the conflation of Islam and terrorism or terrorism and crisis, and the marginalization of minority groups, but as such efforts multiply, they have the potential to improve coexistence among the diverse groups that comprise contemporary "European" society.

Stylistic Features: A Key Component of Media Power

We have seen that while news framing is often a prime focus of studies of news discourse, at a more micro level, stylistic choices play an influential role in shaping the messages conveyed by news texts. Not only framing, but also stylistic choice, "is far from a neutral or inconsequential process" (Freedman 2017: 214). What is more, incorporating stylistic features into a news article is in itself a *desirable* move, as it brings to a predominantly informational text some of the qualities of literature, that is, of good writing, writing that comprises aesthetic elements, writing that draws the reader in and then keeps her there. By all means, use stylistic devices—as long as they do not serve to misrepresent or discriminate. This is unfortunately the case, however, of many of the findings presented in Chapter 4: they continue "a pattern of ... misrepresentation that has been prevalent since 9/11" (214). For example, in the news articles analyzed, Muslims and terrorism were linked, early on in the news cycle, in part due to the background of the perpetrator of the Nice attack; in turn, the attack prompted frequent and lengthy reporting on jihadists, extreme groups, and terrorist events. Moreover, terror was tied to religion, despite the statistics we have seen which show that religion is only infrequently the motivation behind violent attacks in Europe. The "Us" versus "Them" dichotomy was in play, with Western countries portrayed as the noble bastions of democratic values and as victims of a violent, retrograde "Other," or Muslims portrayed as "problem" or "failed" members of society. All of these messages were buoyed by use of the stylistic features of modality, alliteration, and metaphor.

What I would particularly like to concentrate on here, though, is the fact that these messages, like the stylistic choices that underpin them, are highly likely to stoke fear and a sense of threat. Use of modality, for instance, reinforced by frequent violent and negative metaphors and/or made more salient through alliteration, demonstrated that *potential* threats are allowed a "'continuous discursive presence' (Hoskins and O'Loughlin 2009: 107–8) that not only encourages anxiety but can also serve to tether any political activity by Muslims ... to the possibility of future radicalized violence" (Titley 2019: 85). As we saw in Chapter 3, this way of defining political action and engagement on the part of Muslim citizens may keep them from exercising certain rights due to citizens, which may in turn hamper their effective integration. What is more, "fear sells" (boyd and McBride 2014: 177); and mainstream newspapers, whose circulation continues to wane, need to sell. This decrease in readership, coupled with "[t]he technology explosion that has shepherded us into the 21st century," "has magnified the value of attracting an individual's attention" so that media organizations will "go to great lengths to seize focus by any means possible" (177), even when doing so "can pose a challenge to journalism's core values of truth, transparency and community" (177).

Moreover, while "[a]n individual act of fear-mongering causes little damage," "the additive effects of repeated episodes are huge" (boyd and McBride 2014: 178). As the authors point out and as the tenor of the two articles I could not include in my corpus demonstrate, when news stories stoke fear, they not only risk undermining accuracy, they also "fail to tell other stories" (179). In an example that boyd and McBride discuss, such tendentious choices in terms of news content work to the detriment of "youth who seriously need attention, support and help" (179); in the articles in my corpus, the selection of themes leaves out examples of positive coexistence of culturally different groups, the contributions to society of citizens who just happen to be Muslim, or correctives to certain entrenched prejudices, for instance. "For every headline meant to capitalize on fear, an opportunity is lost" (boyd and McBride 2014: 180). In contrast, the "[f]earful messages spread especially far, particularly stories that play into [the] broad cultural anxieties" (181) that have been discussed at length throughout this book. The media's amply demonstrated power to shape politics, policy, and public opinion operates in part through stylistic choices that can contribute to those cultural anxieties, but could also contribute to countering them if stylistic devices were used differently.

The Notion of "Cultural Translation": A Boon for Translation Studies, a Boon for Journalism?

The tenets of cultural translation and cosmopolitanism are valuable ones for Translation Studies. As translation is conceived of not as interlingual, but as intercultural, transfer, and as every "other" is a "text" for each of us to try to decipher, these approaches contribute to a growing trend to broaden the definition of "translation." Together they also position openness to the "other" and tolerant cultural exchange as paramount, and they foreground the experience of the foreign, the effort to understand the foreign, as laudable goals.

In this sense, it is also valuable for the journalist reporting on events abroad for her home audience to think of herself as a translator, as she is mediating between cultures and should—the news principles and guidelines surveyed support this—optimize communication between them, such as by reporting only accurate information, or by avoiding any content or language choices that discriminate against minority groups. If she "translates" well, in line with the ideas underpinning cultural translation, she can challenge the apparent fixity of identities and the apparent validity of certain ideologies. Indeed, her "translation" can serve as a "critique of ideology" (Maitland 2017) or encourage her readers to engage in such a critique. An ideology that might come to be critically examined is one that is prevalent in contemporary "European" societies: that which maintains that Muslims are backward, anti-democratic, violent, terrorists.

To achieve these goals, however, journalists and readers alike must be educated, interpreting subjects, seeking to understand. With respect to the goal of re-presenting the Muslim "Other," and as a result of my findings, I would encourage journalists to try to cultivate in their writing, and thereby in their readers, an "antiessentialist" position on Muslims and Islam. As López García and Bravo López (2008: 979) define it, the antiessentialist view

> denies the total alterity of Islam, the comparison of these two symbolic macro-entities called West and Islam, because it distrusts these identity categories and instead sees collective identities as dynamic, mutable phenomena that carry within them an infinite number of contradictions. Above all, it denies the possibility of establishing a direct link between ethnic origin and cultural identity, beliefs or ways of life.

In fact, before asserting anything on the subject of Islam, the antiessentialist prefers to ask: "Which Islam?" "Whose Islam, from where, during what historical period?" (980). If journalists reporting on violent attacks abroad were to invariably ask such questions, we would see fewer generalizing and negative portrayals of Muslims and Islam in the press. The language, including stylistic choices, would be different; the messages conveyed to the public, more nuanced; the public's resulting interpretations and judgments, better founded; and therefore a contribution could be made to fostering more inclusive "European societies".

Gianni, Giugni, and Michel (2015: 85) emphasize how difficult it is to precisely capture both the literal and the social meaning of the term "Muslim." It encompasses much more than religious affiliation. For the Muslims the authors surveyed, religion was above all both private/personal, and a point of cultural reference, not the prime determiner of their identity. Basically everything the authors learned from their Swiss respondents—that spiritual leaders such as imams carried little sway, that respondents believed that democratic values and laws, as well as the secularity of the state, should be respected, that immigrants, particularly from the Maghreb, were able to integrate successfully on various levels despite important avenues, such as citizenship and voting, being closed to them—flew in the face of the essentialist, rigid, reductive, and negative representations of Muslims that often dominate in the media.

The authors also warn that defining integration as unilateral adaptation to "national values" and then exhorting a minority population—in particular one that is already relatively well-integrated according to various parameters, as is the case of Muslims in Switzerland—to comply, "risks provoking" various kinds of "social reactions" (Gianni, Giugni, and Michel 2015: 116). "For members of the majority," for instance, it may lead to a hardening of identity "in the face of the presumed menace" (116). Moreover, there is a greater risk that "any resistance" at all to adaptation will automatically be interpreted as "a lack of integration" (116). For the Muslim minority, such pressure risks "exacerbating the feeling of discrimination and lack of recognition," which may in turn lead to either a radicalizing of given members' identity or "a tendency toward social and political self-exclusion" (116). Were these things to occur, they could indeed threaten "social cohesion and citizenship, which are essential to the vitality and legitimacy of democratic societies" (116).

The effective "cultural, social and political integration of members of minorities (and not only Muslims) requires their participation in the definition of" the shared cultural, social, and political space (Gianni, Giugni, and Michel 2015: 121). This is necessarily a dynamic, sometimes fraught, and constantly evolving process. It absolutely requires giving more consideration to diversity than the model of integration-by-(pure)-adaptation does. It also requires "fighting against all disrespectful and degrading representations which stigmatize a given cultural group" (122). What does all of this imply? Intercultural dialogue. And translation. Indeed, as the authors observe, encouraging Muslim communities to gather, form associations, and dialogue with social and political authorities "pushes both Muslims and secular institutions to make the effort to *translate* their values into a language the *other* can understand" (127).

Changing Habits for a Changing Landscape?

If journalists were to proceed, to write, as suggested above, they would make more strides toward fulfilling journalism's "social responsibility, which is to contribute to providing information that is balanced and contextualized and provides the public with unbiased elements with which to formulate judgments"

(Piquer Martí 2015: 155). There are various other measures that can be taken, however. The author also suggests, for instance, that "ethical codes need to be reinforced and committees formed that defend truthful and impartial reporting about minorities" (155). These and other measures are discussed below.

The Ethical Journalism Network (EJN) "suggests establishing a body that looks at the ethical and sensitive issues in the media of key nations" (they name the United States and Britain) (Grass 2013). "The reports should highlight examples of good and bad reporting so journalists all over the world can use them as guidelines for their future work." In addition, the EJN's report "recommends international media invest more time, money and manpower in adequate research and communication, and on analyzing the impact their reports can have" (Grass 2013). Working from a large series of concrete examples of news texts that have been evaluated by external experts would surely be a practical and productive way for journalists to develop best practices for how to report on "sensitive" issues such as integration, Islam, Muslims, and terrorism—and to avoid conflating them.

(Regulatory) Bodies with Teeth?

Another move would be to create regulatory bodies "with teeth," or to reinforce existing ones. The regulatory body in the UK that currently adjudicates on press content issues which have recently led to a series of corrections or calls for corrections is the Independent Press Standards Organization (IPSO). The remit of this body is seen as a step in the right direction, but as we already know, there is criticism, and there is room for improvement. First, IPSO needs to become independent in more than name only. Second, it needs to raise quality standards.

> It is not just the right thing to do but a vital commercial imperative if the newspaper industry is going to effectively compete with the chatter of unregulated online news and social media. (Ponsford 2017)

To do so, it also needs to have more power in order to impose "a stronger deterrent to reporting that fails to meet the highest professional standards that members of the press subscribing to IPSO have undertaken to maintain."[1] This is all the more essential as "quality" news, not only tabloids, is guilty of publishing inaccurate news that misrepresents Muslims. A Muslim Council of Britain report (2017: 5) suggests that there should be a means of subjecting media outlets to financial penalties when they publish false, misleading, or Islamophobic news.

The report also calls for "[s]tronger regulation by a truly independent body with the willingness and ability to deter poor standards within the media, as recommended by Lord Leveson," and "[t]raining for journalists" so that they develop "a better understanding of Islam."

The document also provides a whole series of recommendations for changes to procedures and amendments to the Editor's Code. Surprisingly, "under the Code as it currently stands, an article may breach the Public Order Act against incitement to racial or religious hatred but may still not be in breach of the Editors' Code" (Muslim Council of Britain 2017b: 7). For this reason, the MCB argues that despite the importance of safeguarding freedom of expression, "A new provision should be added to the Code prohibiting the incitement to hatred against any group with protected characteristics" (7). This echoes Lord Leveson's recommendations. In a similar vein, the paper suggests that "[a] new provision should be added to the Code prohibiting the levelling of abuse against any vulnerable group unless it can be justified in the public interest" (8). Determining what constitutes abuse is subjective, however, especially considering that the paper maintains that "mere insult" would still be acceptable (7).

According to journalists themselves, internal regulation based on ethical principles and, in particular, accountability (which includes the value of self-regulation) is preferable to external regulation. In their research involving journalists from a number of regions of Spain, presented recently at the International Association for Media and Communication Research (IAMCR) conference in Madrid, Ramon, Mauri, Díaz del Campo, and Rodriguez (2019) investigated Spanish journalists' opinions about in-house Media Accountability Instruments (MAIs), which constitute a means of ensuring accountability without state intervention. As found in an earlier study of journalists from twelve European (including the UK, Switzerland, and Spain) and two Arab countries, in-house stylebooks were seen as the most effective tool, yet even this score was only modest (5.82 on a scale of 1 to 10). Older journalists tended to have more confidence in stylebooks and ombudspersons while newcomers, who embraced accountability the most, considered the section of media websites which presents corporate information as the most effective guarantor of accountability. Moreover, if stylebooks did not receive a terribly high score, this is for two important reasons: time constraints mean they are not properly consulted or comprehensively followed (we saw clear evidence of this), and there is no penalty for non-compliance.

The researchers also organized focus groups with Spanish citizens to examine their knowledge of these accountability mechanisms. There was a clear lack of visibility, and citizens pinpointed the need for media to make the public more aware of them. Journalists and citizens alike were well aware that criticism is healthy. One of the researchers' main conclusions was that media organizations need to revise and update their portfolios of existing MAIs and promote the public's knowledge of them.

On the topic of "audience-inclusive models" of self-regulation, García-Avilés (2019: 272) and his team conducted a study of online accountability measures that looked, among others, at the practices of the online editions of the Spanish news sources studied here, *El País* and *El Mundo*. They found that 45 percent of the media outlets used no online accountability instruments whatsoever; 43 percent used just one (274). They observed that the newsroom blog, while underutilized in the Spanish context, not least because blogs are time-consuming, is a positive tool because it allows journalists to exercise some "autonomy, not just from outside forces but also from the internal control imposed by employers, newsroom practices and the loyalty to colleagues," while also allowing them to explain "to the public the limits" placed on "journalists' decisions" (275). *El País* has a blog, "*El País que hacemos*," which "provides explanations about the paper's coverage, including interviews with the journalists and editors involved in particular news stories" (276). It is not clear, however, how the news stories discussed are selected nor whether reader complaints or other input are addressed. *El País* also incorporated an ombudsperson role in 1985 (277). The study shows that this person's priorities are "issues related to content and editorial aspects," "although other complaints such as gender discrimination and political bias are also prominent" (277). Nevertheless, ombudspersons across Spanish media lack "punitive powers" (278).

Finally, García-Avilés (2019) reminds us that media accountability tools have not been widely taken on board in Spain; that economic and personnel constraints hinder their implementation; and that their use must be coupled with a diplomatic approach based on a willingness to listen, solve problems, and admit shortcomings (280). Accountability tools also need to truly target accountability rather than other goals such as "self-promotion" (281). All in all, though, professional accountability does not seem to have been sufficiently improved.

Rodríguez-Martínez, Mauri-De los Ríos, and Fedele (2017: 70) conclude that "criticism can be considered the best solution to faulty journalistic practice, as well as one of the fundamental aspects of accountability." Given the focus of the press industry on accountability and journalists' own strong recognition of its importance, not only do accountability instruments need to be implemented, evaluated, and updated, but "independent monitoring processes need to be implemented to guarantee [their] neutrality, impartiality and trustworthiness" (Sorsa 2019: 147).

The fundamental problem with all of the above solutions, however, is that if they do not recognize stylistic characteristics as a key driver in cultural (mis)representation of Muslims and Islam in news reporting about terrorism, they cannot identify them, let alone regulate them or encourage journalists toward improved use of stylistic characteristics. It is for this reason that more studies like this one, on other topics, on press from other countries, on more stylistic devices, should be conducted and disseminated.

Various sources discussed above have highlighted the ineffectiveness of certain existing laws in combating misleading, maligning, hate-inciting news content. Not only do these laws need to be reviewed, and not only does the power of bodies like IPSO need to be reinforced; there are other actions that can be taken at the governmental and community levels. A roundtable held at the House of Lords in April 2016 suggested various solutions such as encouraging the circulation of "clear definitions of radicalisation (as terminology) … within the law enforcement and security agencies, and put[ting] in place guidelines to protect individuals from agency profiling"; setting up "a consulting forum led by media and government to facilitate professional communications practices for mosque leaderships, neighbourhood centres, charities, schools and other minority group institutions" to help them "to promote and publish more balanced narratives about their communities"; nominating "a well-recognised figure" such as "a celebrity role model as a Muslim Media Relations officer" and more generally facilitating the visibility of, and engagement with, Muslim role models; and "creating community relations reporters in minority communities."[2] A report by the Muslim Council of Britain also calls for "considering multi-agency co-ordination to stop using the term 'Islamic' or 'jihadi' when describing terrorism in line with [measures taken by] the Obama administration" (Muslim Council of Britain 2016: 4).

In conclusion—and it is much easier said than done, and, depending on the administration in power, not necessarily a priority—more steps need to be taken politically, socially, and economically to educate, to actively deter inaccurate representation, and to further the opportunities and the full inclusion of minority groups in the workplace, in the media, in society. After all, "[i]n developed countries terrorism is more likely to occur in those places where socioeconomic factors such as high unemployment, a lack of faith in democracy and the media […] and negative attitudes towards immigration are widespread" (Warsi [2017] 2018: 76; Institute for Economics and Peace 2019).

Corrections

One way to counter misleading, inaccurate reporting, Islamophobia in reporting or the conflation of terrorism and Islam in reporting is to require corrections of such content. The event entitled "Islam in the Media: Are We Getting It Right?"[3] that took place in London in September 2017 involved discussion of the corrections newspapers have already been required to publish when they emit false or misleading claims about the Muslim community. In response to the question "What would it take for the correction to hit hard?," Miqdaad Versi highlighted the need for a move from "due prominence" to "equal prominence" (described in detail in Muslim Council of Britain 2017b), that is, that the correction should have the same prominence as the original false or misleading claim. He noted, however, that the print press does not like the idea.

With respect to breaking news, "Any material changes to an online news story should be referenced at the top of an article e.g. We previously reported XXX. This was incorrect. It is actually YYY" (Muslim Council of Britain 2017b: 4). In general, "All false stories should be removed with an acknowledgement of the removal. This includes stories published on social media" (4). It is important to be aware, though, that "discriminatory pieces and hate speech against Muslims in *opinion pages* of newspapers … are not covered by the current regulator [IPSO] (in spite of Lord Leveson's recommendations)."[4]

With respect to ruling on corrections called for on the part of newspapers, in particular, the same document (Muslim Council of Britain 2017b) also demonstrates that the requirement in IPSO's code that inaccuracies be "significant" is highly subjective, which has led to clear and unambiguous inaccuracies being ruled by IPSO to be not sufficiently serious to require correction (5). Moreover, according to the paper, "All inaccuracies" [I would stipulate "proven inaccuracies"] "which have been the subject of complaint should be corrected. Any value judgment about 'significance' can be dealt with" effectively if a requirement of "equivalent prominence" is also put into place (6). Where headlines in particular are concerned, "All inaccuracies … should be considered 'significant'. If it was considered important enough to be in a headline then it is clearly significant and central"(6).

Minority Journalists

> If we fail to represent people in our mainstream narratives, they'll switch off. …
> Where are we telling these kids that they can be heroes in *our* story?
>
> (Riz Ahmed, Speech to Parliament,
> Channel 4 annual diversity lecture, March 1, 2017)[5]

According to Josie Dobrin, "Of all the creative industries, … the press is one of the slowest when it comes to diversifying the workforce."[6] In their meta-analysis of (English-language only) studies addressing the treatment of Muslims and Islam in the media, Ahmed and Matthes (2017: 220) highlight the gravity of the current lack of Muslim perspectives in Western news, given that "[t]he Muslim community has over a billion people,[7] and it stretches across six continents encompassing hundreds of cultures (Courbage and Todd 2014)." The absence of this perspective has multiple causes, from failing to consult, include or quote members of the Muslim community when preparing an article, to not hiring journalists from this minority,[8] which may in turn only leave space for narrow and biased "external" views of members of the minority. The authors found that only 9.56 percent of the studies surveyed, or thirty-three, incorporated a Muslim perspective (Ahmed and Matthes 2017: 230).

At the same time, however, as pointed out in the "action points" published following the Cambridge University study of the connections between negative depictions of Muslims in the media and anti-Muslim hostility in the UK,[9] media outlets also need to avoid "ghettoization," that is, over-assigning stories about minorities to minority journalists (and, hence, under-assigning them other types of stories). In fact, the researchers suggest assigning "minority group coverage to non-minority reporters and editors, so as to broaden awareness and avoid 'ghettoisation' of minority coverage" (University of Cambridge 2016). In addition, they call on media organizations to "develop and promote context-sensitive awareness and language use among staff" (University of Cambridge 2016).

Conversely, while in a democracy one cannot silence extreme views due to freedom of speech laws,[10] and while balanced news means representing diverging views, the media should avoid handing extremists a highly visible platform on a silver platter. The terror-group-supporting Anjem Choudary is a case in point, according to Miqdaad Versi (2016b), as broadcasters continue to invite him *without properly contextualizing the persona and the views.*[11] Providing visibility without proper contextualization risks not only fomenting Islamophobia by encouraging people to associate Muslims with extremists, but potentially encouraging terrorism itself. "[Me]dia outlets should not be doing the work of terrorists or spreading their message" (Versi 2016b).

In relation to terrorism reporting more specifically, since it is often linked up with reporting on Muslims and Islam, I have highlighted key questions that journalists can realistically and productively ask about terrorist or other violent events and about their own reporting on them. Seib (2017) reminds us that "[a]nswering such questions requires daily news coverage that consists of more than depictions of scattered chaos." Here is his advice on how this can be done:

- Given that terrorist reporting tends to unquestioningly link up terror and Islam, do not "shy away" from reporting on religion-related themes, as doing so "creates a vacuum of public knowledge that terrorists and anti-Muslim activists and politicians can exploit." I would note that religion-related themes can also be positive.
- Report on Islam regularly, not just when violence happens. If this were the case, "perhaps news consumers would realise that there is far more to Islam than violence. And if antipathy toward Islam were to diminish, terrorists would lose a recruiting tool."
- Report on state-sponsored terrorism. "[T]he news media could play a more forceful role in describing how even purported allies," like Saudi Arabia, "help terrorism take root."
- Avoid understating the sophistication of terrorist groups.
- Scrutinize counterterrorism efforts. "The public needs to know what's working and what isn't."

Following these steps could conceivably lead not only to better understanding and integration of Muslims, but even to a decrease in terrorism.

Social Media

While detailed analysis and discussion of social media are beyond the scope of this study, they are more and more popular as sources of news, especially among young people. I have encountered useful recommendations for improving reporting on Muslims and combating Islamophobia on these platforms. False reports should be removed and their removal, flagged. At the "Islam in the Media" event, Versi insisted that major platforms like Facebook can develop a tool whereby, if a news item is corrected, the account of anyone who has posted the inaccurate news will also receive, and feature as a post, the corrected version. Moreover, the MCB Editorial Code document (2017b: 3) recommends that "[w]herever the Press chooses to publish a headline in isolation e.g. on its front page or social media, care should be taken to ensure that such a headline, when read alone, is not inaccurate or misleading". There is no clear reason why online hate crime should be treated differently than hate crime perpetrated in the public space. Finally, the MCB "Response to the Fake News Inquiry" paper (2017a: 6) recommends "Kitemarks[12] for the trustworthiness of news outlets, determined by an independent panel" as "one means of ensuring that non-verified one-man bands are more easily identified."

Style and "European" Media

It is undeniable that on some levels, news is becoming more and more homogenized. This is evident in the fact that more and more news organizations obtain their news from press agencies—the prevalence of articles from the ATS in my Swiss subcorpus (see Appendix) attests to this—and make very little adjustment before publishing them as their own. My analysis of stylistic features has nevertheless prompted me to question the concepts of a "European" or a "transnational" media. Why? Because the extent to which similarities and differences among national media exist depends upon how their key characteristics are defined, as this has to be done before they can be compared and contrasted. If stylistic features are taken as a key characteristic, there are many differences; by virtue of the different languages in which news is reported in Europe, but also by virtue of the differing weight certain stylistic characteristics may carry in those different languages, or the forms that may predominate in one language versus another. From my corpus, for instance, it appears that alliteration may play a more significant role in English than in French or Spanish in rendering content salient; certain types of metaphor may be common in one language when reporting on the particular themes of Muslims and violence, but completely absent in another language; the type of modality used in one language may tend toward distancing, whereas in another, it may contribute to portraying supposition as fact. Some may see these as inconsequential differences; but as style shapes message, "message" in these cases may turn out differently in one language versus another. In any case, the weight of stylistic features and how they may be *differently distinctive* warrant further research across a greater variety of languages, news sources, and themes.

Conclusion

The role of the journalist has been defined here as that of a translator of culture who narrates not only events but, when those events occur abroad, "other" places and populations for the "home" audience. This role carries both power and responsibility, and fulfilling this role, I hold, therefore requires "ethical reflection" (Maitland 2017, "Introduction," section "What's 'Wrong' with Cultural Translation?").

It is beyond well-established that reporting on Islam and Muslims often paints each in a negative light, including by associating them closely with terrorism and violence when reporting on these types of events. This misleading, inflammatory targeting of a minority group has been recognized (a notable example is Leveson, 2012) and changes called for. While best practices have been proposed (see, for example, Seib 2017), there is a big piece of the "how" of those messages themselves that has not been sufficiently researched: the stylistic features that feed into the negative representations. For practice to change, these factors, too, need to be recognized and remedied.

The power the journalist wields is found not only in the content she conveys but in the forms she chooses; these include stylistic features. The findings of the present study confirm that the stylistic features of modality, alliteration, and metaphor are a non-negligible aspect of "making terrorism mean" (Freedman 2017: 211), and therefore warrant further research.

During a recent lecture at the Reuters Institute for the Study of Journalism on the challenges and future of journalism, Marty Baron, the editor-in-chief of the *Washington Post*, said: "The answer for us [journalists] is clear: Just do our job. Do it honestly, honorably, seriously, fairly, accurately, and also unflinchingly. 'To show, by our work', as David Shribman, editor of the *Pittsburgh Post-Gazette* put it, 'that the truth still matters'" (Baron 2018). This is laudable, but vague. Techniques of reporting that contribute to exacerbating tensions and heightening the sense of threat exist. They are highly questionable. But they sell news. This is one of many thorny questions currently facing journalism that do not have easy answers. In terms of religion and avoiding pre-emptively making terror "about Islam," Seib (2017) has some sage advice: "report on Islam regularly, not just when violence happens." This is indeed the kind of reporting we desperately need more of. It is the means, among other things, for European readers to encounter an "Other" group that is plural, not monolithic; multi-faceted, not one-dimensional; mutable, not fixed; in short, often much like themselves. The result, instead, "of publishing texts which only narrate conflict-laden events which, in turn, are constantly linked to one community is that it constructs an image of Islam and terrorism as intrinsically connected" (Piquer Martí 2015: 143). Moreover, given that in the media, writing is always from the "Us" perspective (Piquer Martí 2015: 141), the Islamophobia present in society necessarily spills over into news articles. According to Piquer Martí, the way that the media portrays (Muslim) immigrants—through un-contextualized, isolated messages always bound up with violence and conflict—coupled with the public's relative ignorance of the Muslim world, encourages negative stereotypes. Thus, whether or not the alternative hypothesis about the perpetrator of the Nice attack, Bouhlel, presented in the *Telegraph* on July 18 (that he was suicidal), marked a turning point in its reporting, that possibility was already unlikely to "stick," given the messages, reinforced by stylistic choices, that had preceded it. Journalists and other news actors need to turn "a critical eye to their complicity in normalizing prejudice" (Allan [2010] 2014: 196); stylistic choices, which play so subtle yet so central a role in shaping cultural representations and public opinion, are a good place to start.

Notes

Chapter 1

1 Sections of this book reproduce parts of three prior publications: articles published online in *Perspectives: Studies in Translation Theory and Practice* (July 5, 2018, ©Taylor & Francis, available online: http://www.tandfonline.com, Doi: 10.1080/0907676X.2018.1478863); *Parallèles* (April 16, 2019, ©Ashley Riggs, available online: https://www.paralleles.unige.ch/en/tous-les-numeros/numero-31-1/riggs/, Doi: 10.17462/para.2019.01.06); and a chapter published in *Intercultural Crisis Communication: Translation, Interpreting and Languages in Local Crises* (2019, C. Declercq and F. M. Federici (eds.), ©Federico M. Federici, Christophe Declercq and Contributors, ISBN: 9781350097056).

2 On that morning, a bucket bomb set by a young Iraqi refugee exploded on a District Line train of the London Underground outside the Parsons Green station.

3 Interestingly, Canel "cites" *El Mundo*, *ABC*, and *El País* directly in English but never mentions that she has translated the content.

4 Unless otherwise indicated, all translations from the Spanish (references and news sources) are my own.

5 https://www.ohchr.org/en/NewsEvents/Pages/DisplayNews.aspx?NewsID=15885&LangID=E

6 Unless otherwise indicated, all translations from the French (references and news sources) are my own.

7 For Spanish online news: https://dircomfidencial.com/medios/ranking-digitales-pais-adelanta-mundo-tras-sumar-trafico-cinco-dias-20170420-0405/; https://www.laboratoriodeperiodismo.org/los-periodicos-con-mas-usuarios-unicos-en-espana/. For Swiss online news: https://www.rts.ch/info/suisse/8533751-la-presse-imprimee-resiste-en-suisse-la-consommation-en-ligne-progresse.html; www.wikipedia.org

8 https://www.notrehistoire.ch/medias/110647

9 The news source is quite liberal when it comes to society and culture, for example, but much less so when it deals with economic and financial topics. https://www.swissinfo.ch/fre/la-couleur-politique-de-la-presse-francophone-en-d%C3%A9bat/29626122

10 The authors also recognize this as a limitation of their own meta-study.

Chapter 2

1   Writing about the Spanish context, Piquer Martí (2015: 140–1) cites 9/11, but also the Gulf wars, as catalysts.

2   https://yougov.co.uk/news/2016/02/19/tracker-islam-and-british-values/

3   https://www.theredcard.org/news/2015/05/20/perception-vs-reality-young-peoples-perceptions-of-society-lead-to-concerns-about-the-potential-development-of-prejudice

4   https://www.met.police.uk/stats-and-data/hate-crime-dashboard/

5   Three days after Andreas Lubitz deliberately flew a plane full of passengers into a mountain, Germany's interior minister Thomas de Maizière announced, "According to the current state of knowledge and after comparing information that we have, he does not have a terrorist background" (Stout, 2015).

6   http://www.observatorioislamofobia.org

7   In his "New(s) racism: A Discourse Analytical Approach" (2000), van Dijk highlights most of the elements in this list when he describes how news reporting incorporates racist biases against foreigners, immigrants, refugees, and minorities.

8   Needless to say, online news content appears with images and other visual media which also play an enormous role in the reading experience. Unfortunately, the examination of non-verbal elements in my corpus was beyond the scope of this book.

9   These were influenced by earlier work from the Hutchins Commission (1947), the Society of Professional Journalists, and the Committee of Concerned Journalists (McBride and Rosenstiel 2014: 5).

10   http://www.ifj.org/about-ifj/ifj-code-of-principles/

11   https://www.theguardian.com/info/2015/aug/05/the-guardians-editorial-code

12   https://www.theguardian.com/guardian-observer-style-guide-a

13   https://www.telegraph.co.uk/about-us/editorial-and-commercial-guidelines/

14   https://www.telegraph.co.uk/style-book/by-letter/

15   https://assets.letemps.ch/sites/default/files/Charte_redactionnelle_v4.pdf

16   https://lecourrier.ch/charte-redactionnelle/

17   Eberwein, Fengler, and Karmasin (2019: 9) point out that in Switzerland, media journalism has largely been phased out due to economic constraints.

18   https://thetrustproject.org/

Chapter 3

1   http://www.bbc.co.uk/languages/european_languages/countries/uk.shtml#sa-link_location=more-story-2&intlink_from_url=https%3A%2F%2Fwww.bbc.

com%2Fnews%2Fworld-europe-18023389&intlink_ts=1563974063201&story_
slot=1-sa

2   https://migrationobservatory.ox.ac.uk/resources/briefings/migrants-in-the-uk-an-
overview/

3   https://www.theguardian.com/education/2015/apr/02/how-manx-language-came-
back-from-dead-isle-of-man; https://www.bbc.com/news/magazine-21242667;
https://en.wikipedia.org/wiki/Manx_language

4   All of the statistics in this paragraph came from the Swiss Confederation website:
https://www.bfs.admin.ch/bfs/de/home/statistiken/bevoelkerung/sprachen-
religionen/sprachen.assetdetail.4542311.html

5   Castilian includes many words of Arabic origin.

6   https://boe.es/buscar/act.php?id=BOE-A-2018-15138

7   https://www.cia.gov/library/publications/the-world-factbook/geos/sp.html

8   Despite distinct phases of Muslim immigration to the UK due to geopolitical
and economic forces—in particular after the Second World War, following the
independence of previous colonies and the importation of cheap labor—most UK
Muslims (67.65 percent) "continue to have ancestral roots in the Indo-Pakistani
subcontinent" (Weller and Cheruvallil-Contractor 2015: 309).

9   S. Rushdie published *The Satanic Verses* in 1988. It caused huge controversy
because it was seen by Muslims the world over as blasphemous toward the prophet
Mohammed (just like publications leading to the later Danish cartoon and *Charlie
Hebdo* affairs).

10   https://humanism.org.uk/campaigns/secularism/constitutional-reform/bishops-in-
the-lords/

11   "As conservative as their traditions and values may be, Muslim immigrants in
Europe, including those who have lived here for generations, tend to vote for
socialist or neo-communist parties" (Cembrero 2016: 297).

12   Religious governance relates to how religious diversity and the relationship between
church and state are managed.

13   Explanation is beyond the scope of this volume. Most of the territory that is now
Spain was under Muslim rule from the eighth to the fifteenth centuries. The first
part of this period was that of al-Andalus, a Muslim kingdom that had its own
"golden age."

14   http://www.legislation.gov.uk/ukpga/2000/11/section/1

15   https://www.boe.es/biblioteca_juridica/codigos/codigo.php?id=038_Codigo_
Penal_y_legislacion_complementaria&tipo=C&modo=2

16   Nevertheless, his party ended up being ousted less than a year later following a
huge financial scandal.

17   Cembrero (2016: 196) actually compares Spain unfavorably to the UK, noting that
the latter has published 116 pages of its anti-radicalization plan, while the former
has divulged only a fourteen-slide PowerPoint.

18 Among the indicators of cultural pluralism in the study were "Allowance of dual nationality, Cultural requirements for naturalization (e.g., language skills, … evidence of cultural and social assimilation), … Immigrant consultative bodies on the national" and local levels, "Mother tongue teaching in public schools, Cultural requirements for the granting of residence permits (e.g., language skills, other knowledge of the host society), Programs in immigrant languages in public broadcasting" (Michalowski and Burchardt 2015: 107).

19 Indicators of religious pluralism included "Muslim consultative bodies," "Right of Muslim female teachers," and "Muslim students to wear a headscarf in public schools, Allowance of ritual slaughtering of animals according to the Islamic rite," "Existence of Muslim cemeteries and separate sections of cemeteries," "Muslim chaplains in prisons" and "in the military" (Michalowski and Burchardt 2015: 107).

20 The full transcript of his speech is available online: https://www.gov.uk/government/speeches/pms-speech-at-munich-security-conference

21 They are referring to violent, ethnically motivated riots that took place in Oldham, in the northwest of England.

22 See one reference here: https://www.theguardian.com/uk-news/2017/sep/17/parsons-green-tube-bomb-police-arrest-second-man. Interestingly, an innovative project called "British Muslim Values" (https://britishmuslimvalues.wordpress.com) demonstrated that Muslim values show immense overlap with those predominating in British society.

23 http://www.mipex.eu/united-kingdom

24 https://cordis.europa.eu/project/rcn/89092/factsheet/en

25 I deliberately use the word "group" rather than "wave," which is logical in light of the stylistic analysis in Chapter 4.

26 https://www.bfs.admin.ch/bfs/de/home/statistiken/kataloge-datenbanken/tabellen.assetdetail.7226813.html

27 https://appsso.eurostat.ec.europa.eu/nui/submitViewTableAction.do

28 A model "with many political parties, distinct in their ideological orientations, ranging over a wide political spectrum and including 'antisystem' parties on the right and left" (Hallin and Mancini 2004: 130).

29 They define political parallelism as "the degree and nature of the links between the media and political parties or, more broadly, the extent to which the media system reflects the major political divisions in society" (21). Importantly, this characteristic also makes Britain an exception among the countries fitting under the Liberal Model, which is apparently one of "neutral professionalism" (197). One has to wonder whether the phenomenon "neutral commercial press" (67) really exists.

30 https://www.cam.ac.uk/research/news/media-fuelling-rising-hostility-towards-muslims-in-britain

31 It is noteworthy that to evaluate the level of Islamophobic content, the observatory uses eight indicators provided by the UK's Runnymede Trust (1997).

Chapter 4

1   As we have seen, Conservatives began rolling it back when they returned to power under David Cameron (prime minister from 2010 to 2016).

2   Arthur Goldhammer made a different translation choice in in his 1958 *The Algerian Chronicles* ("the bloody marriage of terrorism and repression").

3   In contrast, TG1 and TG3 refer to "homegrown militants," part of the *Guardian*'s recognition that extremism in France has a complex background.

4   The tenor of the allusions, however, is not reported. Other texts across the corpus quote people who knew Bouhlel as highlighting his *lack* of religiosity.

5   Marianne symbolizes the victory of the French Republic and the values of *liberté*, *égalité*, and *fraternité*.

Chapter 6

1   http://www.pressgazette.co.uk/dossier-of-20-inaccurate-uk-news-stories-about-muslims-revealed-with-warning-coverage-fuels-the-far-right/

2   http://www.cam.ac.uk/research/news/media-fuelling-rising-hostility-towards-muslims-in-britain

3   https://www.ebrd.com/news/events/islam-in-the-media-are-we-getting-it-right-.html

4   https://www.theguardian.com/commentisfree/2017/jan/23/uk-media-misrepresents-muslims-islam-prejudice-press

5   https://www.facebook.com/Channel4News/videos/10154616232846939/

6   http://www.bbc.co.uk/mediacentre/proginfo/2017/39/press-for-diversity

7   Seib (2017) notes that a "religion of 1.6 billion people is being defined in public discourse by the acts of the few who spill blood in a Manchester arena or a Baghdad marketplace" (http://en.ejo.ch/ethics-quality/superficial-speculative-hysterical-outdated-terror-reporting-must-change).

8   In an article in the *Independent*, Miqdaad Versi (2016a) also highlighted this issue: "Less than 0.5 percent of journalists in the UK are Muslim. No wonder[] so many misleading stories make the cut."

9   https://www.cam.ac.uk/research/news/media-fuelling-rising-hostility-towards-muslims-in-britain

10 However, as Versi (2016b) notes, the Human Rights Act does allow for "limits to free speech including incitement to violence" (http://www.independent.co.uk/voices/anjem-choudary-sentence-isis-terrorism-links-guilty-lee-rigby-media-blame-a7195286.html).

11 http://www.independent.co.uk/voices/anjem-choudary-sentence-isis-terrorism-links-guilty-lee-rigby-media-blame-a7195286.html
12 *OED*: "a quality mark, similar in shape to a kite, granted for use on goods approved by the British Standards Institution."

References

Abad Liñan, J. M. (2018), "España es el tercer país con un mayor abandono del cristianismo de Europa," *El País*, December 27. Available online: https://elpais.com/sociedad/2018/12/26/actualidad/1545833978_509115.html (accessed January 27, 2020).

Agence télégraphique suisse/B. O. I. (2017), "La consommation d'informations en ligne dépasse celle de la TV et la radio," *RTS Info*, October 23. Available online: https://www.rts.ch/info/sciences-tech/9021941-la-consommation-d-informations-en-ligne-depasse-celle-de-la-tv-et-la-radio.html (accessed January 27, 2020).

Ahmed, S., and J. Matthes (2017), "Media Representation of Muslims and Islam from 2000 to 2015: A Meta-analysis," *International Communication Gazette*, 79 (3): 219–44. Doi: 10.1177/1748048516656305

Allan, S. ([2010] 2014), "Journalism and the Culture of Othering," *Brazilian Journalism Research*, 10 (2): 188–203.

Amiraux, V., and A. Fetiu (2017), "After the Drama: The Institutionalisation of Gossiping about Muslims," in G. Titley, D. Freedman, G. Khiabany, and A. Mondon (eds.), *After Charlie Hebdo: Terror, Racism and Free Speech*, 63–78, London: Zed Books.

Antichan, S., and Jarvis, L. (2017), "'Counter-terrorism Policies Play an Important Role in Shaping a National Identity Narrative': Conversation with Lee Jarvis," *The Conversation*, December 6. Available online: http://theconversation.com/counter-terrorism-policies-play-an-important-role-in-shaping-a-national-identity-narrative-conversation-with-lee-jarvis-88680 (accessed January 27, 2020).

Antón, M. (2011), "Consideraciones sociolingüísticas sobre el bilingüismo hispano-árabe en Ceuta (España), *Revista Internacional de Lingüística Iberoamericana*, 9 (2): 121–41. Available online: https://www.jstor.org/stable/pdf/41678474.pdf?refreqid=excelsior%3Aacbc5aa9c666c177d76ee7dec2cb96eb (accessed January 27, 2020).

Arnold, D. (2019), "Involvement of Private and Civil Society Actors in Media Regulation Processes: A Comparison of All European Union Member States," in T. Eberwein, S. Fengler and M. Karmasin (eds.), *Media Accountability in the Era of Post-truth Politics: European Challenges and Perspectives*, 181–95, London and New York: Routledge.

Astor, A. (2015), "Governing Religious Diversity amid National Redefinition: Muslim Incorporation in Spain," in M. Burchardt and I. Michalowski (eds.), *After Integration: Islam, Conviviality and Contentious Politics in Europe*, 247–65, Weisbaden: Springer VS. Doi: 10.1007/978-3-658-02594-6. Retrieved from https://books.google.ch.

Baker, M. (2006), *Translation and Conflict: A Narrative Account*, New York and London: Routledge.

Baker, M. (2007), "Reframing Conflict in Translation," *Social Semiotics*, 17 (2): 151–69. Doi: 10.1080/10350330701311454

Baker, P., C. Gabrielatos, and T. McEnery (2013), *Discourse Analysis and Media Attitudes: The Representation of Islam in the British Press*, Cambridge, UK: Cambridge University Press.

Barbero, I. (2016), "Citizenship, Identity and Otherness: The Orientalisation of Immigrants in the Contemporary Spanish Legal Regime," *International Journal of Law in Context*, 12 (3): 361–76. Doi: 10.1017/S1744552316000252

Baresch, B., S. Hsu, and S. Reese ([2010] 2012), "Studies in News Framing," in S. Allan (ed.), *Routledge Companion to News and Journalism Studies*, 637–47, New York: Routledge.

Baron, M. (2018), "When a President Wages War on a Press at Work," Reuters Memorial Lecture, Reuters Institute for the Study of Journalism, University of Oxford, February 16. Transcript available online: https://reutersinstitute.politics.ox.ac.uk/sites/default/files/2018-02/Marty%20Baron%20Reuters%20Memorial%20Lecture%2016th%20Feb%202018.pdf (accessed January 27, 2020).

Barnett, S. (2016), "IMPRESS vs IPSO: A Chasm, Not a Cigarette Paper," *Press Gazette*, October 28. Available at https://www.pressgazette.co.uk/impress-vs-ipso-a-chasm-not-a-cigarette-paper/ (accessed May 6, 2020).

Bassets, M. (2017), "Francia vuelve a preguntarse sobre qué es la laicidad," *El País*, November 25. Available online: https://elpais.com/elpais/2017/11/24/opinion/1511544926_700420.html (accessed January 27, 2020).

Bauman, Z., and C. Bordoni (2014), *State of Crisis*, Cambridge, England: Polity.

Baumgarten, S., and C. Gagnon (eds.) (2008), *Translating the European House: Discourse, Ideology and Politics—Selected Papers by Christina Schäffner*, Newcastle upon Tyne: Cambridge Scholars Publishing.

Bazzi, S. (2014), "Foreign Metaphors and Arabic Translation: An Empirical Study in Journalistic Translation", *Journal of Language and Politics*, 13 (1): 120–51.

Bednarek, M. (2010), "Evaluation in the News. A Methodological Framework for Analysing Evaluative Language in Journalism," *Australian Journal of Communication*, 37 (2): 15–50.

Bednarek, M., and H. Caple (2012), *News Discourse*, London and New York: Bloomsbury.

Beliveau, R., O. Hahn, and G. Ipsen (2011), "Foreign Correspondents as Mediators and Translators between Cultures: Perspectives from Intercultural Communication Research in Anthropology, Semiotics and Cultural Studies," in P. Gross and G. G. Kopper (eds.), *Understanding Foreign Correspondence*, 129–63, New York: Peter Lang.

Bertrand, C.-J. (2000), *Media Ethics and Accountability Systems*, New Brunswick: Transaction.

Bettison, N. (2009), "Preventing Violent Extremism: A Police Response," *Policing*, 3 (2): 129–38.

Bialostosky, D. (2017), *How to Play a Poem*, Pittsburgh, PA: University of Pittsburgh Press. Retrieved from https://books.google.ch.

Bielsa, E. (2016a), *Cosmopolitanism and Translation: Investigations into the Experience of the Foreign*, London: Routledge.

Bielsa, E. (2016b), "La traducción en los medios de comunicación: una perspectiva cosmopolita," in M. R. Martín Ruano and A. Vidal Claramonte (eds.), *Traducción, medios de comunicación, opinión pública*, 17–34, Granada: Comares.

Bielsa, E. (2018), "Translation and Cosmopolitanism," in F. Fernández and J. Evans (eds.), *Routledge Handbook of Translation and Politics*, 110–24, London: Routledge.

Bielsa, E., and C. W. Hughes (eds.) (2009), *Globalization, Political Violence and Translation*, Basingstoke: Palgrave Macmillan.

Bielsa, E., and S. Bassnett (2009), *Translation in Global News*, London and New York: Routledge.

Birkenstein, J., A. Froula, and K. Randell (2010), *Reframing 9/11: Film, Popular Culture and the "War on Terror,"* New York: Continuum.

Boase-Beier, J. (2006), *Stylistic Approaches to Translation*, Manchester: St Jerome Publishing.

Boase-Beier, J. ([Print 2011] 2012), "Stylistics and Translation," in K. Malmkjaer and K. Windle (eds.), *The Oxford Handbook of Translation Studies*, Oxford: Oxford University Press. Doi: 10.1093/oxfordhb/9780199239306.013.0006

boyd, d., and K. McBride (2014), "The Destabilizing Force of Fear," in K. McBride and T. Rosenstiel (eds.), *The New Ethics of Journalism: Principles for the 21st Century*, 177–88, Los Angeles: Sage.

Brownlie, S. (2010), "Representing News from France," in C. Schäffner and S. Bassnett (eds.), *Political Discourse, Media and Translation*, 32–54, Newcastle upon Tyne: Cambridge Scholars.

Bugnot, M.-A. (2012), "Traduction des discours sur l'islam dans la presse de France et d'Espagne," *Meta*, 57 (4): 977–96.

Burchardt, M., and I. Michalowski (2015), "After Integration: Islam, Conviviality and Contentious Politics in Europe," in M. Burchardt and I. Michalowski (eds.), *After Integration: Islam, Conviviality and Contentious Politics in Europe*, 3–16, Weisbaden: Springer VS. Doi: 10.1007/978-3-658-02594-6

Canel, M.-J. (2012), "Communicating Strategically in the Face of Terrorism: The Spanish Government's Response to the 2004 Madrid Bombing Attacks," *Public Relations Review*, 38 (2): 214–22. Doi: http://dx.doi.org/10.1016/j. pubrev.2011.11.012

Canel, M.-J., and K. Sanders (2010), "Crisis Communication and Terrorist Attacks: Framing a Response to the 2004 Madrid Bombings and 2005 London Bombings," in W. T. Coombs and S. J. Holladay (eds.), *The Handbook of Crisis Communication*, 449–66, Chichester, West Sussex: Wiley-Blackwell.

Cembrero, I. (2016), *La España de Alá*, Madrid: La Esfera de los Libros.

Cesari, J. (2004), *When Islam and Democracy Meet*, New York: Palgrave.

Cheng, J. (2015), "Islamophobia, Muslimophobia or Racism? Parliamentary Discourses on Islam and Muslims in Debates on the Minaret Ban in Switzerland," *Discourse and Society*, 26 (5): 562–86. Doi: 10.1177/0957926515581157

Cheruiyot, D. (2019), "Media Criticism in an African Journalistic Culture: An Inventory of Media Accountability Practices in Kenya," in T. Eberwein, S. Fengler, and M. Karmasin (eds.), *Media Accountability in the Era of Post-truth Politics: European Challenges and Perspectives*, 284–97, London and New York: Routledge.

Chesterman, A. (1995), "Ethics of Translation," in M. Snell-Hornby, Z. Jettmarová, and K. Kaindl (eds.), *Translation as Intercultural Communication*, 147–57, Amsterdam: John Benjamins.

Chuquet, H., and M. Paillard (1987), *Approche linguistique des problèmes de traduction anglais-français*, Paris: Ophrys.

Conway, K. (2005), "Assessing Apparently Equivalent Translations in the News Media," *Meta: journal des traducteurs/Meta: Translators' Journal*, 50 (4). Doi: 10.7202/019834ar

Conway, K. (2010), "News Translation and Cultural Resistance," *Journal of International and Intercultural Communication*, 3 (3): 187–205. https://doi.org/10.1080/17513057.2010.487219

Conway, K. (2012), "Cultural Translation, Long-form Journalism, and Readers' Responses to the Muslim Veil," *Meta: journal des traducteurs/Meta: Translators' Journal*, 57 (4): 997–1012. Doi: 10.7202/1021229a

Conway, K. (2015), "What Is the Role of Culture in News Translation? A Materialist Approach," *Perspectives: Studies in Translatology*, 23 (4): 521–35. http://id.erudit.org/iderudit/019834ar

Cottle, S. ([2011] 2012), "Global Crises and World News Ecology," in S. Allan (ed.), *Routledge Companion to News and Journalism*, 473–84, London and New York: Routledge.

Courbage, Y., and E. Todd (2014), *A Convergence of Civilizations: The Transformation of Muslim Societies around the World*, New York: Columbia University Press.

Crespo Fernández, E. (2008), "El léxico de la inmigración: atenuación y ofensa verbal en la prensa alicantina," in M. M. Lirola (ed.), *Inmigración, discurso y medios de comunicación*, 45–64, Alicante: Instituto Alicantino de Cultura Jan Gil Albert, Diputación Provincial de Alicante.

Culler, J. (1997), *Literary Theory: A Very Short Introduction*, Oxford: Oxford University Press.

D'Amato, G. (2015), "How Foreigners Became Muslims: Switzerland's Path to Accommodating Islam as a New Religion," in M. Burchardt and I. Michalowski (eds.), *After Integration: Islam, Conviviality and Contentious Politics in Europe*, 285–301, Weisbaden: Springer VS. Doi: 10.1007/978-3-658-02594-6

Davier, L. (2009), "Polyphonie dans le discours journalistique: une étude comparative de la presse anglophone et francophone," *ASP*, 56: 67–88.

Davier, L. (2013), "Le rôle du transfert interlinguistique et interculturel dans la coconstitution d'un problème public par les agences de presse: Le cas de la votation antiminarets," PhD Thesis, University of Geneva, Switzerland, and University Sorbonne Nouvelle, Paris.

Davier, L. (2015), "'Cultural Translation' in News Agencies? A Plea to Broaden the Definition of Translation," *Perspectives*, 23 (4): 536–51. http://dx.doi.org/10.1080/090 7676X.2015.1040036

Davier, L. (2017), *Les enjeux de la traduction dans les agences de presse*, Lille: Septentrion.

Davier, L., and Conway, K. (eds.) (2019), *Journalism and Translation in the Era of Convergence*, Amsterdam/Philadelphia: John Benjamins.

D'hulst, L., M. Gonne, T. Lobbes, R. Meylaerts, and T. Verschaffel (2014), "Towards a Multipolar Model of Cultural Mediators within Multicultural Spaces. Cultural Mediators in Belgium (1830–1945)," *Belgisch Tijdschrift voor Filologie en Geschiedenis/Revue Belge de Philologie et d'Histoire*, 92 (4): 1255–75.

Doyle, N. J. (2011), "Lessons from France: Popularist Anxiety and Veiled Fears of Islam," *Christian-Muslim Relations*, 22 (4): 475–89. Doi: 10.1080/09596410.2011.606194

Eberwein, T., S. Fengler, and M. Karmasin (2019), "Theory and Practice of Media Accountability in Europe: An Introductory Overview," in T. Eberwein, S. Fengler, and M. Karmasin (eds.), *Media Accountability in the Era of Post-truth Politics: European Challenges and Perspectives*, 3–17, London and New York: Routledge.

El-Madkouri Maataoui, M. (2006), "El Otro entre Nosotros: el musulmán en la prensa," in M. Lario Bastida (ed.), *Medios de comunicación e inmigración*, 98–123, Alicante: CAM Obra Social.

El-Madkouri Maataoui, M., and M. Taibi (2006), "Medios de comunicación, opinión y diversidad (social y cultural). Reflexiones en torno al fenómeno migratorio", in M. Lario Bastida (ed.), *Medios de comunicación e inmigración*, 126–43, Alicante: CAM Obra Social.

El País (2014), El País: *Libro de Estilo*, Mexico City: Aguilar/Santillana Ediciones Generales, S.A.

Encyclopaedia Britannica Online (2019), "Spain." Encylopaedia Britannica Inc. Available at https://www.britannica.com/place/Spain (accessed May 6, 2020).

Eliassi, B. (2013), "Orientalist Social Work: Cultural Otherization of Muslim Immigrants in Sweden," *Critical Social Work*, 14 (1): 33–47.

Esser, A. (2012), "European Media: Structures, Policies and Identity," *European Journal of Communication*, 27 (2): 203–6. Doi: https://doi.org/10.1177/0267323112441293

Ettema, J. S. ([2010] 2012), "News as Culture," in S. Allan (ed.), *The Routledge Companion to News and Journalism*, 289–300, London: Routledge.

European Commission against Racism and Intolerance (2016), *ECRI Report on the United Kingdom* (*Fifth Monitoring Cycle*), October 4. Strasbourg: ECRI Secretariat, Council of Europe. Available online: https://www.coe.int/en/web/european-commission-against-racism-and-intolerance/united-kingdom (accessed January 27, 2020).

Europol (2019), *European Union Terrorism Situation and Trend Report 2019*. Available online: https://www.europol.europa.eu/activities-services/main-reports/terrorism-situation-and-trend-report-2019-te-sat (accessed January 27, 2020).

Eyerman, R. (2008), *The Assassination of Theo Van Gogh: From Social Drama to Cultural Trauma*, Durham, NC: Duke University Press.

Fairclough, N. (1989), *Language and Power*, London: Longman.

Feddersen, A. (2013), "Public Discourse on Muslims and Foreigners," MA Thesis, University of Geneva, Switzerland. Available online: https://archive-ouverte.unige.ch/unige:35314 (accessed January 27, 2020).

Federici, F. M. (ed.) (2016), *Mediating Emergencies and Conflicts. Frontline Translating and Interpreting*, London: Palgrave Macmillan.

Fengler, S., T. Eberwein, G. Mazzoleni, and C. Porlezza (eds.) (2014), *Journalists and Media Accountability: An International Study of News People in the Digital Age*, New York: Peter Lang.

Fiddian-Qasmiyeh, E., and Y. M. Qasmiyeh (2010), "Muslim Asylum-seekers and Refugees: Negotiating Identity, Politics and Religion in the UK," *Journal of Refugee Studies*, 23 (3), 294–314.

Freedman, D. (2017), "Media Power and the Framing of the *Charlie Hebdo* Attacks," in G. Titley, D. Freedman, G. Khiabany, and A. Mondon (eds.), *After Charlie Hebdo: Terror, Racism and Free Speech*, 209–22, London: Zed Books.

Gallardo San Salvador, N. (2012), "De pateras o de cómo la embarcación utilizada por la inmigración irregular se convierte en fuente de creación neológica: aspectos sociolingüísticos de la neología especializada de las migraciones en la prensa," *Neology in Specialized Communication*, 18 (1): 128–48.

García-Avilés, J. A. (2019), "Examining Media Accountability in Online Media and the Role of Active Audiences: The Case of Spain," in T. Eberwein, S. Fengler, and M. Karmasin (eds.), *Media Accountability in the Era of Post-truth Politics: European Challenges and Perspectives*, 270–83, London and New York: Routledge.

Gianni, M. (2010), *Vie musulmane en Suisse: Profils identitaires, demandes et perceptions des musulmans en Suisse: rapport réal. par le Groupe de recherche sur l'islam en Suisse (GRIS): 2ème édition du rapport 2005, complétée de l'analyse de Stéphane Lathion*, Berne-Wabern: Commission fédérale des étrangers CFE.

Gianni, M., M. Giugni, and N. Michel (2015), *Les Musulmans en Suisse: Profils et intégration*, Lausanne: Presses polytechniques et universitaires romandes.

Gould, R. (2015), "Islam Returns to Spain: Religious Diversity, Political Discourse and Women's Rights," *Islam and Christian-Muslim Relations*, 26 (2): 165–82. Doi:10.1080/09596410.2014.997964

Granados Martínez, A. (2006), "Medios de comunicación, opinión y diversidad (social y cultural). Reflexiones en torno al fenómeno migratorio," in M. Lario Bastida (ed.), *Medios de comunicación e inmigración*, 61–83, Alicante: CAM Obra Social.

Grass, K. (2013), "The Innocence of the Media? Media and Political Violence," *European Journalism Observatory*, July 30. Available online: http://en.ejo.ch/ethics-quality/innocence-media-journalists-hate-speech-political-violence (accessed January 27, 2020).

Grieves, K. (2012), *Journalism across Boundaries: The Promises and Challenges of Transnational and Transborder Journalism*, New York: Palgrave Macmillan.

Halliday, M. A. K. (1976), "Modality and Modulation in English," in G. Kress (ed.), *Halliday: System and Function in Language*, 189–213, London: Oxford University Press.

Hallin, D. C., and P. Mancini (2004), *Comparing Media Systems: Three Models of Media and Politics*, Cambridge: Cambridge University Press.

Hernández Guerrero, M. J. (2010), "Las noticias traducidas en el diario *El Mundo*: El trasvase transcultural de la información," in *Translating Information*, R. A. Valdeón (ed.), 51–85, Oviedo: Universidad de Oviedo.

Hernández Guerrero, M. J. (2011), "Presencia y utilización de la traducción en la prensa española," *Meta: Translator's Journal*, 56 (1): 101–18. Doi: 10.7202/1003512ar

Hewson, L. (2011), *An Approach to Translation Criticism: Emma and Madame Bovary in Translation*, Amsterdam/Philadelphia: John Benjamins.

Hodgson, J. (2018), "Key Reading: Sarah Maitland's 'What Is Cultural Translation' (2017)," *Cultural Translation Research Blog*, March 29. Available online: http://bcmcr.org/culturaltranslation/2018/03/29/key-reading-sarah-maitlands-what-is-cultural-translation-2017/ (accessed June 6, 2020).

Hoksbergen, H. W., and J. N. Tillie (2012), *EURISLAM Survey-data & Codebook*. Available online: https://doi.org/10.17026/dans-xx7-5x27 (accessed January 27, 2020).

Hoskins, A., and B. O'Loughlin (2009), "Media and the Myth of Radicalization," *Media, War & Conflict*, 2 (2): 107–10.

Hussain, A. J. (2007), "The Media's Role in a Clash of Misconceptions: The Case of the Danish Muhammad Cartoons," *The Harvard International Journal of Press/Politics*, 12 (4): 112–30.

Hussain, E. (2007), *The Islamist: Why I Joined Radical Islam in Britain, What I Saw Inside, and Why I Left*, London: Penguin.

Institute for Economics & Peace (2019), *Global Terrorism Index 2019: Measuring the Impact of Terrorism*. Sydney, November 2019. Available online: http://visionofhumanity.org/app/uploads/2019/11/GTI-2019web.pdf (accessed May 12, 2020).

Karlsson, M., and J. Strömbäck (2009), "Freezing the Flow of Online News: Exploring Approaches to the Study of the Liquidity of Online News," *Journalism Studies*, 11 (1): 2–19.

Kapsaskis, D. (2019), "*What Is Cultural Translation?*" [Review], *Translation Studies*: 1–4. https://doi.org/10.1080/14781700.2018.1559762

Kelly, D. (1997), "Prensa e identidad nacional: la imagen de España en la prensa británica," PhD Thesis, Universidad de Granada, Granada, Spain. Available online: https://digibug.ugr.es/handle/10481/14433 (accessed January 27, 2020).

Kelly, D. (1998), "Ideological Implications of Translation Decisions: Positive Self- and Negative Other Presentation," *Quaderns: Revista de traducció*, 1: 57–63.

Kenny, D. (2001), "Corpora in Translation Studies," in M. Baker (ed.), *Routledge Encyclopedia of Translation Studies*, 50–3, London: Routledge.

Keown, C. (2017), "*What Is Cultural Translation?* by Sarah Maitland, (2017)," *New Voices in Translation Studies*, 17: 137–42.

Khiabany, G., and M. Williamson (2012), "Terror, Culture and Anti-Muslim Racism," in D. J. Freedman and D. K. Thussu (eds.), *Media and Terrorism: Global Perspectives*, 134–50, London: Sage.

Kundnani, A. (2017), "Extremism, Theirs and Ours: Britain's 'Generational Struggle'," in G. Titley, D. Freedman, G. Khiabany, and A. Mondon (eds.), *After Charlie Hebdo: Terror, Racism and Free Speech*, 146–61, London: Zed Books.

Lakoff, G., and M. Johnson (1980), "Conceptual Metaphor in Everyday Language," *The Journal of Philosophy*, 77 (8): 453–86. Retrieved from www.jstor.org

Le Poder, M.-E. (2012), "Perspective sociolinguistique des emprunts de l'anglais dans la section économique du quotidien espagnol *El País*," *Babel*, 58 (1): 377–94.

Leveson Inquiry (2012), *An Inquiry into the Culture, Practices and Ethics of the Press. Executive Summary*, London: HMSO.

Llaneras, K. (2019), "El auge de Vox y otras cuatro claves del sondeo," *El País*, November 3. Available online: https://elpais.com/politica/2019/11/02/actualidad/1572707413_764384.html (accessed January 27, 2020).

López García, B., and F. Bravo López (2008), "Un intento de clasificación: el Islam en el imaginario español," in J. García Roca and J. Lacomba Vázquez (eds.), *La inmigración en la sociedad española: una radiografía multidisciplinar*, [pre-print version, 961–89], Madrid: Ministerio de Trabajo y Asuntos Sociales/Suárez Barcala, S.L.

Maitland, S. (2017) [Kindle version], *What Is Cultural Translation?*, Bloomsbury Advances in Translation, London: Bloomsbury.

Matejka, L. ([1929] 1986), "On the First Russian Prolegomena to Semiotics," in V. N. Vološinov, *Marxism and the Philosophy of Language*, trans. L. Matejka and I. R. Titunik, 161–74, Cambridge, MA: Harvard University Press.

Maussen, M. (2009), *Constructing Mosques: The Governance of Islam in France and the Netherlands*, Amsterdam: Amsterdam School for Social Science Research.

Maussen, M. (2015), "Institutional Change and the Incorporation of Muslim Populations: Religious Freedoms, Equality and Cultural Diversity," in M. Burchardt and I. Michalowski (eds.), *After Integration: Islam, Conviviality and Contentious Politics in Europe*, 79–104, Weisbaden: Springer VS. Doi: 10.1007/978-3-658-02594-6

McBride, K., and T. Rosenstiel (2014), "Introduction. New Guiding Principles for a New Era of Journalism," in K. McBride and T. Rosenstiel (eds.), *The New Ethics of Journalism: Principles for the 21st Century*, 1–6, Los Angeles: Sage.

McLaughlin, M. (2011), *Syntactic Borrowing in Contemporary French: A Linguistic Analysis of News Translation*, Oxford: Legenda.

Michalowski, I., and M. Burchardt (2015), "Islam in Europe: Cross-National Differences in Accommodation and Explanations," in M. Burchardt and I. Michalowski (eds.), *After Integration: Islam, Conviviality and Contentious Politics in Europe*, 105–25, Weisbaden: Springer VS. Doi: 10.1007/978-3-658-02594-6

Miranda, J., and C. Camponez (2019), "European Models of Journalism Regulation: A Comparative Classification," in T. Eberwein, S. Fengler, and M. Karmasin (eds.), *Media Accountability in the Era of Post-truth Politics: European Challenges and Perspectives*, 18–35, London and New York: Routledge.

Misson, J. (2014), "Que fait la Suisse contre le terrorisme?" *tink.ch*, September 19. Available online: https://tink.ch/fr/?s=que+fait+la+suisse+contre (accessed January 27, 2020).

Modood, T. (2007), *Multiculturalism*, Cambridge: Polity.

Moore, M., and G. Ramsay (2013), *IPSO: An Assessment*, London: Media Standards Trust.

Munday, J. (2007), "Translation and Ideology: A Textual Approach," *The Translator*, 13 (2): 195–217.

Muñoz-Calvo, M., and C. Buesa-Gómez. (eds.) (2010), *Translation and Cultural Identity: Selected Essays on Translation and Cross-cultural Communication*, Newcastle upon Tyne: Cambridge Scholars.

Muslim Council of Britain (2016), *Written Evidence Submitted by the Muslim Council of Britain for the Hate Crime and Its Violent Consequences Inquiry by the Home Affairs Committee*. Available online: http://data.parliament.uk/writtenevidence/committeeevidence.svc/evidencedocument/home-affairs-committee/hate-crime-and-its-violent-consequences/written/40384.html (accessed January 27, 2020).

Muslim Council of Britain (2017a), *Response to "Fake News" Inquiry by the Culture, Media and Sport Parliamentary Committee*, London: Muslim Council of Britain.

Muslim Council of Britain (2017b), *MCB's Response to Editor's Code of Practice— Committee Consultation*, March 3. Available online: https://mcb.org.uk/mcb-updates/mcbs-response-to-editors-code-of-practice-committee-consultation/ (accessed January 27, 2020).

Nash, M. (2005), *Inmigrantes en nuestro espejo*, Barcelona: Icaria.

Ofcom (2017), "News Consumption in the UK: 2016," June 29. Available online: https://www.ofcom.org.uk/__data/assets/pdf_file/0016/103570/news-consumption-uk-2016.pdf (accessed June 6, 2020).

Office for National Statistics (2013), *Immigration Patterns of Non-UK Born Populations in England and Wales in 2011*. Report by the UK government. Available online:

https://webarchive.nationalarchives.gov.uk/20160107164635/http://www.ons.gov.uk/ons/dcp171776_346219.pdf (accessed June 6, 2020).

Office for National Statistics (2018), *English Language Skills*. Report by the UK government. Available online: https://www.ethnicity-facts-figures.service.gov.uk/uk-population-by-ethnicity/demographics/english-language-skills/latest (accessed January 27, 2020).

Ogan, C. L. Willnat, R. Pennington, and M. Bashir (2014), "The Rise of Anti-Muslim Prejudice: Media and Islamophobia in Europe and the United States," *The International Communication Gazette*, 76 (1): 27–46.

O'Halloran, K. (2010), "Investigating Metaphor and Ideology in Hard News Stories," in S. Hunston and D. Oakey (eds.), *Introducing Applied Linguistics: Concepts and Skills*, 97–107, London and New York: Routledge.

Olohan, M. (2004), *Introducing Corpora in Translation Studies*, New York: Routledge.

Osgood, C. E., G. J. Succi, and P. H. Tannenbaum (1957), *The Measurement of Meaning*, Urbana: University of Illinois Press.

Owunna, M. (2015), "Terrorists Killed 2,000 People in Nigeria Last Week. So Why Doesn't the World Care?" *Mic*, January 12. Available online: https://www.mic.com/articles/108192/terrorists-killed-2-000-people-in-nigeria-last-week-so-why-doesn-t-the-world-care (accessed January 27, 2020).

Piquer Martí, S. (2015), "La islamophobia en la prensa escrita española: aproximación al discurso periodístico de *El País* y *La Razón*," *Dirāsāt Hispānicas. Revista Tunecina de Estudios Hispánicos*, 2: 137–56.

Ponsford, D. (2017), "Newspaper Stories Misrepresenting Islam Would Not Be Tolerated if They Were about Judaism, Regulator IPSO Needs to Step In," *Press Gazette*, January 27. Available online: https://www.pressgazette.co.uk/newspaper-stories-misrepresenting-islam-would-not-be-tolerated-if-they-were-about-judaism-regulator-ipso-needs-to-step-in/ (accessed January 27, 2020).

Price, S. (2017), "The Event of Terrorism: Ambiguous Categories and Public Spectacle," *Television and New Media*, 19 (2): 163–9.

Purdam, K. (2000), "The Political Identities of Muslim Local Coucillors in Britain," *Local Government Studies*, 26 (1): 47–64.

Purdam, K. (2001), "Democracy in Practice: Muslims and the Labour Party at the local level," *Politics*, 21 (3): 147–57.

Ramon, X., M. Mauri, J. Díaz Del Campo, and R. Rodriguez (2019), "A Disconnect from Media Accountability? Spanish Journalists' and Citizens' Perceptions of In-house Traditional and Innovative Instruments," Paper presented at the International Association for Media and Communication Research (IAMCR) conference, Madrid, Spain.

Ramsay, G., and M. Moore (2019), "Press Repeat: Media Self-regulation in the United Kingdom after Leveson," in T. Eberwein, S. Fengler, and M. Karmasin (eds.), *Media Accountability in the Era of Post-truth Politics: European Challenges and Perspectives*, 84–99, London and New York: Routledge.

Rane, H., J. Ewart, and J. Martinkus (2014), *Media Framing of the Muslim World: Conflicts, Crises and Contexts*, Basingstoke and New York: Palgrave Macmillan.

Ravazzolo, E. (2017), "La langue de la presse économique française et italienne: spécificités linguistiques et stratégies rhétorico-pragmatiques," in U. Wienen, L. Sergo, T. Reichmann, and I. Gutiérrez Aristizábal (eds.), *Translation und Ökonomie*, 139–62, Berlin: Frank & Timme.

Reese, S. (2001), "Framing Public Life: A Bridging Model for Media Research," in S. Reese, O. Gandy, and A. Grant (eds.), *Framing Public Life*, 7–31, Mahwah, NJ: Erlbaum.

Rice-Oxley, M. (2016), "Reporting on Atrocities: It Is Vital That We Measure Every Word with Care," The *Guardian*, July 29. Available online: https://www.theguardian.com/membership/2016/jul/29/reporting-on-atrocities-it-is-vital-that-we-measure-every-word-with-care (accessed January 27, 2020).

Riggs, A. (2014), "Thrice upon a Time: Feminist Fairy-tale Rewritings by Angela Carter and Emma Donoghue, and Their French Translations," PhD Thesis, Faculty of Translation and Interpreting, University of Geneva, Switzerland.

Riggs, A. (2018), "The Role of Stylistic Features in Constructing Representations of Muslims and France in English Online News about Terrorism in France," *Perspectives*: 1–19. Doi: 10.1080/0907676X.2018.1478863

Riggs, A. (2019a), "How Terrorism Is 'Made to Mean', or Why We Should Study Stylistic Features of News," *Parallèles*, 31 (1): 57–74.

Riggs, A. (2019b), "On France, Terrorism, and the English Press: Examining the Impact of Style in the News," in F. M. Federici and C. Declercq (eds.), *Intercultural Crisis Communication: Translation, Interpreting, and Languages in Local Crises*, 193–215, London: Bloomsbury Academic.

Rodríguez-Martínez, R., M. Mauri-de Los Ríos, and M. Fedele (2017), "Criticism in Journalism as an Accountability Instrument: The Opinion of Spanish Journalists," *Communication & Society*, 30 (1): 57–72.

Rorty, R. (1989), *Contingency, Irony, and Solidarity*, New York: Cambridge University Press.

Runnymede Trust (1997), *Islamophobia: A Challenge for Us All*, London: Runnymede Trust. Available online: www.runnymedetrust.org/companies/17/74/Islamophobia-A-Challenge-for-Us-All.html (accessed January 27, 2020).

Runnymede Trust (2017), *Islamophobia: Still a Challenge for Us All. A 20th-anniversary Report*, London: Runnymede Trust.

Saner, M., and V. Wyss (2019), "Strengthening Media Accountability through Regulated Self-regulation: The Swiss Model," in T. Eberwein, S. Fengler, and M. Karmasin (eds.), *Media Accountability in the Era of Post-truth Politics: European Challenges and Perspectives*, 150–61, London and New York: Routledge.

Schäffner, C. (2012), "Rethinking Transediting," *Meta: journal des traducteurs/Meta: Translators' Journal*, 57 (4): 866–83.

Schäffner, C. (2013), "Discourse Analysis," *Handbook of Translation Studies* Online, 4: 47–52. Available online: https://benjamins.com/online/hts/articles/dis1 (accessed January 27, 2020).

Schäffner, C. (2014), "Umbrellas and Firewalls: Metaphors in Debating the Financial Crisis from the Perspective of Translation Studies," in D. R. Miller and E. Monti (eds.), *Tradurre figure/Translating Figurative Language*, 64–84, Bologna: Bononia University Press.

Schäffner, C., and S. Bassnett (eds.) (2010), *Political Discourse, Media and Translation*, Newcastle upon Tyne: Cambridge Scholars.

Seib, P. (2017), "Superficial, Speculative, Breathless: Outdated Terrorism Reporting Must Change," *EJO—European Journalism Observatory*, June 6. Available online: https://en.ejo.ch/ethics-quality/superficial-speculative-hysterical-outdated-terror-reporting-must-change (accessed January 27, 2020).

Sherwood, H. (2017), "Press publishing 'consistent stream' of inaccurate stories about Muslims," January 19. Available at https://www.theguardian.com/world/2017/jan/19/press-publishing-consistent-stream-of-inaccurate-stories-about-muslims (accessed May 6, 2020).

Simpson, P. (1993), *Language, Ideology and Point of View*, London and New York: Routledge.

Sorsa, K. (2019), "Public Value and Shared Value through the Delivery of Accountability," in T. Eberwein, S. Fengler, and M. Karmasin (eds.), *Media Accountability in the Era of Post-truth Politics: European Challenges and Perspectives*, 135–49, London and New York: Routledge.

Sousa Ribeiro, A. (2004), "The Reason of Borders or a Border Reason? Translation as a Metaphor for Our Times," *Eurozine*, January 8. Available online: https://www.eurozine.com/the-reason-of-borders-or-a-border-reason/ (accessed January 27, 2020).

Stetting, K. (1989), "Transediting—A New Term for Coping with the Grey Area between Editing and Translating," in G. Caie, K. Haastrup, A. L. Jakobsen, J. E Nielsen, J. Sevaldsen, H. Specht, and A. Zettersten (eds.), *Proceedings from the Fourth Nordic Conference for English Studies*, 371–82, Copenhagen: University of Copenhagen.

Stout, D. (2015), " Here's What We Know about the Germanwings Co-pilot Andreas Lubitz," *Time* magazine, March 27. Available online: https://time.com/3761151/andreas-lubitz-germanwings-co-pilot-background/ (accessed January 29, 2020).

Suárez-Villegas, J. C., R. Rodríguez-Martínez, M. Mauri-Ríos, and A. López-Meri (2017), "Accountability and Media Systems in Spain: Real Impact and Good Practices in Spanish Media," *Revista Latina de Comunicación Social*, 72: 321–30. Doi: 10.4185/RLCS-2017-1167. http://www.revistalatinacs.org/072paper/1167/17en.html

Thornton, T. P. (1964), "Terror as a Weapon of Political Agitation," in H. Eckstein (ed.), *Internal War*, 71–99, New York: Free Press.

Titley, G. (2017), "Introduction: Becoming Symbolic: From '*Charlie Hebdo*' to 'Charlie Hebdo,'" in G. Titley, D. Freedman, G. Khiabany, and A. Mondon (eds.), *After Charlie Hebdo: Terror, Racism and Free Speech*, 1–27, London: Zed Books.

Titley, G. (2019), *Racism and Media*, London: Sage.

University of Cambridge (2016), "Media fuelling rising hostility towards Muslims in Britain," University of Cambridge website, April 28. Available online: https://www.cam.ac.uk/research/news/media-fuelling-rising-hostility-towards-muslims-in-britain (accessed July 4, 2020).

Vaarakallio, S. (2010), "Veiled Phobias: The French Republican Dress Code," Reuters Institute Fellowship Paper, University of Oxford. Available online: https://reutersinstitute.politics.ox.ac.uk/our-research/veiled-phobias-french-republican-dress-code (accessed January 27, 2020).

Vacca, A. (2013), "Protection of Minority Languages in the UK Public Administration: A Comparative Study of Wales and Scotland," *Revista de Llengua i Dret*, 60: 50–90.

Valdeón, R. A. (2007), "Ideological Independence or Negative Mediation: *BBC Mundo* and *CNN* en Español's (Translated) Reporting of Madrid's Terrorist Attacks," in M. Salama-Carr (ed.), *Translating and Interpreting Conflict*, 99–118, Amsterdam: Rodopi.

Valdeón, R. A. (2009), "Euronews in Translation: Constructing a European Perspective for/of the World," *Forum*, 7 (1): 123–53.

Valdeón, R. A. (ed.) (2010), *Translating Information*, Oviedo: Universidad de Oviedo.

Valdeón, R. A. (2018), "On the Use of the Term 'Translation' in Journalism Studies," *Journalism*, 19 (2): 252–69. https://doi.org/10.1177/1464884917715945

Valdeon, R. A. (2019), "Ad Hoc Corpora and Journalistic Translation Research: BBC News and BBC Mundo's Coverage of Margaret Thatcher's Death and Funeral," *Across Languages and Cultures*, 20 (1): 79–95. Doi: 10.1556/084.2019.20.1.4

van Dijk, T. (2000), "New(s) Racism: A Discourse Analytical Approach," in S. Cottle (ed.), *Ethnic Minorities and the Media: Changing Cultural Boundaries*, 33–49, Milton Keynes: Open University Press.

van Doorslaer, L. (2010a), "The Double Extension of Translation in the Journalistic Field," *Across Languages and Cultures*, 11 (2): 175–88. Doi: 10.1556/acr.11.2010.2.3

van Doorslaer, L. (2010b), "Journalism and Translation," in *Handbook of Translation Studies*, Y. Gambier and L. van Doorslaer (eds.), 180–4, Amsterdam and Philadelphia: John Benjamins.

van Doorslaer, L. (2012), "Translating, Narrating and Constructing Images in Journalism with a Test Case on Representation in Flemish TV News," *Meta: journal des traducteurs/Meta: Translators' Journal*, 57 (4): 1046–59.

Van Hoof, H. V. (2008), "Rime et allitération dans les langues française et anglaise," *Meta*, 53 (4): 899–906. https://doi.org/10.7202/019654ar

Versi, M. (2016a), "Why the British Media Is Responsible for the Rise in Islamophobia in Britain," *The Independent*, April 4. Available online: https://www.independent.

co.uk/voices/why-the-british-media-is-responsible-for-the-rise-in-islamophobia-in-britain-a6967546.html (accessed July 4, 2020).

Versi, M. (2016b), "Anjem Choudary inspired terrorists around the world – and the media shares some of the blame," The *Independent*, October 17. Available online: https://www.independent.co.uk/voices/anjem-choudary-sentence-isis-terrorism-links-guilty-lee-rigby-media-blame-a7195286.html (accessed July 4, 2020).

Vološinov, V. N. ([1929] 1986), *Marxism and the Philosophy of Language*, trans. L. Matejka and I. R. Titunik, Cambridge, MA: Harvard University Press.

Wagman, D. (2006), "Los medios de comunicación y la criminalización de los inmigrantes," in M. Lario Bastida (ed.), *Medios de comunicación e inmigración*, 202–13, Alicante: CAM Obra Social.

Wales, K. (2001), *A Dictionary of Stylistics*, 2nd edn, Harlow, UK: Pearson Education Ltd.

Warsi, S. ([2017] 2018), *The Enemy Within: A Tale of Muslim Britain*, London: Penguin Random House.

Weller, P., and S. Cheruvallil-Contractor (2015), "Muslims in the UK," in M. Burchardt and I. Michalowski (eds.), *After Integration: Islam, Conviviality and Contentious Politics in Europe*, 303–25, Weisbaden: Springer VS. Doi: 10.1007/978-3-658-02594-6

White, P. R. R. (1997), "Death, Disruption and the Moral Order: The Narrative Impulse in Mass Media 'Hard News' Reporting," in F. Christie and J. R. Martin (eds.), *Genre and Institutions: Social Processes in the Workplace and School*, 100–33, London: Cassell.

Williams, K. (2011), *International Journalism*, London: Sage.

Women and Equalities Committee, House of Commons (2016), *Employment Opportunities for Muslims in the UK. Second Report of Session 2016–17*, London. Available online: https://publications.parliament.uk/pa/cm201617/cmselect/cmwomeq/89/89.pdf (accessed January 27, 2020).

Wyss, V. (2013), "Auf dem Weg zur Anreizregulierung: Der Blick auf das Schweizer Modell," in die medienanstalten—ALM GbR (ed.), *Programmbericht 2013: Fernsehen in Deutschland. Programmforschung und Programmdiskurs*, 111–23, Berlin: Vistas.

Wyss, V., and G. Keel (2009), "Media Governance and Media Quality Management: Theoretical Concepts and an Empirical Example from Switzerland," in A. Czepek, M. Hellwig and E. Nowak (eds.), *Press Freedom and Pluralism in Europe. Concepts and Conditions*, 115–28, Chicago: University of Chicago Press.

Zelizer, B. (2015), "Terms of Choice: Uncertainty, Journalism, and Crisis," *Journal of Communication*, 65 (5): 888–908. Doi: 10.1111/jcom.12157

Zhang, M., H. Pan, X. Chen, and T. Luo (2015), "Mapping Discourse Analysis in Translation Studies via Bibliometrics: A Survey of Journal Publications," *Perspectives: Studies in Translatology*, 23 (2): 223–39. Doi: 10.1080/0907676X.2015.1021260

Appendix: List of Articles in the Corpus

Abbreviation	Source	Date	Short title	Author
TG1	*Guardian*	07.15.16	Why does France keep getting attacked?	Burke, J.
TG2		07.17.16	Police and academics search Nice attacker's history for a motive	Burke, J.
TG3		07.16.16	As horror strikes again, all eyes are on how France reacts	Nougayrède, N.
TG4		07.17.16	François Hollande pleads for unity amid anger over Nice attack	Chrisafis, A.
TG9		07.15.16	From Charlie Hebdo to Bastille Day: France reels after new deadly attack	Rawlinson, K., Chrisafis, A., and Dodd, V.
TG10		07.15.16	84 dead after truck rams Bastille Day crowd in Nice	Chrisafis, A., and Dehghan, S. K.
TG11		07.15.16	"My daughters saw bodies. Lots of them": Witnesses recall Nice truck attack	Fischer, S.
TG12		07.15.16	France attack: Use of truck in Nice demonstrates evolving nature of threat	Burke, J.
TG13		07.15.16	France stunned after truck attacker kills 84 on Bastille Day in Nice	Chrisafis, A., Fischer, S., and Rice-Oxley, M.
TG14		07.15.16	Nice attack is a crisis for presidency of François Hollande	Chrisafis, A.
TG15		07.16.16	Nice attack bewilders Mohamed Lahouaiej-Bouhlel's relatives	Stephen, C.
TG16		07.16.16	Nice truck attack: Islamic State claims responsibility	Jones, S., Chrisafis, A., and Davies, C.

Abbreviation	Source	Date	Short title	Author
TGObs17	***Guardian/ Observer***	07.16.16	Tourism will not give in to terror, but the industry faces a rethink	Doward, J.
DT5	***Telegraph***	07.15.16	Nice terror attack: Europe "faces summer of copycat attacks"	Farmer, B.
DT6		07.16.16	Nice attack: Truck driver who killed 84 named – the news as it unfolded on Friday, July 15	Boyle, D., Morgan, T., Chazan, D., Turner, C., Willgress, L., Allen, P., … Millward, D.
DT7		07.17.16	Bataclan brought us together—but this attack in Nice will drive a wedge into France	Moutet, A.-E.
DT8		07.18.16	Mourners spit and throw rubbish on "hate memorial" at spot Bastille Day terrorist was killed	Morgan, T., Turner, C., Willgress, L., and Allen, P.
DT18		07.15.16	The Nice terror attack shows just how easy it is to commit an atrocity— and how hard it is to stop one	Coughlin, C.
DT19		07.15.16	How the terror in Nice unfolded: Driver told police he was delivering ice creams – but instead delivered murder on a massive scale	Mendick, R.
DT20		07.15.16	The crumb of comfort from the Nice attack is that even terrorists who plot alone can be stopped	Blair, D.
DT21		07.15.16	Analysis: Nice truck attack shows France's acute vulnerability to terrorism	Blair, D.
DT22		07.16.16	The best defence against terrorism is to show that it does not work as a way of changing government policy or public perception	Barrett, R.

Abbreviation	Source	Date	Short title	Author
DT23		07.18.16	Who is the Nice terror attack suspect? Everything we know so far about Mohamed Lahouaiej Bouhlel	Samuel, H., and Morgan, T.
DT24		07.18.16	French PM booed at Nice tribute for victims of terror attack	Samuel, H., Chazan, D., Turner, C., and Willgress, L.
DT25		07.18.16	Nice terrorist attack on Bastille Day: Everything we know so far on Monday	Henderson, B., and Sabur, R.
DT26		07.15.16	How religion can drive someone to slaughter his fellow citizens—and believe they deserve it	Meleagrou-Hitchens, A.
DT27		07.15.16	The Nice terror attack is why Donald Trump might win	Stanley, T.
LT1	*Le Temps*	07.15.16	L'attentat de Nice et les tensions en mer de Chine assombrissent le sommet Europe-Asie	AFP
LT2		07.15.16	Attentat de Nice: un maximum d'effets avec un minimum de moyens	Dubuis, E.
LT3		07.15.16	Attentat de Nice: l'exécutif socialiste est sous le feu des critiques de l'opposition	AFP
LT4		07.16.16	Attentat de Nice: quatre hommes en garde à vue	AFP
LT5		07.17.16	L'auteur de l'attentat avait repéré les lieux avec son camion	AFP
LT6		07.17.16	Pourquoi l'attentat de Nice est (peut-être) en train de changer la France	Werly, R.
LT7		07.18.16	Face aux attentats, le risque du déni français	Werly, R.
LT8		07.18.16	A Nice, le jour se lève sur une nuit de sang	Werly, R.

Abbreviation	Source	Date	Short title	Author
LT9		07. 18.16	Attentat de Nice: des médias français sont critiqués pour avoir diffusé des images choquantes	AFP
LT10		07. 18.16	Le quinquennat et la terreur	Werly, R.
LT11		07.18.16	Pour François Molins, l'enquête de tous les dangers	Werly, R.
LT12		07.18.16	Cette «guerre» qui fracture la société française	Werly, R.
TDG1	*La Tribune de Genève*	07.15.16	Les attaques en France depuis janvier 2015	(afp/nxp)
TDG2		07.15.16	Un véhicule lancé pour tuer: une arme déjà utilisée	(ats/nxp)
TDG3		07.15.16	Témoins et Niçois racontent le chaos	(afp/nxp)
TDG4		07.15.16	L'attaque frappe une ville mondialement connue	(ats/nxp)
TDG5		07.15.16	«Daech espère des représailles contre les musulmans»	Kuhn, G.
TDG6		07.15.16	L'Espagne va plus contrôler les zones touristiques	(afp/nxp)
TDG7		07.15.16	Nice, un terreau de radicalisation islamiste	(afp/nxp)
TDG8		07.15.16	Des touristes suisses rentrent déjà	(ats/nxp)
TDG9		07.15.16	Le portrait de l'auteur présumé de l'attentat se dessine	(ats/nxp)
TDG10		07.15.16	Le maire de Genève a condamné un «attentat odieux»	Mabut, J.-F.
TDG11		07.15.16	Dumoulin et Froome terminent la 13e étape en force	(afp/nxp)
TDG12		07.15.16	La Suisse en deuil après l'attaque	(ats/nxp)

Abbreviation	Source	Date	Short title	Author
TDG13		07.15.16	La France à nouveau frappée par un attentat	(afp/cbx/nxp)
TDG14		07.15.16	Un terroriste sème la mort face à la Baie des Anges	Bot, O. and Kuhn, G.
TDG15		07.16.16	Deuil national de trois jours en France	(afp/nxp)
TDG16		07.16.16	Daech revendique la tuerie de Nice	(afp/nxp)
TDG17		07.16.16	La France confrontée à un nouveau type d'attentat	(ats/nxp)
TDG18		07.16.16	Appel aux volontaires pour la réserve opérationnelle	(ats/nxp)
TDG19		07.16.16	Premières indemnisations pour les victimes	(afp/nxp)
TDG20		07.17.16	L'enquête se poursuit, le gouvernement se défend	(afp/nxp)
TDG21		07.17.16	Une fillette de 6 ans d'Yverdon (VD) a péri dans le carnage	(ats/nxp)
TDG22		07.17.16	Un nouveau coup dur pour le tourisme en France	(ats/nxp)
TDG23		07.17.16	Sécurité: Le conseiller d'Etat genevois Pierre Maudet plaide pour une meilleure formation des policiers	Sassoon, G.
TDG24		07.17.16	L'attentat de Nice accroît les tensions politiques	(afp/nxp)
TDG25		07.18.16	Huée et surenchère politique après le drame à Nice	Cuénod, J.-N. (Paris)
TDG26		07.18.16	La piste d'un acte prémédité se précise	(ats/nxp)
LC1	*Le Courrier*	07.15.16	Le bilan devrait encore s'alourdir à Nice – Deux Suisses tués	ATS

Abbreviation	Source	Date	Short title	Author
LC2		07.15.16	Pluie de larmes sur Nice	Jacolet, T.
LC3		07.16.16	Une lutte peu efficace	Jacolet, T.
LC4		07.18.16	Un terroriste venu de nulle part	Unknown
LC5		07.17.16	Après Nice, la fuite en avant	Koessler, C.
LC6		07.15.16	Au moins 84 morts et plus de 200 blessés à Nice	ATS
LC7		07.15.16	Un attentat perpétré avec un camion a fait au moins 84 morts à Nice	ATS
LC8		07.15.16	Attentat de Nice: Festivals et spectacles annulés en France	ATS
LC9		07.15.16	Les liaisons entre la Suisse et Nice maintenues	ATS
LC10		07.15.16	Un attentat perpétré avec un camion a fait plus de 80 morts à Nice	ATS
EP1	*El País*	07.15.16	El atentado de Niza obliga a Brasil a revisar la seguridad de los Juegos	Moniz, G.
EP2		07.15.16	"El Tour debe seguir"	Arribas, C.
EP3		07.15.16	Francia, bajo la amenaza del terror	Sánchez-Vallejo, M. A.
EP4		07.15.16	Francia, un país en estado de emergencia	Ferluga, G.
EP5		07.15.16	Interior mantiene el nivel 4 de alerta y califica de "yihadista" el ataque de Niza	Ortega Dolz, P.
EP6		07.15.16	La UE admite estar ante un fenómeno terrorista difícil de controlar	Abellán, L.
EP7		07.15.16	La unidad entre los partidos se resquebraja tras la matanza	Yárnoz, C.
EP8		07.15.16	Los vehículos como arma de guerra de los lobos solitarios	Agencies

Abbreviation	Source	Date	Short title	Author
EP9		07.15.16	Minuto de silencio en el Ayuntamiento, Comunidad y la Delegación del Gobierno por el atentado de Niza	Escandón, P.
EP10		07.15.16	Obama destaca la "resistencia extraordinaria" de Francia	Faus, J.
EP11		07.15.16	Por qué el Estado Islámico odia a Francia	Vicente, Á.
EP12		07.15.16	¿Por qué Niza?	Amón, R.
EP13		07.15.16	Rajoy convoca el pacto antiterrorista para dar respuesta global a la amenaza tras el atentado en Niza	Casqueiro, J.
EP14		07.15.16	Rajoy, Sánchez, Iglesias y Rivera expresan su conmoción por el atentado	EFE
EP16		07.16.16	El ISIS se responsabiliza de la matanza de Niza	Yárnoz, C.
EP17		07.16.16	Exteriores busca a 11 españoles sin localizar tras el atentado de Niza	Gonazález, M.
EP18		07.16.16	La fiscalía teme que el retroceso bélico del ISIS recrudezca los atentados en Europa	Pérez, F. J.
EP19		07.16.16	Lo que se sabe del atentado en Niza	Unkown
EP20		07.17.16	Alcohol, hachís y juego, las aficiones del autor de la masacre	Verdú, D. (special correspondent)
EP21		07.17.16	Le Pen acusa de blando al Gobierno porque no expulsa a los islamistas radicales	Yárnoz, C.
EP22		07.17.16	Los héroes que intentaron detener al atacante de la Riviera	Unknown
EP23		07.18.16	"Lleva 5 armas a C.", escribió por SMS el terrorista de Niza minutos antes del atentado	Yárnoz, C.

Abbreviation	Source	Date	Short title	Author
EP24		07.18.16	El pequeño Kilian y otras vidas rotas	Teruel, A.
		07.18.16	Francia afronta el terror de nuevo cuño	Yárnoz, C.
EP26		07.18.16	Francia agota las opciones legales contra el terror	Yárnoz, C.
EP27		07.18.16	Golpe a la ciudad más vigilada	Teruel, A.
EP29		07.18.16	Jugando a los bolos con nosotros	Basterra, F. G.
EP30		07.18.16	La Asamblea francesa advierte de la amenaza del lobo solitario	Cañas, G.
EP31		07.18.16	La masacre ataca directamente al sector turístico	Verdú, D.
EP32		07.18.16	Las víctimas del atentado de Niza	Teruel, A.; Verdú, D. (special correspondents)
EP33		07.18.16	Niza y los lobos de Mustafá	Irujo, J. M.
EP34		07.18.16	Niza, el caladero yihadista de Francia	Verdú, D.
EP35		07.18.16	Pitidos a Valls y tensión máxima en el minuto de silencio en Niza	Teruel, A.
EP36		07.18.16	"Sufría un principio de psicosis y alteración de la realidad"	Verdú, D.
EP37		07.18.16	Una familia diezmada por la masacre	Teruel, A.
EP38		07.18.16	Valls alerta del riesgo de que el ISIS logre fracturar a la sociedad francesa	Cañas, G.
EM1	*El Mundo*	07.15.16	Atentado en Niza: al menos 84 muertos y 50 heridos críticos en un ataque terrorista con un camión	Valderrama, M. D.; Hernández, M. (Paris; Madrid)
EM2		07.15.16	El embajador de Francia en España no descarta que aún pueda haber víctimas españolas en Niza	Sanz, L. A.

Abbreviation	Source	Date	Short title	Author
EM3		07.15.16	Atentado en Niza: El fiscal confirma la muerte de 84 personas y eleva a 202 el número de heridos	Unknown
EM4		07.15.16	España mantiene el nivel 4 de alerta y Rajoy ofrece toda la cooperación para erradicar la "locura criminal"	Cruz, M.; Lázaro, F.
EM5		07.16.16	España ofrece 100 militares más para la lucha contra el Estado Islámico	Lázaro, F.
EM6		07.15.16	Hollande dice que se tomaron "todas las medidas" de seguridad en Niza	Agencies
EM7		07.15.16	Interior refuerza la seguridad en centros turísticos, fronteras y lugares de máxima afluencia	Lázaro, F.
EM8		07.15.16	Atentado en Niza: qué se sabe hasta ahora	Unknown
EM9		07.15.16	Testigos del atentado en Niza: "Los restos volaban por todos lados, un caos absoluto, la gente gritaba"	Valderrama, M. D.
EM10		07.15.16	Un atentado con tintes yihadistas cometido por un delincuente común	Martín, I. J. (Rabat)
EM11		07.15.16	Una familia encuentra a su bebé tras el atentado gracias a Facebook	EFE (Paris)
EM12		07.16.16	Analfabetos del Corán en busca de expiación	Escrivá, Á.
EM13		07.16.16	El Estado Islámico reivindica el atentado de Niza	Hernández Velazco, I. (special correspondent, Nice); Carrión, F. (Cairo)
EM14		07.16.16	El padre del autor del atentado en Niza: "Mi hijo tuvo problemas mentales"	Martín, I. J. (Rabat)

Abbreviation	Source	Date	Short title	Author
EM15		07.16.16	Francia, objetivo prioritario	Sahagún, F.
EM16		07.16.16	El autor de la masacre: "Llevo helados para la fiesta"	Hernández Velasco, I. (special correspondent, Nice)
EM17		07.16.16	Niza, un nido yihadista en Francia	AFP
EM18		07.16.16	Niza, 31 ataques terroristas en 40 años	Guisado, P.; Lepetit, N.
EM19		07.16.16	Niza, ciudad fantasma	Valderrama, M. D.
EM20		07.16.16	El paseo de los muertos	Ferrero, J.
EM21		07.16.16	Previsible e imprevisible	Alonso, R.
EM22		07.16.16	Una hostelera en Niza: "Hemos perdido 11.000 euros en 24 horas"	Valderrama, M. D.
EM23		07.16.16	Atentados "low cost", pero de alto rendimiento	Baños, P.
EM24		07.17.16	El atentado terrorista da oxígeno al Frente Nacional	Valderrama, M. D. (Paris)
EM25		07.17.16	El autor del atentado de Niza pidió en un mensaje "más armas" antes de perpetrar el ataque	Agencies
EM26		07.17.16	Fuerzas de seguridad y hospitales, en ruinas a días de Río 2016	Pomi, A. M. (Rio de Janeiro)
EM27		07.17.16	Manuel Valls: "El IS busca la confrontación, la guerra civil"	Valderrama, M. D. (Paris)
EM28		07.18.16	Atentado en Niza: el asesino tenía fotos de Charlie Hebdo, Bin Laden y el IS en su teléfono	EFE (Paris)
EM29		07.18.16	Valls desvela que Francia frustró un atentado "muy mortífero" justo antes de la Eurocopa	EFE (Paris)
EM30		07.15.16	Atentado en Niza: un ataque con la firma del Estado Islámico	Carrión, F. (Cairo)

Abbreviation	Source	Date	Short title	Author
EM31		07.15.16	El vehículo como "arma de guerra", una idea de Al Qaeda ya usada en Francia	Rojas, A. (Madrid); Carrión, F. (Cairo)

Index